Borchert Field

As this view makes clear, Borchert Field was very much a neighborhood ball-park. COURTESY OF EGON GROTHE

Borchert Field

~

Stories from Milwaukee's Legendary Ballpark

Bob Buege

WISCONSIN HISTORICAL SOCIETY PRESS

Published by the Wisconsin Historical Society Press
Publishers since 1855

The Wisconsin Historical Society helps people connect to the past by collecting, preserving, and sharing stories. Founded in 1846, the Society is one of the nation's finest historical institutions.

Order books by phone toll free: (888) 999-1669
Order books online: shop.wisconsinhistory.org
Join the Wisconsin Historical Society: wisconsinhistory.org/membership

Photographs identified with WHi or WHS are from the Society's collections; address requests to reproduce these photos to the Visual Materials Archivist at the Wisconsin Historical Society, 816 State Street, Madison, WI 53706.

Front cover photos: top, Otto Borchert (the man at right in the suit and hat) knew how to fill his ballpark in the 1920s—let kids in free for a day. Photograph courtesy of the Milwaukee County Historical Society. Bottom left and bottom right, Richard Lulloff Collection. Spine: Richard Lulloff Collection. Back cover: Brewers schedule courtesy of Paul F. Tenpenny

wisconsin history.org

Printed in the United States of America
Designed by Ryan Scheife/Mayfly Design

21 20 19 18 17   1 2 3 4 5

To my dad, who lit the flame

Contents

Borchert's Orchard

Okay, so it wasn't Yankee Stadium. But it had a short right-field line, just like the park where Maris slammed number 61. The Yankees played here a bunch of times, too. The Bambino, the Iron Horse, Joltin' Joe, the Mick—they all played in Borchert Field.

Casey Stengel managed in Borchert Field, for more than one club. He managed the Milwaukee ball club, and his team won the pennant. He was not universally popular, though, and he got fired. Just like in the Big Apple.

The man acclaimed as the world's greatest athlete in the 1912 Olympic Games, Jim Thorpe, didn't get along in Gotham City,

Old Glory waves in front of Borchert Field's left-center-field fence while long shadows signal the game must end soon. PHOTOGRAPH COURTESY OF THE MILWAUKEE COUNTY HISTORICAL SOCIETY

so he was farmed out to play ball in Borchert Field (called Athletic Park at the time) for a season. He and his family took up residence a fly ball away. A few years later he returned and played pro football there.

Just like in the famous ballpark in the Bronx, visiting ballplayers included the greatest heroes of the game: Teddy Ballgame, the Say-Hey Kid, Stan the Man, even native son Bucketfoot Al, known locally as the Duke of Mitchell Street. They all showed off their talents in Borchert Field.

So did Eddie Mathews and Lew Burdette, stars of the 1957 World Series. Eddie smashed a grand slam and the next day was demoted to Atlanta. And owner Bill Veeck learned how to be a promotional genius in Borchert Field. He conceived and perfected many of his stunts in the old wooden ballpark at Eighth and Chambers.

Just like the House That Ruth Built, Borchert Field hosted non-baseball events also, some in the sports field, some not. Boxing and wrestling matches were big. So were football games at every level.

The Green Bay Packers played in Borchert Field, in league games, not exhibitions. Sometimes they were the home team; other times they were the visitors. Curly Lambeau's guys held Yankee Stadium's team, the ones sportscaster Chris Berman likes to call the New York Football Giants, without a first down. Somehow, the Packers still lost. Anything was possible in Borchert Field.

Major league baseball's winningest manager, and the runner-up, appeared there. The greatest hitter who ever lived and the best ballplayer both performed at Eighth and Chambers. The first driver to intentionally roll a car over did so inside Borchert's wooden confines. The finest woman athlete the world has ever seen rode a donkey there. The ugliest man in the world—and no one disputed the claim—grappled there.

Borchert Field's manual scoreboard in right-center field kept the score, advertised the sponsors, and stood watch over a variety of activities. HISTORIC PHOTO COLLECTION / MILWAUKEE PUBLIC LIBRARY

Jackie Price caught fly balls in his jeep and took batting practice while hanging upside down. Ralph Cutting's goat kept the lawn trimmed. Cuckoo Christensen read the newspaper while playing the outfield. The man who ordered the dropping of the atomic bomb on Hiroshima gave a speech standing near the ballpark's home plate. Every night for two weeks, Mount Vesuvius erupted behind second base and probably scared neighborhood dogs out of their wits.

A person lucky enough to live on Milwaukee's near north side between 1888 and 1952 could experience the world without ever leaving the neighborhood.

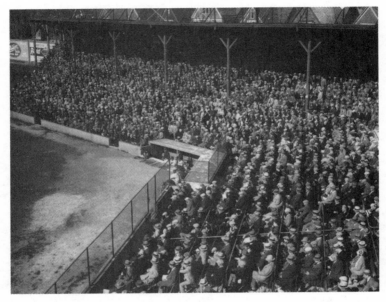

The photographer must have hung from the rafters to capture this full house and one of Borchert Field's unusual angled dugouts. PHOTOGRAPH COURTESY OF THE MILWAUKEE COUNTY HISTORICAL SOCIETY

1

This Old House

Athletic Park, later named Borchert Field, was Milwaukee's major sports venue for 64 years. It was built entirely of wood in less than three months in the same year in which Ernest Lawrence Thayer's poem "Casey at the Bat" first caught the public's fancy. At the time, the United States had only 38 states. The cost of the project was roughly $40,000, all private money, the lion's share of which went for the purchase of five acres of land on Milwaukee's north side, bounded by North Seventh and Eighth Streets and West Chambers and Burleigh Streets.

Like New York's Polo Grounds, Athletic Park filled a rectangular city block, producing very short distances to the foul poles and a deep center field. The dugouts were angled in the middle, and the grandstands behind and alongside home plate were U-shaped. As a result, fans could not see the entire playing field. As Minneapolis Millers owner Mike Kelley so aptly explained, to see a game in Milwaukee's park you needed to buy two admissions, one on the first-base side today and one on the third-base side tomorrow.

Built for Milwaukee's Brewers of the Western Association, Athletic Park opened for business on May 20, 1888. An "immense" crowd of 6,000, the city's largest for a ballgame, packed the premises for the dedication and the Brewers' 9–5 victory over St. Paul.

The standing-room crowd in Athletic Park on Labor Day 1909 filled the perimeter of the outfield. As this postgame view illustrates, they were not a tidy bunch. COURTESY OF MILWAUKEE PUBLIC MUSEUM

The park served for nine seasons but became redundant when Milwaukee Baseball Park (also known as Lloyd Street Grounds) was constructed. In 1897 the facility was converted to a National Guard drill ground and horse stable. With the formation of the American Association in 1902, park owner Harry Quin retrofitted it for baseball. It remained so for half a century.

In 1919 a group of Milwaukee investors purchased the Brewers, ballpark included, for a reported $87,000. Foremost among these was Otto Borchert, who bought two-sevenths of the stock. On November 20, 1921, Borchert acquired an additional two-sevenths, giving him a controlling interest in the club. In 1925 he bought out his last partner and took total ownership.

Otto Borchert was a Milwaukee native, the son of a brewery executive who nevertheless went his own path and, as a traveling salesman, became a wealthy man. His introduction to baseball began as a youngster when he sold peanuts at the Wright Street ballpark at 12th and Wright. He later became a Brewers batboy. As an adult he enjoyed many sports, including boxing and billiards, but especially baseball. As the Brewers' owner he liked attending ballgames in Athletic Park, carrying a stylish cane and decked out in his signature swallowtail suit jacket. "Swallowtail Otto" reveled in the mockery heaped on him by rowdy fans as he made his way across the diamond before each game and climbed the stairs to his box on the roof of the grandstand.

On the eve of the 1927 home opener, at the Brewers' annual preseason banquet, Otto was the main speaker on the program. While addressing the gathering of 600 in the Milwaukee Elks' Clubhouse and a live radio audience, Borchert suffered a stroke and died within minutes. His final words were, "I always made it a point to be loyal to my employers." The scheduled opening series with the Toledo Mud Hens was postponed out of respect.

Borchert's widow, Idabel Borchert, inherited the franchise, including the ballpark, and appointed herself team president. Her knowledge of baseball was limited, so she left all major decisions to her late husband's friend, confidant, and attorney, Henry J. Killilea. The following January, Killilea purchased the Brewers from Mrs. Borchert for $280,000, probably more than the team was worth. Killilea was looking out for the interests of his good friend's wife.

Henry Killilea was a high-profile lawyer in Milwaukee who along with his brother Matthew had owned the Brewers of the Western League. They had hired Connie Mack as manager from 1897 through 1900. Along with Mack, Ban Johnson, and Charles Comiskey, they had founded the American League in a clandestine meeting in room 185 of Milwaukee's Republican Hotel on March 5, 1900. In 1903 Henry Killilea owned the Boston Red Sox, who won the inaugural World Series. He later served as the attorney of Ban Johnson and the American League.

Besides providing Mrs. Borchert with a generous sale price for the Brewers, Killilea sweetened the transaction even further.

He allowed her to retain title to Athletic Park, which he renamed Borchert Field as soon as he bought the ball club. Killilea then used all his legal skills to hammer out an iron-clad 25-year lease for Mrs. Borchert's ballpark. The terms of the document were, to say the least, extraordinary.

First, the annual rent that Mrs. Borchert received was $8,500, with a sliding scale that would increase it annually by increments of $100 until it reached $10,000. This does not sound like anything today, but the median per capita income in 1928 was under $1,000. What's more, the ball club's owner had to pay all costs of maintenance, insurance, and taxes. If the structure were destroyed by fire, the club owner had to pay to rebuild. Failure to fulfill any of these conditions would cause the ownership of the entire franchise to revert to Idabel Borchert.

And then the coup de grâce—under no condition could the Milwaukee ball club operate on any piece of earth except Borchert Field during the life of the lease, which would expire in 1953. If the Brewers moved away from Borchert Field, even for one day, the franchise ownership would be taken over by Idabel Borchert. In other words, the Milwaukee Brewers were held hostage for 25 years, thanks to Otto Borchert's lawyer, Henry Killilea.

Borchert Field was the oldest park in the American Association, which had been formed in 1902, and it showed. Its wooden seats were splintered and rotted in places. In November 1935, *Milwaukee Journal* sports editor R. G. Lynch wrote a column in which he said that Borchert Field would soon be condemned. Writing with the assurance and authority that his position warranted, he said the park needed extensive repairs before the next season. The ballpark predated zoning, but a city ordinance stated that the cost of repairing any building could not exceed 50 percent of its assessed valuation at the time the area was zoned. Lynch concluded with a bold prediction: "The end of Borchert Field is in sight."

Lynch was off by 17 years. Idabel Borchert's lease held firm

In the championship season of 1936, Brewers fans stood in long lines to buy tickets to watch their heroes. RICHARD LULLOFF COLLECTION

despite evidence that the stadium was falling apart. On November 11, 1940, a blizzard collapsed a section of the outfield wall. A few days before the 1944 home opener, a windstorm flattened the entire left-field fence from the foul pole to the corner in left center. The wooden barrier was resurrected the day before the opening pitch. Famously, two months later half the grandstand roof blew off during a game. For its final eight years of existence, Borchert Field proudly stood topless.

Besides the twin dangers of splinters and the threat of imminent collapse, the ballpark constantly faced one other potential calamity: fire. Fortunately that never occurred on a large scale. Bill Topitzes, who as a youngster was hired by Bill Veeck to be a clubhouse boy, gopher, and general helper, remembered, "Part of our duties was, we'd go underneath the stands and see if a cigarette had dropped between the cracks in the floor and started a fire. There were hoses around to put out the little fires."

In the first decade of the 20th century, the local "bugs" (fans) walked across the playing field after the game to reach their exit of choice. PHOTOGRAPH COURTESY OF THE MILWAUKEE COUNTY HISTORICAL SOCIETY

Borchert Field hosted its final season in 1952. With the construction of Milwaukee's new County Stadium nearly complete, and with Mrs. Borchert's lease finally coming to its close, the Brewers held a ceremony between games of a doubleheader against Indianapolis on August 26, 1952. Mayor Frank Zeidler put a match to the lease while Mrs. Borchert and Brewers general manager Red Smith, along with Brewers legal adviser Robert Cannon, stood by. The crowd spontaneously broke into a chorus of "Auld Lang Syne." The ashes of the lease were placed into a receptacle and solemnly hauled away in a horse-drawn hearse.

Beginning in March 1953, even before the snow had melted away, a crew of workers armed with crowbars dismantled Borchert Field. Signs were put up offering "free kindling," and scavengers carried away the remains. After the demolition the site became a children's playground. Today interstate highway I-43 passes over the once-hallowed ground.

2

Pioneer in a New Park

In 1961 Major League Baseball initiated its first expansion in 60 years. The American League added two new franchises, the Los Angeles Angels and the Washington Senators. The new Senators filled a vacancy created when the old Senators, owned by Calvin Griffith, packed up their bats and moved to Minneapolis–St. Paul, adopting the name Minnesota Twins.

Calvin Griffith was the nephew and adopted son of Clark Griffith, who owned the sometimes-good, sometimes-awful Washington Senators from 1920 to 1955. Clark, an American League pioneer whose name identified Washington's ballpark for four decades, was inducted into the Baseball Hall of Fame in Cooperstown in 1946 as an executive. His credentials as a ballplayer, however, are also substantial and worthy of mention. As a five-foot six-inch right-handed hurler, the Old Fox notched 237 victories in the big leagues, surpassing 20 wins seven times in eight seasons.

Unlike many ball club owners, Clark Griffith was not born with the proverbial silver spoon in his mouth. He was raised in the wilderness of central Missouri after the Civil War, in the days when Jesse James and his gang were running loose in the territory. By the time he was 10 he was earning his keep trapping fur-bearing animals. Only after his family moved to Bloomington, Illinois, did

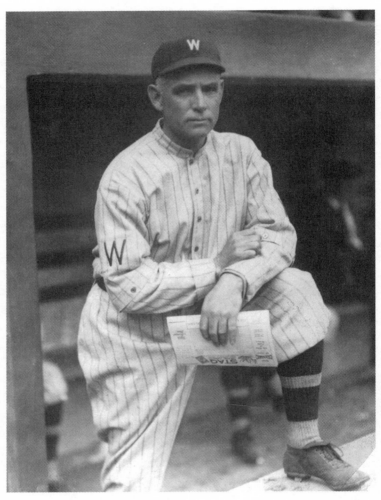

Washington Senators manager Clark Griffith stares out from the dugout. He later became the club's owner. NATIONAL BASEBALL HALL OF FAME LIBRARY, COOPERSTOWN, NY

he discover that (a) there was a game called baseball, and (b) he had a knack for playing it.

In 1888 the Milwaukee Creams (dubbed "Brewers" by the *Milwaukee Sentinel* on August 4 of that year) signed the 18-year-old Griffith to a contract to pitch in the new Western Association, which had been formed the previous winter. To provide a venue for its games, the club purchased five acres of land on Milwaukee's north side—one city block—and ordered the construction of a wooden ballpark. Athletic Park cost upwards of $42,000, most of it for the acquisition of the property. Work on the new stadium began in late March and was completed as required by Opening Day on May 20. The *Milwaukee Journal* proclaimed that the only ballpark larger was New York's Polo Grounds. George Walthers, nephew of Milwaukee pioneer Solomon Juneau, was appointed head groundskeeper. The Milwaukee club provided an appropriate curtain-raiser for their new playground by defeating the St. Paul Apostles, 9–5.

On July 8, 1888, the sports world was abuzz with reports that Hattie Leslie, a 20-year-old stage performer whose act consisted of sparring with her husband, had challenged 24-year-old professional golfer Alice Leary to a prize fight, the first ever advertised between female combatants. The fistic bout, illegal in the United States, eventually took place on September 16 on Navy Island on the Canada side of the Niagara River, witnessed by a scant gathering of 50. Mrs. Leslie, weighing in at 168 pounds, was knocked down twice and had her nose smashed, but she rallied and KO'd her 148-pound opponent in the seventh round with a hard right to the jaw. In a tragic footnote, the victorious Leslie—real name: Libbie Spann—died of typhoid pneumonia on September 28, 1892, during a scheduled one-week engagement at the People's Theater in Milwaukee.

Of less prurient interest but perhaps greater significance in the sporting world, on that same July 8 Clark Griffith made his professional pitching debut for the Milwaukee Creams in Athletic Park against the Sioux City Corn Huskers. The Huskers had been in the league for only a week, having replaced the bankrupt St. Louis Whites. Such comings and goings were not uncommon in the early days of professional base ball (two words, as it was then spelled). During the course of its inaugural season, the Western Association featured 10 different teams in its eight-team league, including the Chicago Maroons, the Davenport Onion Weeders, and the pennant-winning Des Moines Prohibitionists. Three clubs failed to finish the season, and all 10 played a different number of games.

On that Sunday afternoon, Clark Griffith took the mound and began his march toward the Hall of Fame. A light drizzle greeted him and lingered through most of the contest. Griffith was not a stylish pitcher, but he was a determined competitor. He did everything he could (all of it legal at the time) to make the baseball unhittable—he cut it, scuffed it, and applied every available substance to its surface, including saliva, dirt, perspiration, and whatever he happened to be chewing at the time. Years later he would claim to have invented the screwball.

Despite being the home team, the Milwaukeeans batted first. Until 1950 the host club had its choice, and before 1900 they often chose to take the first turn at bat. Leadoff hitter Tom Forster grounded to the third baseman, who threw wide of first for an error. Center fielder Jimmy McAleer ripped a double to the wall in center, scoring Forster, and the floodgates were open. The Creams scored three times in the first inning.

Griffith led off the home second by taking five successive bad pitches and being awarded first base. At that time five balls outside the strike zone constituted a base on balls. The rules of the game were in flux: two years earlier a walk had required seven bad pitches, and in 1879, nine. Griffith quickly scored, followed by two of his mates. In the third inning Milwaukee again scored three runs. As the unnamed baseball writer of the *Milwaukee Sentinel* explained in the florid prose style of his era, "It began to look as though each inning would have a triune termination."

Meanwhile, Milwaukee's young right-hander did his best to hold the visitors in check under the sloppy conditions. He struggled to control the wet ball, walking five and releasing three wild pitches, and his club committed four errors. On this day, though, it hardly mattered. The Beer City bunch belted 15 base hits and scored 16 runs, with Griffith himself producing a pair of base knocks and scoring twice. Every batter on Griffith's team scored at least once, except left fielder Bobby Lowe. This was somewhat ironic because Lowe was probably their best hitter. (Playing for the Boston team in the National League on May 30, 1894, Lowe would become the first major leaguer to hit four home runs in one game.)

Griffith pitched the complete game, allowed only one earned run, and fanned 10 batters while winning 16–4. He pitched the rest of that season plus two more in Athletic Park as a Milwaukee Brewer. In 1891 he joined the big-league St. Louis Browns.

3

Gay Nineties

Eighteen ninety-two was a screwed-up year. The island of Western Samoa moved the International Date Line and in so doing created two consecutive days of Monday, July 4. The Chicago World's Fair, called the Columbian Exposition to commemorate the 400th anniversary of the year Christopher Columbus sailed the ocean blue (1492), wouldn't open its gates until May 1, 1893. And the Milwaukee Brewers abruptly ended their 1892 season three months early, after which Harry Quin, who had purchased Athletic Park from the Creams' owners after the 1888 season, laid a quarter-mile cinder bicycle track inside his stadium to capitalize on the two-wheeled craze that was sweeping the country.

In the early decades of baseball, teams came and went. In 1891 the Milwaukee Brewers had competed in the Western Association until mid-August. With team owners struggling to meet their payrolls, the league fell apart. The Brewers took advantage of the opportunity to take the place of Cincinnati in the American Association, considered a major league at the time. The Brewers enjoyed the better part of two months as a big-league ball club. By spring the American Association had disappeared from the landscape, so Milwaukee's club joined the newly constituted Western League (not Association, you understand).

Katharine Wright (far right), sister of Wilbur and Orville, was a pioneer among "lady bicyclists" and a role model for wheel women like those who made Athletic Park their hangout in 1893. PUBLIC DOMAIN

The Western League organized a schedule in two three-month segments. The first half ended on June 30. The second finished on September 30. The winners of each half would then play each other in a postseason playoff. The Brewers, under the leadership of manager Charlie Cushman, put a respectable team on the Athletic Park diamond, equal to or better than every opponent except one—the force known colloquially as Jupe Pluvius (that is, rain). By Decoration Day the Milwaukee club had suffered through 20 rainouts, including eight in a row at the beginning of June. The Brewers were a second-place outfit but trailed the league-leading Columbus Solons, who had played nine more games.

Besides inclement spring weather, the Western League encountered other obstacles. The league's talent was not distributed evenly among its eight teams, resulting in a lack of competitive balance. Rival leagues seeking ballplayers led to threats of labor strikes and raids on team rosters. In addition, assorted blue laws kept some teams from playing games on Sundays, generally one of the top days for attendance. One such incident occurred on May 22, when police in Toledo walked onto the field during the ninth inning and arrested both the Toledo and Columbus players and their managers and coaches. Bail was set at $1.50 per man and was promptly paid by management. The alleged scofflaws were acquitted in a court of law in June, but Toledo discontinued games on the Sabbath.

At the season's midpoint the new Western League quickly began to unravel. On July 7 two clubs, those in Fort Wayne and Milwaukee, disbanded. As the *Milwaukee Sentinel* aptly described it in its announcement of the collapse, "There isn't enough left of the Western League to make a decent funeral." A week later the rest of the league closed up shop. Representatives of National League teams swooped down on Milwaukee to offer contracts to now-unemployed Brewers. The ballplayers were ripe for the picking—they were all owed at least three weeks' pay. When they approached the club secretary for their overdue wages, all they received was the remainder of the final game's receipts. They divided $18 equally among the entire team.

Athletic Park sat mostly idle the rest of the summer. Quin staged some amateur and semipro ballgames to supplement the stadium's new status as a hangout for "wheelmen" on their bikes. A ballgame between Milwaukee County officials and a team of local reporters brought in a crowd of around 200. The place didn't really come alive, though, until September.

From September 1 through September 17, every night except Sunday and Monday, Athletic Park was magically transformed into one of the world's most horrible natural disasters. The event was called "The Last Days of Pompeii." This traveling extravaganza, put on by James Pain and Sons of Manhattan Beach, featured 300 actors and extras, all clad in the garb of ancient Rome.

Some carried swords and raced in chariots. Ballet dancers performed while Hugo Bach's military band provided music. The scenery was spectacular, especially the huge artificial lake upon which swans and ducks glided lazily. Every day 15 men worked to rebuild the sets.

The star of the evening, however, was always Mount Vesuvius. "The sleeping volcano begins to smoke," said the *Milwaukee Sentinel*, "and in a few moments it is belching forth fire and smoke in such torrents that the people sit absolutely awe-stricken."

Tuesdays were children's nights. Through the wonders of electricity (a large percentage of the audience had no electric service in their homes), fiery pigeons winged their way across the lake, an acrobatic monkey performed somersaults, and an elephant named Jumbo walked across a burning stage.

As if that were not enough, the pyrotechnic display for which the presenters were best known concluded the night's entertainment. Utilizing electricity and more than half a ton of gunpowder, Pain and his boys proceeded to light up the sky while exploding rockets terrified every dog and cat within a five-mile radius. In the end, "Houses fall and the great temple of Isis crumbles to a shapeless ruin." All this for 50 cents' general admission. The most amazing part of the evening was that the wooden structure of Athletic Park, unlike the city of Pompeii, survived.

In 1893 Milwaukee had no baseball team to call its own. With few exceptions, the warm days of summer were given over to the wheelmen. At season's end, though, on the first and third days of October, ballpark owner Quin put together a pair of exhibition baseball games involving the best baseball club in the land, the three-time champions of the National League, the Boston Beaneaters.

Boston's opponents in these non-league contests were called the American All-Stars, and they indeed met the challenge of that moniker. Three men from their lineup are today enshrined

in Cooperstown. At third base they had George Davis, one of
the top left-side infielders in the 1890s. In right field they had
Baltimore's Joe Kelley, a .305 hitter who soared to .393 in 1894.
Stationed at first base they boasted Jake "Eagle Eye" Beckley, a
.303 hitter for Pittsburgh. Besides the Hall of Fame material, on
the mound the All-Stars presented 22-year-old right-hander Kid
Carsey, a 20-game winner for the Phillies. At shortstop the Stars
had a .304 hitter from Louisville, Voiceless Tim O'Rourke. He
had acquired his nickname after a wayward pitch struck him in
the throat, rendering him unable to speak above a loud whisper.

Unable to speak at all was All-Star center fielder Dummy Hoy,
whose given name, William, was seldom used. In the cruel and
politically incorrect world of baseball, every American Indian
was called Chief, and every deaf player, including Hoy, was called
Dummy. He was one of the shortest men ever to compete in the
big leagues, standing just five-foot-four. He could play, though,
covering his position with speed and grace and batting above .290
in most years. Hoy had made his professional debut at Oshkosh,
80 miles up the road from Athletic Park.

Of course Boston had not won three pennants in a row using
scotch tape and mirrors. Like the All-Stars, they also put a trio of
future Hall of Famers on the field, not counting Hugh Duffy, who
didn't play, and manager Frank Selee. One was Duffy's partner,
left fielder Tommy McCarthy. In tandem McCarthy and Duffy
were known as the Heavenly Twins, primarily for their exceptional defensive skills. Another was pitcher Kid Nichols, a Madison native who won 34 games for the Beaneaters in 1893 and 361
in his career.

Boston's third future Hall of Famer in the lineup, Big Ed Delahanty, was something of a mystery. His presence was mysterious
because he was not a member of the Boston club. He was a Philadelphia Phillie, and a great one. One of five Delahanty brothers
who played in the major leagues, Big Ed was the dominant power

hitter of the 1890s. He nearly won the mythical triple crown in 1893, leading in home runs and runs batted in while finishing third in batting at .368. Why the Beaneaters would want Delahanty playing for them is obvious. Why he replaced Duffy in center field is unknown and not really important.

The Sunday game on October 1 was strictly a blowout. Kid Nichols was unhittable, and the Bostons cruised to a 10–1 victory in a contest made very uncomfortable by a cold, steady rain in front of about 500 hardcore fans. Two days later the teams played again with the same lineups except for two different pitchers. The rain subsided but the temperature dipped even lower. Fewer than 100 frigid spectators showed up for what proved to be an interesting match, won by the All-Stars, 9–6. Dummy Hoy paced the victors with four hits, including a triple.

Ed Delahanty never played for Boston again. His departure from the world of baseball remains even more of a conundrum than his presence in the Beaneaters' outfield. On July 2, 1903, after a drinking binge, Big Ed was traveling by rail from Detroit to New York. He became disorderly and was put off the train by the conductor near the International Railway Bridge over the Niagara River. In almost total darkness Ed stumbled partway across the bridge, reportedly scuffled with a night watchman, and under circumstances never made clear, tumbled into the water. His nearly naked body was found a week later 20 miles downstream, at the foot of the Canada side of Niagara Falls.

The two star-studded ballgames with which Athletic Park concluded 1893 served as a perfect segue to the return of baseball there in April 1894. Under president Matthew Killilea, the Brewers joined the revamped Western League. They finished eighth in an eight-team league.

4

Major League

During the fall and winter of 1913–14, just a few months before the outbreak of the War to End All Wars, an amazing aggregation of ballplayers, mostly from the Chicago White Sox and the New York Giants, played an around-the-world tour to spread the popularity of baseball.

On their trip they gambled in Monte Carlo, shook hands with King George V, rode camels to the Great Pyramids, and received a private audience with Pope Pius X. Among the athletes in the group were Tris Speaker, Germany Schaefer, Jim Thorpe, and half a dozen other future Hall of Famers. The leaders of the two teams, the bankrollers and babysitters, were Chisox owner Charles "the Old Roman" Comiskey and Giants manager John "Little Napoleon" McGraw.

Comiskey and McGraw had been on opposite sides as players in the American Association in 1891. Derisively called the Beer and Whiskey League because concessionaires sold alcoholic beverages at their games (National League parks did not), the American Association was a second major league, in competition with the National League, from 1882 through 1891.

The AA's Cincinnati club—commonly called Kelly's Killers in deference to their manager, King Kelly—suffered from poor fan support in 1891 and folded in mid-August, with the strange contractual provision that they would rejoin the league the following season. To fulfill the remainder of Cincinnati's schedule, the Milwaukee Brewers summarily quit the struggling Western Association and signed on with the American Association on August 17.

The Brewers did not play a home game for their first three weeks. When they finally appeared in Athletic Park on September 10, they looked like the greatest ball club on the planet. Behind a barrage of 24 base hits, augmented with 14 bases on balls and three hit batsmen, Milwaukee's new major leaguers embarrassed the visiting Washington Nationals, 30–3. Contributing to the visitors' futility was their horrible fielding. They committed eight errors, including four by the outfielders, allowing the Brewers to score 20 unearned runs.

On September 16 the Baltimore Orioles visited Athletic Park for what would be their only time in the stadium's long history. Their catcher was future Hall of Fame inductee Wilbert Robinson. Playing the shortstop position for the Birds, and batting ninth, one slot below the pitcher, was an 18-year-old bundle of fury named John McGraw. The youngster showed promise of a fine career, but few could foresee that he would become one of baseball's legendary figures. In three decades as manager of the New York Giants, he led his club to 10 pennants and more victories than anyone except Connie Mack.

McGraw had been discovered, managed, and given tutelage in ball playing by a shadowy figure named Alfred Lawson. As one of Al Lawson's American All-Stars, young McGraw accompanied the team on an exhibition tour of Cuba in January 1891. The All-Stars wore bright yellow jerseys, and McGraw was small and very quick, so the islanders dubbed him "El Mono Amarillo," the Yellow Monkey. After returning to the mainland, Lawson told a reporter that McGraw was "one of the coming stars of the profession."

Lawson himself also enjoyed a noteworthy future. He would become a cult figure who attempted during the Great Depression to change the monetary standard of the United States. He also founded a bizarre institution of higher learning. Generations of travelers between Milwaukee and Chicago beginning in the 1950s were confronted and puzzled by a large horizontal sign alongside Highway 41 that read "University of Lawsonomy." Lawson boasted that he was the discoverer of the Law of Penetrability, whereby all matter throughout space is moved about continuously by the power of suction and pressure. Lawson also established a Lawsonian Religion.

By 1894 the Orioles had earned a reputation as a rough, tough, dirty bunch of bullies. Even on such a ball club, McGraw stood out as more ruthless, brutal, and brawling. He often directed vile curses toward umpires and opposing pitchers. Although he stood just a bit over five and a half feet tall (hence his nickname, Little Napoleon), he was quick to fight anyone, to spike an infielder, to gouge an opponent's eyes. He sometimes took advantage of the averted gaze of the lone umpire—baseball employed only one at that time—and obstructed a base runner by pushing him, tripping him, or grabbing the man's belt. As rival Charlie Comiskey said, "Why, it was an awful thing for a man to undertake a journey round the bases when some of these teams were playing." Then he added, "They play much nicer, cleaner ball nowadays," referring to 1904.

On May 15, 1894, McGraw engaged in a notorious fight with Boston outfielder Tommy Tucker. When Tucker slid into third base with spikes high, McGraw applied a hard tag and kicked his rival in the head for good measure. A vicious battle ensued, during which the wooden grandstand behind home plate caught fire, probably from a discarded cigarette. Spectators fixed their attention on the on-field fisticuffs and ignored the growing blaze around them. Ultimately the fire destroyed nearly the entire

Charlie Comiskey began his baseball career at age 16 with the amateur Milwaukee Alerts. He became a major league first baseman, manager, and owner, and a founder of the American League. WIKIMEDIA COMMONS

structure, then spread to the surrounding neighborhood. One hundred seventy buildings suffered damage and 1,900 people were left homeless.

The John McGraw that Milwaukee fans ("bugs," they were called then) witnessed in mid-September 1891 did not entirely resemble the devil incarnate that he would soon become. For one thing, he was an 18-year-old rookie with only three weeks under his big-league belt. For another, the two games he played in Athletic Park were distinctly one-sided. Baltimore lost the first contest, 11–4, as McGraw went hitless in three trips and walked once. Both teams committed five errors, not a large number in an age when some fielders still chose not to wear a glove. Nevertheless, only five of the Brewers' runs were earned. The game was so wanting for drama that the fans' chief source of interest seemed to be umpire Bob Ferguson, making his first appearance in Milwaukee. Ferguson was well known for his custom of not wearing a mask when he worked. As the *Milwaukee Sentinel* described it, this "kept the spectators in a constant state of fear lest they should see an umpire's corpse carried off the field."

The next afternoon was even worse for the Orioles. McGraw singled twice, but he also committed three errors. Second baseman Joe Walsh fumbled four, and the Baltimore total of 10 errors gave Milwaukee 11 runs they did not deserve, leading to a 16–6 thumping. The Brewers banged 17 hits, with Abner Dalrymple, Jimmy Canavan, and Bob Pettit recording three apiece.

After the Brewers replaced Cincinnati in the American Association, they played their first 15 games on the road. They came out ahead in just five of those. In Athletic Park, it was a different story. Their two victories over Baltimore gave them a 7–1 record on the home stand. They may have benefited from the friendly environment, but they also continued to strengthen their roster. The night before the Orioles came to town, for example, former Cincinnati right-hander Willard "Grasshopper" Mains joined the Milwaukee club after recuperating at home from a sore arm. Unable to secure a room in any of the downtown hotels, Grasshopper had to bunk for the night with teammate Harry Vaughn. One wonders if every hotel in town was really booked solid or if the innkeepers would not accept a ballplayer.

The Brewers concluded their brief major league season with a three-game series in Athletic Park against the second-place St. Louis Browns. Charlie Comiskey managed the Browns and also played first base. His club boasted an exceptional trio of outfielders: left to right, Tip O'Neill, Dummy Hoy, and future Hall of Famer Tommy McCarthy.

On Sunday, October 11, the two clubs split a doubleheader. The season ended on Monday, and not a day too soon. The weather was cold, even for a city accustomed to the cooling breezes off Lake Michigan. As the *Milwaukee Journal* scribe so elegantly phrased it, "Baseball, like tomatoes, should be harvested before frost sets in." Roughly 100 cranks (fans) showed up, but by game time, 3:00, none of the Browns had. The Comiskey men walked through the gates about 3:15, then took the usual pregame warm-ups, so the game did not begin much before 4:00.

The contest ended 12–9 in favor of the Browns. The score might have gone higher, but only seven innings were completed before darkness crept over the diamond. Milwaukee catcher Harry Vaughan led his team with a single, a triple, and a home run. Comiskey paced the visitors with three hits. The major excitement of the afternoon occurred in the fourth inning with the Browns at bat. A disputed fair ball allowed two runs and enraged the guys in Milwaukee uniforms. They descended like wolves on hapless umpire Kilpatrick and would not relent. Finally the man in blue reached the end of his tolerance and left the premises. Former Brewers hurler Clark Griffith was discovered in the grandstand and was conscripted to put on the mask for the last few innings of the season.

By 1892 the American Association was defunct. Charlie Comiskey had become the player-manager of the Cincinnati club in the newly expanded National League. McGraw and his Orioles teammates had also joined the National League, albeit as the league's worst ball club. Milwaukee lost its major league status and had to be content as members of the new Western League.

In 1900 Comiskey came back to Milwaukee and made history. On the night of March 5, he and four other men secretly convened in room 185 of the Republican Hotel at what is now Third and Kilbourn and incorporated the American League, with Milwaukee as one of the clubs.

5

Tragedy of the Rube

In the late 1800s the name Rube was applied to any man considered to be a country bumpkin. It was not intended as a compliment.

George Edward Waddell, a fire-balling southpaw, was the prototypical Rube, but he was much more. Writer Lee Allen wrote of Waddell: "In 1903 he began the year sleeping in a firehouse in Camden, New Jersey, and ended it tending bar in Wheeling, West Virginia. In between those events he won 21 games for the Philadelphia Athletics, played left end for the Business Men's Rugby Football Club of Grand Rapids, Michigan, toured the nation in a melodrama called 'The Stain of Guilt,' courted, married, and separated from May Wynne Skinner of Lynn, Massachusetts, saved a woman from drowning, accidentally shot a friend through the hand, and was bitten by a lion."

Calling Waddell eccentric would be like calling Marilyn Monroe pretty. He was known to leave the ballpark during a game to join a parade or follow a fire engine. One time in Brooklyn he did not turn up for a game in which he was supposed to pitch. He was discovered shooting marbles with some kids. In a similar situation when Rube was pitching for Connie Mack's Athletics, his teammates located him near the fairgrounds, playing leapfrog with some neighborhood boys. He wrestled alligators in Florida.

He seldom wore underwear. He was often paid in dollar bills, one per day, to keep him from blowing his entire salary all at once. He was unable to pitch in the World Series in 1905 after injuring his shoulder trying to punch a hole in teammate Andy Coakley's straw hat because he was wearing it after Labor Day.

The Rube was taunted mercilessly by opponents, fans, and sometimes teammates. *The Sporting News* described him as "a man with an infant's brain." Had he lived a century later, he might have been labeled autistic or in some way mentally challenged. Despite raging alcoholism and having to endure a lifetime of cruelty, Waddell achieved 193 major league victories, 50 shutouts, a career earned run average of 2.16, and 349 strikeouts in one season, still the record for American League lefties. In 1946 he received enshrinement in Cooperstown by the Hall of Fame Veterans Committee.

On August 27, 1899, Milwaukee residents had their choice between two remarkable entertainments: Buffalo Bill's famous Wild West Show, including a detachment of Teddy Roosevelt's Rough Riders recently returned from fighting the Spanish-American War, or Rube Waddell and the Grand Rapids Rustlers of the Western League contesting Connie Mack's Milwaukee Brewers at Milwaukee Park at 16th and Lloyd Streets. Colonel Cody and his frontier extravaganza arrived at five o'clock that morning via the Chicago and North Western Railroad. Five hours later they paraded their wagons and horses through Milwaukee's business district in full regalia. No one can be certain, but it seems unimaginable that Waddell would have allowed himself to miss such a spectacle. Nevertheless, by three forty-five that afternoon the erratic southpaw was on the mound in the Lloyd Street Grounds. His left-field teammate that afternoon was another future Hall of Famer, Wahoo Sam Crawford.

This was not the Rustlers' day. Waddell was battered for 14 base hits and thoroughly outpitched by Brewers right-hander

Rube Waddell was tormented throughout his life by people who had no understanding of his mental deficiencies, thinking he was merely eccentric.
PUBLIC DOMAIN

Bill Reidy. Waddell actually did his best work with his bat, getting a single and a double, but he allowed three runs in the opening inning and ended up losing, 5–1.

The following season found Waddell pitching for Pittsburgh in the National League. On July 8 his shenanigans finally exceeded the club's level of tolerance, and they suspended him. On July 25 Milwaukee manager Connie Mack found Rube playing sandlot ball in rural Pennsylvania and, with the Pirates' blessing, signed him to pitch for the Brewers in the new American League.

In five weeks as a Milwaukee Brewer, Waddell won 10 games and lost three, threw 12 complete games, and sported an amazing 1.05 ERA. His most notable performance occurred on August 19 in Chicago against Charlie Comiskey's White Stockings. In the first game of a Sunday doubleheader, Rube labored 17 innings to defeat the home club, 3–2. He was so pleased with himself that he turned a handspring after the final out.

The second game was, by mutual consent owing to impending darkness, a five-inning contest. Mack, sensing an opportunity, offered his star southpaw a deal. He would give Waddell three days off to go fishing at Pewaukee Lake while the Brewers traveled to Kansas City if he would keep pitching for five more innings. The Rube, who would rather fish than eat, accepted at once. He proceeded to throw five shutout innings and beat the Chicagos again, 1–0.

Two nights later lightning struck a dairy barn near Pewaukee. Who should show up to help fight the blaze but Rube Waddell. Thanks largely to his efforts, 40 head of livestock and several pieces of farm machinery were saved. Interviewed afterward by a *Milwaukee Sentinel* reporter, the slightly singed left-hander explained, "I'm a peach at a fire. There is nothing I like better than to fight fires." Except maybe fishing.

During the next decade Waddell distinguished himself as one of the top hurlers in the major leagues. On May 5, 1904, he was the losing pitcher in Cy Young's perfect game. On Independence Day 1905, Rube and the immortal Cy hooked up again, this time in an epic battle that Waddell finally won, 4–2, in 20 innings. Both men pitched the entire game, which was the second game of a double-header. Waddell had also retired the final two batters of the first game. For years to come Rube would swap the baseball from that famous game in exchange for drinks from friendly bartenders. He probably traded hundreds, using any baseball that was handy.

On June 1, 1911, Waddell returned to Milwaukee, this time in Athletic Park as the ace of the American Association champion Minneapolis Millers. His big-league days were over. On this afternoon, however, he showed that he still had strength in his arm. Although the "lively" new ball, with more rubber in the center and more velocity off the bat, was the talk of the sporting world—Millers manager Joe Cantillon predicted it would be the "death of the game"—Waddell had no trouble shutting down the slumping Brewers, striking out nine and walking just one.

A year later he came back to Athletic Park, recording five outs in relief in a game the Millers lost to the Brewers, 6–5, on June 18. Alcohol and age (35) seemed to be taking their toll on his stamina. The Rube admitted to a doctor that he had consumed a quart and a pint of whiskey every day for 15 years.

On June 20 Waddell tried again. He entered the game with one out in the ninth, the Millers leading 5–4, and Brewers on first and second. The role of the closer was many decades in the future, but teams often brought in their best starting pitcher to quell a rally. Waddell had done it many times.

But not this time. His first offering was a wild pitch that advanced the runners to second and third. On a 2-and-0 pitch right fielder Newt Randall laced a single to right, scoring both runners and sending the Athletic Park crowd to the exits in a gleeful mood.

Rube was living in the Ohio River community of Hickman, Kentucky, in 1913 when the town was threatened by floodwaters.

Volunteers, including Rube, piled thousands of sandbags in a vain attempt to reinforce the town's levee. After standing in icy water for hours at a time, the unfortunate pitching giant developed pneumonia, and his health spiraled downward. According to *Sporting Life,* on November 18, 1913, Waddell was picked up while wandering the streets in St. Louis, exhausted and suffering from "consumption." He was not able to speak above a whisper. Friends provided him with enough money to take the train to San Antonio. He died penniless in a Texas sanatorium on April Fools' Day 1914.

6

Send in the Clowns

Milwaukee Braves manager Charlie Dressen once sent catcher Bob Uecker to the minor leagues, telling him, "There is no room in baseball for a clown." Dressen was wrong.

Baseball has employed a number of notable jesters. Four of them plied their trade in Milwaukee's minor league ballpark. Each possessed exceptional athletic ability, yet each left a legacy not of on-field stardom but of buffoonery.

The American Association originated in 1902, with the Milwaukee Brewers as a charter member. They played their home games in Athletic Park, while concurrently the Milwaukee Creams of the newly established Western League made their home in Milwaukee Park, commonly called the Lloyd Street Grounds, located scarcely a mile to the southwest. The mainstay of the Brewers pitching staff in their initial season was a jug-eared, supple-faced 25-year-old left-hander named Nick Altrock. He won 28 games that year despite the Brewers' lowly seventh-place standing.

On Sunday, August 3, the redoubtable southpaw's mound efforts were nothing short of heroic. In the first game of a doubleheader with the Indianapolis Indians, Altrock hurled a two-hitter and allowed two runs, neither of them earned, in a 7–2 Milwaukee victory. Still feeling strong, Altrock persuaded his manager, shortstop Billy Clingman, to let him work the second contest as well. He then pitched a nine-inning, four-hit complete game, losing 3–0 as his teammates failed to produce any offensive support. Milwaukee baseball "cranks" who missed Altrock's iron-man performance may have had a good reason. Simultaneously, across town at the Lloyd Street Grounds, Madison native Kid Nichols, already a 329-game winner with Boston in the National League, was busy striking out nine Creams hitters in a 2–2 tie called after 12 innings to allow Nichols and the other Kansas City Blue Stockings to catch a train.

In 1906 Altrock won 21 games to help the Chicago "Hitless Wonders" (the White Sox) win the pennant and the World Series, beating the crosstown Cubs in six games. In the Series, Altrock twice pitched against future Hall of Famer Mordecai "Three Finger" Brown, beating him 2–1 in the opener and losing, 1–0, in Game Four.

On July 4, 1912, the American flag was flown for the first time over Athletic Park. Two days later, Altrock, back in the American Association with the Kansas City Blues, pitched there against his former club. He was hit hard and did not survive the fifth inning. The next day he started on a new career path.

Inspired by having watched a film of world featherweight boxing champ Johnny Kilbane, Altrock took the field between games of a doubleheader and sent the crowd into hysterics. At that moment, he invented a shadowboxing routine that he would use for the next four decades in stadiums throughout the country. After exchanging punches with himself for a round or two, he wound up and hurled a huge roundhouse blow that landed on his own chin and knocked him out. Fans could not get enough of it.

Everyone enjoyed Nick's show except Kansas City owner Patsy Tebeau, who promptly released him. Clark Griffith signed Altrock to be the Washington Senators' first-base coach and designated entertainer. He retained that job through 1953. In the nation's capital, he did his pantomimes, juggled, mimicked the umpires with mirror-like accuracy, and, most popular of all, chased butterflies. Maybe monarchs and fritillaries were more plentiful then, but the lepidopteran creatures seemed drawn to Altrock as if by a magnet. He, in turn, fascinated his audiences by interacting with the winged beauties, sometimes playing catch and release.

Beginning in 1919 Altrock teamed with another former pitcher, Al Schacht, to create the baseball equivalent of Laurel and Hardy. During the off-season they performed on vaudeville stages, and they displayed their shtick at every World Series from 1921 to 1933. On June 20, 1933, when the Washington Senators visited Borchert Field for an exhibition game with the Brewers, Altrock and Schacht, the latter in a top hat and swallowtail coat, cavorted on the field and kept the Beertown crowd laughing.

On the last day of the Senators' pennant-winning 1924 season, the 48-year-old Altrock pitched the final two innings in relief. In his only at-bat of the season, he belted a triple, becoming the oldest player ever to hit a three-bagger. Nine years later he pinch-hit in the first-place Washington's finale, becoming, at age 57, the oldest player in major league history (since exceeded by Satchel Paige and Minnie Minoso). Those records, however, are entirely obscure. Altrock's legacy is simpler: he was the first man to make a career as a baseball clown.

Another funnyman who wore a Milwaukee Brewers uniform during the Deadball Era was Herman "Germany" Schaefer. On May 10, 1904, in Athletic Park, the hometown nine took on the Louisville Colonels. The unseasonably frigid weather held the official attendance down to 250, but the Brewers batters showed no ill effects. They produced 11 base hits in a 7–6 victory. Leading the hit parade was shortstop Germany Schaefer with a double, a triple, and a home run, driving in four runs. He also made several sensational fielding plays while wearing a glove not much larger than his hand.

After the season, the Brewers sold Schaefer to the Detroit Tigers. He had been known for having a sense of humor, but in the major leagues his penchant for comedy and "street theater" rose to new heights. During a game in Cleveland, with rain pelting down but the umpire unwilling to suspend play, Schaefer borrowed a raincoat and a pair of rubber boots from a friendly fan, then strolled to his infield position and waited for a reaction. The man in blue stopped the game.

In 1906 in Chicago's South End Park, Schaefer entered the game as a pinch hitter. He bowed deeply to the grandstand, then introduced himself. "I am Germany Schaefer," he said, "the world's greatest batsman." The crowd responded with hoots and catcalls, but the world's greatest batsman smacked a two-run homer. As he did his home-run trot, he slid artfully into each base. After a beautiful headfirst dive into home, he brushed himself off and announced loudly, "Ladies and gentlemen, this concludes my afternoon performance."

Schaefer's reputation as a comedian continued to grow. On August 11, 1911, his Senators hosted the New York Highlanders. With the score tied in the 11th inning, a man on third, and one out, the New York manager, Hal Chase, ordered his pitcher to walk Clyde Milan. Schaefer was the next scheduled batter. Throughout the intentional base on balls, Schaefer performed a monologue for the spectators. After ball one, Germany announced loudly, "Ladies and gentlemen, the young man is making the mistake of his life." The crowd laughed. After ball two: "Evidently the young man has not perused the American League batting averages lately." A similar remark followed ball three. Then as Milan ambled toward first base, Schaefer doffed his cap and shouted, "Open the exits, ushers! Folks, get ready to leave. I will now proceed to break up the game by hitting the first pitch to left field for a single." He did. The people in the seats went crazy.

Schaefer teamed with Nick Altrock for a couple of zany seasons and trod the boards of the nation's theaters even longer. Schaefer's career inspired an MGM musical motion picture, *Take Me Out to the Ballgame*, costarring Gene Kelly, Frank Sinatra, and Esther Williams.

Nothing Schaefer ever accomplished, however, could overshadow the one feat for which he will forever be remembered: he stole first base. Detroit Tigers teammate Davy Jones described the event in Lawrence Ritter's book *The Glory of Their Times*. By Jones's account he was on third base and Schaefer was on first. In those days teams commonly attempted a double steal in that situation, with the runner on first trying to draw the catcher's throw to second so the man on third could score.

In this instance, Schaefer stole second, but the catcher held the ball. The double steal had been thwarted. On the next pitch, Schaefer let out a scream and sprinted back toward first base, sliding in safely as the catcher again made no throw. Not a man to give up easily, Schaefer broke toward second base on the next pitch. Davy Jones claimed the catcher finally made a throw and that he and Germany were both safe. So was Schaefer's reputation as a screwball. Major League Baseball later changed its rules to prevent a runner from proceeding clockwise around the bases.

Walter "Cuckoo" Christensen was another off-kilter jester of the ball diamond whom Milwaukee fans enjoyed. Standing barely five and a half feet tall, Christensen played in the outfield for the Cincinnati Reds during the 1926 and 1927 seasons. In the former year he batted a healthy .350 and led the league in on-base percentage, a statistic that of course did not exist at the time.

The Brewers signed Christensen after he was released by the Mission Reds of the Pacific Coast League. In his first game in Borchert Field, on June 17, 1930, he jogged out to his position in left field, alongside Pickles Gerken in center, then did handsprings like a hyperactive teenager. The fans loved him immediately. Because outfielders have lots of free time waiting for something to happen, Cuckoo filled those idle moments by goose-stepping in circles or doing his patented staggering act. He lurched around the field like a monster in deep mud. On those occasions when he could persuade his fellow fielders to join the act, the spectators were overcome with glee.

The irrepressible Cuckoo rarely missed an opportunity to have fun and create levity. He sometimes carried a newspaper with him to the outfield, then opened it wide and read the comics while watching the action through a hole sliced in the center of the paper. In the late innings of an exhibition game in Milwaukee against Babe Ruth and the Yankees, Cuckoo smoked a cigar and donned a fireman's helmet. He was also a comedian away from the ballpark. In December 1931 for a charity benefit at Wauwatosa's Tosa Theater, he painted his face black and impersonated Al Jolson singing "Mammy." That sort of humor was not considered offensive in those distant days.

⌇

Unlike the three previously described entertainers, Jackie (also called Johnny) Price was not technically funny. Nevertheless, fans who witnessed his performances could not help but laugh and smile. He was simply amazing. He was an athletic freak.

As a skinny minor leaguer in the mid-1930s, Price received sage advice from people like Casey Stengel and Bill Veeck: find another line of work to fall back on. Rather than take it as an insult, Price went to work perfecting a baseball-related repertoire of acrobatics, prestidigitation, and physical wizardry. He dropped

The amazing Jackie Price performed stunts with a bat and ball that no one else could do. PHOTOGRAPH COURTESY OF THE MILWAUKEE COUNTY HISTORICAL SOCIETY

out of baseball for seven years and took to heart the old show-biz joke, "Can you tell me how to get to Carnegie Hall?" The reply: "Practice, practice, practice." He did, in the process suffering 17 finger fractures and innumerable dislocations.

What Price developed during those years of intense training was a half-hour program that astounded audiences everywhere.

Price caught fly balls while standing on a jeep. RICHARD LULLOFF COLLECTION

He strapped metal hooks on his ankles and hung upside down from a bar. At first the blood rushing to his head prevented him from remaining that way more than a minute. Gradually he conditioned himself so he could stay suspended that way for up to 20 minutes. From that position he could drive pitches to the outfield or throw to the bases. He caught throws while lying supine on the ground. He held three baseballs in one hand, then in one motion tossed each one to a different fielder. He balanced upside down on a bat. He caught fungoes inside his shirt or his trousers. He drove a jeep around the outfield, steering with one hand while catching fly balls with the other. Using a slingshot, he launched baseballs out of the park from home plate or drove into the field and caught them in his vehicle. He caught baseballs in the unbuttoned fly of his pants. To top it off, he handled live snakes while doing many of his tricks.

The Brewers bought Price from the Columbus Red Birds on June 14, 1945. He didn't get into a game for more than a week, but he performed his show for Miller Brewery Night on June 25. On the final day of the regular season, he added a new wrinkle by playing one inning at each of the nine positions.

In the first round of the playoffs, Price played each game as the Milwaukee shortstop. He was the hero of Game Two, blasting a game-winning two-out triple in the 11th inning. Unfortunately, in Game Three he quickly turned to goat, committing four errors, two of them in the ninth inning of a 3–1 defeat. Jackie Price excelled at every phase of baseball except actually playing baseball.

He made one more appearance in Borchert Field. On August 30, 1946, Bill Veeck's Cleveland Indians played an exhibition game against Veeck's old club, the Milwaukee Brewers. Price played a few innings at shortstop. One other baseball clown also appeared in that game, also for the Indians. Veeck's favorite jester, the rubber-faced human pretzel Max Patkin, cavorted along the foul line during the contest and then pinch-hit in the ninth inning for Pat Seerey. Max failed to get a hit, but he garnered a ton of laughs. He also coached at third base for the Brewers in a game with the Saints on June 24, 1952.

~

No discussion of baseball clowns would be complete without mentioning the Ethiopian Clowns, also known at various times as the Cincinnati or Indianapolis Clowns. A team that combined

Negro Leagues talent with vaudeville-caliber physical comedy, the Clowns won the 1941 national semipro title while also amusing the crowds. On the evening of August 18, 1941, they brought their antics to Borchert Field. The Clowns adopted strange names for their players—Selassi, Wahoo, Tarzan, and Showboat, to name a few—and they won over their audiences with skillful shenanigans that earned them a reputation as "the Harlem Globetrotters of baseball." They played a pregame "shadowball" inning in which no ball was used, just slow-motion pantomime of a pretend ballgame by all nine men. They also played pepper, a rapid-fire exchange of the baseball that approximated the Globetrotters' sleight of hand with a basketball.

On June 23, 1942, the Clowns returned to Borchert. This time their catcher, Lloyd Bassett (also known as Pepper), caught one full inning while seated in a rocking chair behind home plate. When they came back on July 16, 1943, they brought along Richard King, called King Tut, a gangling funnyman wearing an enormous fielder's glove. Tut had a gift for creating uproarious laughter in a way that might be compared with Max Patkin. And on September 2, 1947, their star attraction was basketball genius Goose Tatum, who developed many of his hardcourt routines on the baseball diamond. So big an attraction was Tatum that the Clowns had a standing guarantee: if for any reason Goose Tatum did not show up and perform his comedy act, spectators could receive a full refund. He showed up.

7

Iron Man

In baseball an "iron man" is a ballplayer with exceptional endurance. Lou Gehrig became the "Iron Horse" because he never missed a game for almost 14 years. Most appropriately, the nickname has also been applied to Joe "Iron Man" McGinnity, a New York Giants pitcher at the dawn of the 20th century. The right-handed Irishman actually acquired his famous moniker long before reaching the major leagues, back when he worked in a foundry. In August 1903 he hurled both ends of a doubleheader on three separate occasions, winning all six games and providing a baseball context for his colorful appellation that he carried all the way to the Hall of Fame.

The Milwaukee Brewers in 1909 had their own version of an iron man hurler. His parents named him Ulysses Simpson Grant McGlynn in honor of the famous Civil War general. McGlynn's teammates and fans simply knew him as Stoney, a tribute to his endurance on the mound. That season he established an American Association record for innings pitched, 446 in 64 games. His exaggerated sidearm motion, bordering on an underhand delivery, allowed him to pitch frequently, and he did so without apparent strain. He claimed that he never suffered a sore arm. His secret, he explained, was that after each appearance he would put

BREWER SLAB STAR WHO WON TWO GAMES IN AN AFTERNOON

Stoney McGlynn.

Stoney McGlynn PUBLIC DOMAIN

his pitching arm and shoulder under a hot shower, almost to the point of scalding his skin.

Before he became a Brewer, Stoney pitched three seasons in the National League for the St. Louis Cardinals, 1906–1908. On September 29, 1906, and again on July 31, 1907, Stoney went head-to-head with Joe McGinnity in battles of famed iron men.

In each instance the future Hall of Fame enshrinee was the victor, but Stoney's teammates were at least partially to blame, committing three errors in both of the games. The 1907 campaign was by far Stoney's most notable in the big leagues. Pitching for a terrible St. Louis club, worst in the league, he finished with a dismal 14–25 record, this despite the fact that he allowed fewer than three runs per nine innings. He led the National League in starts, complete games, and innings pitched, 42 more than the great McGinnity. In addition, Stoney cemented his reputation by hurling both games of a doubleheader in Cincinnati on June 3 and twice pitching complete games on consecutive days in August.

In spring of 1909 Stoney could not come to terms with Cardinals management. Instead Milwaukee manager John McCloskey signed him for the Brewers. Milwaukee had never come close to a pennant in the American Association, but with McGlynn leading the way, the Brewers stayed in contention throughout the season. In Stoney's April 16 debut in Athletic Park, he worked nine strong innings against the St. Paul Saints in a 1–1 tie ended by rain.

May 2 found the Brewers at home once more against the Saints, with McGlynn back on the mound. A crowd of more than 5,000 enthusiastic rooters came out to see Milwaukee's pitching sensation, and he did not disappoint. He gave up just four harmless singles in winning his fourth straight start and his third consecutive shutout, along with several successful relief appearances in between. The game was twice threatened by heavy bursts of snow that were loudly cheered by the spectators. The local bugs didn't mind a little wintry weather—their heroes were in first place, and the Stone-Armed Kid was invincible.

While in Kansas City in late May, the Brewers acquired a lucky charm they thought might propel them to the pennant. It was a 14-year-old "little colored lad," as the *Milwaukee Journal* described him, whom the ballplayers picked up off the street. They named him Snowball and made him their official mascot. It should be noted that baseball players have always been among the most superstitious creatures on the planet. In 1909 they believed in the power of certain people—especially prized were young African American boys, cross-eyed children, and teenaged humpbacks like Louis Van Zelst of Connie Mack's A's—to bring them good luck. Nevertheless, the fact that they could pick up a child and travel with him to far-flung cities seems, even in that period of history, bizarre.

The Brewers had a precedent for Snowball. In 1896, when they were part of the Western League, the team had co-opted a young "colored" boy, also in Kansas City, and made him their mascot. Manager Larry Twitchell's club promptly lost 11 games in a row and dumped their lucky charm.

In 1909 Snowball also failed to produce the desired results. Milwaukee won just one game under his influence. On June 12 as they were leaving Indianapolis for Louisville, the ballplayers took up a collection, bought Snowball a train ticket, and gave him his unconditional release. In fairness to the unfortunate lad, it should be reported that Stoney had injured his leg and missed several starts during Snowball's brief tenure. Stoney remained out of the lineup until June 30. In Athletic Park on that day he fired a one-hit shutout, the only blemish being a bloop single by rival pitcher John Halla.

On July 21 McGlynn made perhaps his finest effort of the season. He started and won both games of a doubleheader with the Louisville Colonels. In the first game, leading 9–1 after seven innings, Stoney retired for a quick shower while southpaw Jimmy Wacker finished up on his behalf. Stoney then returned and hurled the complete second game, finally winning, 3–2, in 10 innings, putting the Brewers just half a game out of first place.

In mid-September Milwaukee was still running neck and neck with Louisville in the American Association race. McGlynn let his manager know that he would be available every day if called upon. On September 13 he pitched 11 innings against Louisville without allowing a run. Darkness ended the affair in a scoreless tie. Two days later Stoney labored through both ends of a doubleheader, winning the first, 5–2, but losing the nightcap, 1–0, in a six-inning contest truncated by darkness. On September 16 he started his third game in two days. However, in the first inning his spikes caught on the pitching rubber and he sustained a painful injury that forced him to leave after the third out. Manager McClosky feared that Stoney's season was over, but he surprised everyone and returned after two days of recuperation to shut out Indianapolis, 1–0, his 13th shutout of the season.

A rash of injuries handicapped the Brewers at season's end. They finished second, two games behind the Colonels. Milwaukee fans would have to wait four more years before enjoying a pennant, by which time Stoney had retired and taken a job as a lifeguard on Manitowoc's public beach. He continued to play sandlot ball, pitching for the final time in 1931 in the Manitowoc County League. He was 65 years old. He made his last return to Borchert Field on August 25, 1938, to help celebrate the MVP season of ace right-hander Whitlow Wyatt. Three years later Stoney died at his home in Manitowoc.

8

Wordsmith

In the earliest days of the 20th century, John and Lelah Vaughan's teenaged son Manning liked to join other boys in peeking through knotholes in the wooden fence at the Lloyd Street Grounds to watch baseball games. During the summer before Vaughan's senior year at South Division High School, the park was demolished. By that time he had already begun writing high school sports articles for the *Milwaukee Sentinel*.

After graduating in June of 1905, Vaughan continued to work for the newspaper's sports department. In 1907 sports editor Tom Chivington resigned to become president of the American Association. Although not yet old enough to vote, Vaughan succeeded Chivington and embarked on one of the most notable careers in the annals of Milwaukee sports journalism. He worked for the Sentinel until 1924, when he switched over to the rival *Milwaukee Journal*.

Vaughan covered a variety of athletic endeavors—boxing, college football, wrestling—but his real love was baseball. In a quarter century of chronicling America's pastime, he crafted accounts of more than 4,000 ballgames. Besides World Series and the occasional major league tilt, he traveled with the Brewers to their road games, including an annual trip to their spring training facility in Hot Springs, Arkansas. Nearly half of the games he saw, though, were Milwaukee's league games in Athletic Park, later Borchert Field. Vaughan generally watched from the press coop atop the wooden grandstand, and his face was a familiar sight to ballpark visitors.

Among all those thousands of innings, Vaughan felt privileged to witness many outstanding performances. He was on hand for eight no-hitters, including five thrown by Milwaukee hurlers and one tossed by the great Smoky Joe Wood. On July 16, 1913, he endured a 19-inning struggle in Athletic Park that lasted nearly four hours. Jack Ferry of the Columbus Senators pitched the complete game, scattering 18 base hits and striking out two while the Brewers employed four different moundsmen in gaining a 6–5 victory. Ferry's 18-hit job stood in stark contrast to the previous afternoon's effort by former Chicago Cubs star Leonard "King" Cole, who allowed Milwaukee no hits in nine innings. Actually, 1913 was one of Vaughan's favorite years of covering baseball. The Brewers won their first American Association pennant. He said that team was one of the best minor league clubs ever.

Vaughan's skill as a journalist lay not in making an interesting game sound appealing but in creating an entertaining account of a dull or routine contest. He harbored strong opinions about how baseball should be conducted and played. He was well known for his fanciful wit and his ability to criticize without seeming unduly harsh or negative. Occasionally, however, his self-restraint failed.

Writing about a game in Athletic Park on August 19, 1911, Vaughan pulled no punches. He blasted the "nauseating umpiring by Bumpire Hayes, who spoiled every chance Milwaukee had of winning by his atrocious work back of the log." He went on to say "his putrid work in Milwaukee looks like nothing but downright cussedness." He accused Hayes of boasting that he would "get the goats of several Milwaukee players." Vaughan insisted he did "not believe in panning umpires, but Hayes' work bears an investigation by the health authorities."

Vaughan was renowned for his humor and colorful use of language. He described a ninth-inning base hit that broke up a no-hitter: "A white pill flashed its way to right field—a perfect hit, all wool and a yard wide—and with it went Glenn Liebhardt's prayer for the distinction that goes with a no hit game."

On August 18, 1911, Brewers first baseman Tom Jones was beaned in a game with the Minneapolis Millers. "The impact was frightful," Vaughan wrote, "and the sound could be heard all over the park. For a moment it was feared that the blow had proved fatal." This near-tragic moment allowed no levity, but in subsequent sentences Vaughan returned to form. He explained the vicious rivalry between the two teams and stated that before the end of the fifth inning, five players "had been placed hors du combat [*sic*]." Then he added, "From here to the finish the only excitement was furnished by the doctors, the human ambulances, and the farcical umpiring of Bumpire Hayes."

Like other writers, Vaughan tried to avoid repetition by using synonyms or alternate phrases. Describing Brewers pitcher Joe Hovlik and his arsenal of spitballs (legal at the time), Vaughan penned these lines: "Hovlik turned loose a great array of spitters," although "seven hits were collected off the damp shoots." In another game he called Hovlik "the Iowa sprinkling cart" and said that he "put on the damp goods in copious gobs."

Perhaps more than anything else, Vaughan loved to assign nicknames to teams, players, and even owners. The 1912 Brewers manager was future Hall of Famer Hugh Duffy. Vaughan dubbed Duffy's club the "Duffydils." The Athletic Park announcer who shouted introductions through a megaphone was Charley Fichtner, but thanks to Vaughan he became "Silver Lips." Happy Felsch (whose name the *Sentinel* customarily misspelled that season by omitting the *s*), a native of Milwaukee's heavily Germanic north side, was referred to as "the pride of the wooden shoe country." Lou Gehrig became "the crown prince of the Slug dynasty."

Similarly, Milwaukee southsider Al Simmons was given the moniker "the Duke of Mitchell Street." And Brewers owner Otto Borchert was "the Dutchman" or, because he frequently sported a swallowtail tuxedo, cut short in front with two tails behind, "Swallowtail Otto." Receiving a nickname from Manning Vaughan was considered a badge of honor.

In the days before political correctness, seemingly every journalist employed ethnic stereotypes. Vaughan was no exception, and today, some of his phrases would be considered slurs. His nickname for first baseman Joe Hauser borrowed the German pronoun *unser*, meaning "our," and appended it to Milwaukee's dialectical version of Joe to create "unser Choe from the wooden shoe district." The "Unser Choe" part stuck to him for life.

One other of Vaughan's Deutschisms became a permanent part of Borchert Field lore. Any home run slammed out of the park and across the street was said to land in Mrs. Hasenpfeffer's front yard or porch. That terminology was adopted by scribes and broadcasters and utilized proudly long after Vaughan had left the scene.

Sometimes the verbally playful Vaughan would meld his daily baseball report with current events. On June 20, 1912, the biggest news in the country concerned Teddy Roosevelt, William Howard Taft, and Fighting Bob La Follette wrangling for the presidential nomination at the Republican National Convention in Chicago. Vaughan's Milwaukee Brewers story that afternoon featured Minneapolis pitcher Rube Waddell, a notorious alcoholic. Vaughan referred to him as "the presidential candidate of the Prohibition ticket." In the same paragraph, Vaughan related that Milwaukee hurler John Nicholson, "the famous son of Scandinavia, did not look his best and the opposition seated a delegate in the opening inning."

As much as any baseball writer, Vaughan was conversant with and comfortable employing the colorful jargon of the national

Presidential candidate Al Smith signs his name at the Milwaukee Press Club in 1928. To his left, in the dark-rimmed glasses, is Press Club president Manning Vaughan. PHOTOGRAPH COURTESY OF THE MILWAUKEE COUNTY HISTORICAL SOCIETY

pastime. His language may sound overbaked today, but readers in those days before mass media relished it. Describing a doubleheader sweep of the Kansas City Blues on Labor Day 1913, he wrote: "Johnny Hughes and John Beall ... labored like true sons of toil Monday and thanks to a pair of knockout wallops delivered by this duo, the charging Brewers leaped ahead another peg in the mad chase for the A.A. muslin. In the morning combat Beall delivered a home run that cooked the goose, while a Hughes double, worth its weight in gold, broke the hearts of the Kawmen in the second."

On another occasion Vaughan painted a picture of a home run by the American Association's leading slugger of the 1911 season: "one cyclonic lick from the wagon tongue of the demon fence buster, Mr. Gavvy Cravath, spilled the beans."

On April 7, 1932, Vaughan died as a result of a skull fracture suffered in a fall in his hotel room in Memphis. He was just 45 years old.

On January 19, 1954, at Milwaukee's first Diamond Dinner following the franchise shift of the Braves from Boston, Eddie Mathews received the award as the club's Most Valuable Player of 1953, presented by the Milwaukee chapter of the Baseball Writers' Association of America. It was named the Manning Vaughan Award.

9

Georgia Peach

Player-manager Pep Clark's 1914 Milwaukee Brewers repeated as champions of the American Association. That accomplishment earned them the right to compete in a postseason series with the Birmingham Barons of the Southern Association, the winners to receive bragging rights as baseball's minor league champions of the world.

One day before the visitors from Alabama reached Milwaukee, however, the Brewers played host to a more illustrious ball club. The Detroit Tigers of the American League spent part of their October 2 travel day performing in Athletic Park. The Tigers had two games at home with the Cleveland Indians left on their schedule, but an exhibition game in Milwaukee brought in more money than a home game and compensated well for the inconvenience.

The Tigers' manic manager, Hughie Jennings, was worth the price of admission all on his own. Milwaukee fans had seen Jennings before, at the end of September 1891. He was the shortstop of the Louisville Colonels when they visited Athletic Park during the Brewers' brief experience as a major league club in the American Association. Later he became the shortstop on the great Baltimore Orioles teams of the mid-1890s. Jennings approached the game with energy and finesse. One year he batted .401 with his all-out, take-one-for-the-team attitude. On the diamond the man was fearless, ever willing to stand in front of a 90-mile-an-hour fastball if it would put him on base. In the years 1894 through 1898 he was hit by a pitch 202 times. Well over a century later he still holds the major league records for most times hit by a pitch both in a single game and in a career.

He paid a price. Concussions were little known and scarcely understood in the 19th century, but he no doubt suffered far more of them than any person should. In 1897 Jennings was beaned in the third inning by Amos Rusie, whose pitch velocity had earned him the nickname the Hoosier Thunderbolt. The ball struck Jennings near his temple and rendered him briefly unconscious. After he revived, he stayed in the game, but he collapsed shortly afterward. He remained hospitalized and comatose for four days, yet he returned to baseball and continued to crowd the plate for another five seasons. Several years after the Rusie incident, Jennings unknowingly dived into an empty swimming pool. In 1911 he suffered a skull fracture and concussion in a near-fatal car wreck. Fans who watched Jennings in the third-base coaching box in Athletic Park were seeing a medical miracle, a walking testament to the resilience of the human cranium.

What the Milwaukee fans witnessed along the baseline was part mime, part sound-effects machine, and 100 percent entertainment. Jennings produced a perpetual stream of hoots, shouts, and piercing two-fingered whistles. He carried on a constant conversation with the people in the stands. His trademark "Ee-yah!" echoed throughout the ballpark. His other signature move involved waving both arms while repeatedly raising his right knee, giving the appearance of a whooping crane attempting flight. He also plucked handfuls of grass, over and over, until the area surrounding the coach's box had been entirely defoliated. Describing Jennings as colorful far understates his behavior. He was elected to the Hall of Fame in 1945, long after his death at age 58.

⌒

Jennings had numerous fine ballplayers that he penciled into the lineup in Athletic Park that afternoon, including future Hall of Fame outfielder Wahoo Sam Crawford. Those men, however, played no role in attracting a large and boisterous crowd to Milwaukee's splintery ballpark on a weekday afternoon in early autumn. The healthy turnout can be explained in two words: Ty Cobb.

Ty Cobb and Shoeless Joe Jackson (shown here with footwear on) were the two leading hitters in the American League in 1913. PUBLIC DOMAIN

Everyone in the ballpark knew about Cobb and wanted to see him in person. Folks followed Cobb's exploits through the newspapers and were keenly aware of his reputation as the greatest ballplayer in the country. He came to Milwaukee batting .368 and was two days away from earning his eighth consecutive batting title. Not too many years previous he had led his Detroit club to three straight American League pennants.

But what really drew people to see Cobb with their own eyes was his reputation of being a fury in spikes, a relentless, no-holds-barred competitor who would do anything to win. His teammates reportedly hated him. His opponents feared him. No one, however, questioned Cobb's skills on the diamond. For example, on July 12, 1911, he had stolen second, third, and home on three consecutive pitches.

Cobb often got his name in the newspaper, in the sports pages or otherwise. His most notorious incident occurred just over two years before he visited Milwaukee. It had stayed in the news for two weeks, so Beertown readers knew the whole story.

On May 15, 1912, the Tigers were playing in New York's Hilltop Park. A heckler named Claude Lueker was seated with friends behind third base. Lueker had a history of yelling insults at Cobb. Some of these reportedly made reference to the fact that Cobb's mother had shot and killed Cobb's beloved father during Cobb's rookie season with the Tigers. On this occasion the loud-mouthed Cobb-hater is believed to have shouted racial slurs and disparaged Cobb's mother as an unfaithful wife.

By the sixth inning Cobb had heard enough. Enraged, he leaped over the railing, entered the grandstand, and proceeded to beat the heckler viciously about the head and neck. As it turned out, the foul-mouthed Lueker had been the victim of an industrial accident that cost him all of one hand and three fingers of the other. Lueker's disability made Cobb appear to be not the victim of verbal abuse but a heartless monster. League president

Ban Johnson, who happened to witness the attack, suspended Cobb indefinitely.

Cobb's teammates generally despised him, but in this matter they supported him. They refused to take the field the next day, vowing not to return until Cobb did. This marked Major League Baseball's first labor action. Ultimately Johnson reduced the indefinite suspension to 10 days and a $50 fine, so the ballplayers returned to their jobs. In the one game that the players had boycotted, students from St. Joseph's college, semipro players, and two Detroit coaches filled all nine positions in a farcical 24–2 loss to Connie Mack's Philadelphia A's in Shibe Park.

Predictably, in the Athletic Park exhibition, Cobb was not only the main attraction but also the star of the show. The Georgia Peach struck out in the first inning but ripped four straight hits after that. He showed none of his customary competitive fire, instead bantering good-naturedly with fans seated near the diamond. He did show his vaunted foot speed, though. In the third inning he lined a gapper and legged out a stand-up triple. When Brewers shortstop Joe Berg casually received the throw from the outfield and momentarily turned his head, Cobb, who had stopped at third, dashed toward the plate. The surprised shortstop fired the ball home, but his throw was off target and Cobb scored.

Cobb's third base hit of the game was a routine single that one-hopped to Happy Felsch in left field. The Tigers center fielder took off at the crack of the bat, as he always did, and never slowed down. He slid feetfirst into second but was tagged out on a close play. Had this been an American League contest, two things would have been different. Ty's spikes would have been aimed higher, and the umpire's decision would have drawn a strong argument. This being an exhibition, Cobb trotted calmly to the dugout.

For the record, the Tigers defeated the Brewers, 6–5. Most likely the 6,000 spectators either did not notice or soon forgot. None of them ever forgot the day they saw Ty Cobb in Athletic Park.

10

A Touch of Ginger

On Wednesday night, November 28, 1951, one of the most illustrious and diverse groups of athletic celebrities ever assembled in one place gathered inside the new Milwaukee Arena. The event was the inaugural ceremony of the Wisconsin Athletic Hall of Fame, attended by 800 paying dinner guests and, among many others, the Green Bay Packers' Lumberjack Band. The stars presented for induction that evening, 14 in all including four deceased, were legends.

Gridiron standouts Pat O'Dea (the Kicking Kangaroo), Don Hutson, Ernie Nevers, Clarke Hinkle, and Bob Zuppke greeted the audience. Olympic sprinter Ralph Metcalfe had his plaque unveiled by no less a runner than Jesse Owens. Wrestler Ed "Strangler" Lewis was introduced by fellow grappler Verne Gagne. Eighty-eight-year-old Connie Mack made the journey to Milwaukee to pay tribute to Al Simmons, called by Mack "my greatest player."

The most poignant moment of the evening, though, was the presentation of wheelchair-bound Clarence "Ginger" Beaumont. He had arrived by ambulance from his home in Rochester, Wisconsin, 30 miles southwest of Milwaukee. During the previous few years he had twice suffered debilitating strokes that restricted his movement. Beaumont had been the first batter in the first

Ginger Beaumont (seated) examines a photograph at his 1951 induction to
the Wisconsin Athletic Hall of Fame. The first three standing gentlemen from
the left are Cy Young, Connie Mack, and Deacon Phillippe. BURLINGTON
HISTORICAL SOCIETY

World Series game, back in 1903. On hand to remove the shroud
from his plaque were the opposing pitchers from that historic initial interleague battle, Beaumont's Pittsburgh teammate Deacon
Phillippe and Red Sox ace Cy Young.

Beaumont had begun his major league career with the Pirates
in 1899. From 1900 through 1906 he was a teammate of the immortal Honus Wagner. Wagner hit over .300 for 15 straight years
and won eight NL batting titles, but in 1902 it was Beaumont who
led not only the Pittsburgh club but also the National League,
hitting .357. For his accomplishment he received a free pair of
shoes. Ginger also led the league in base hits four times, including
a record three consecutive seasons.

By 1907 Beaumont's knees were used up and his foot speed
had fled. The Pirates traded him to the Boston Beaneaters (soon

to become Doves). Following three seasons in the Hub, he finished his big-league career with the pennant-winning Chicago Cubs of Tinker to Evers to Chance.

Born in 1876, the son of a butcher, Beaumont got his start in baseball playing on amateur and semipro teams around Wisconsin: Rochester, East Troy, Waupun. While at Waupun he was spotted by Tom Andrews, a Milwaukee sportswriter and sometime boxing promoter. Andrews in turn told his friend Connie Mack, then managing the Milwaukee Brewers in the Western League, about the speedy young man. Mack auditioned Beaumont in a pair of exhibition games on August 8 and 9, 1898, against the Chicago Unions, an itinerant black team that the *Milwaukee Journal* called "the colored champions of Chicago." The young man performed well, and beginning on August 23 and for the remaining four weeks of the season, Ginger was the Milwaukee left fielder.

With the Brewers, success arrived at once. In his first game in the Lloyd Street Grounds, Beaumont walked twice, sacrificed, singled, homered, and stole second base. One week after his Western League debut the local paper wrote, "The playing of Beaumont is surpassing anything that Mack had anticipated. He does something brilliant each day." The next afternoon he slammed a single and a three-run home run, both in the first inning. Two days later he was again the star of the show with three singles and a double besides being hit by a pitch. His heroics helped the Brewers slip into first place.

Not everyone was pleased with Beaumont's everyday excellence. His parents, Thomas and Mary, were God-fearing people who believed baseball on the Lord's Day was blasphemy. To preserve tranquility in the family, Ginger assumed the name of a nonplaying teammate each Sunday. In his first three Sabbath appearances he borrowed the identity of George Nicol; the next time it was William "Farmer" Weaver. Of course Ginger's folks never attended a Sunday game, and if they read a box score from one, their boy's name was absent. The Almighty gave no sign of disapproval. Ginger batted .348 on Sundays. Overall in his four weeks as a Milwaukee Brewer, he batted .361 and earned a place in the Pittsburgh Pirates lineup for 1899.

Beaumont put the finishing touch on his 12-season career in the majors by pinch-hitting three times in the 1910 World Series for the losing Chicago Cubs. In his final appearance he batted for hurler Ed Reulbach, drew a base on balls, and scored on a hit by Frank Schulte. After the Series the Cubs released Beaumont.

Down but not out, Beaumont accepted an invitation to join the 1911 St. Paul Saints in the American Association in late June. He played center field and had just a so-so year at the plate. On July 23, his 35th birthday, he hit a game-tying ninth-inning home run against Toledo in a contest ultimately called on account of darkness. On September 10 in St. Paul's Lexington Park, he belted his final home run as a professional, a grand slam against the Brewers in a 6–3 victory.

Perhaps fittingly, Beaumont ended his professional baseball career in the city where it began—Milwaukee. With the Saints and Brewers running neck and neck in the battle for the first division (fourth place), the teams faced off in a pair of double-headers in Athletic Park on September 30 and October 1, the last weekend of the season. The clubs split the first twin bill, with Milwaukee winning the first game, 7–2, then losing the second, 2–0. The Brewers really had only two reliable hurlers, who between them had thrown nearly 600 innings since Opening Day. One of these aces, Tom Dougherty, worked both games on Saturday, not an unusual feat in that era but nonetheless a Herculean effort.

In Dougherty's 2–0 defeat, the home crowd thought the Brewers were victims of inept umpiring. They were not alone in that belief. In the sixth inning Milwaukee had runners on second and third with two out. Brewers shortstop Phil Lewis hit a line drive up the middle. Second baseman Barry McCormick knocked it down and threw to first. In a close play, base umpire Jerry Eddinger called Lewis out to end the inning. Both Lewis and his manager, Jimmy Barrett, confronted the man in blue, berating him vehemently. Then Lewis retrieved his glove and trotted to his position.

Eddinger, however, ordered Lewis off the diamond. Instead the incensed infielder raced toward the umpire and pummeled him with a series of blows before other players could intervene. Finally a half-dozen police officers appeared on the scene and escorted the assailant to the clubhouse. A sports reporter covering the game described it as "the worst thing ever pulled off on the local diamond," but Lewis was back in the lineup the next afternoon. Some people speculated that Lewis would face a suspension, perhaps for life, but in fact he played five more years with the Brewers.

The even split meant that Milwaukee needed two victories on Sunday to overtake Beaumont's Saints. To accomplish that, Manager Barrett called on his other workhorse, Stoney McGlynn. What ensued, though, was by one newspaper account "the most disgraceful piece of work that has been seen at the local ball orchard" and "an insult to the great national game."

Several times the St. Paul players created excuses to stall and delay the game. Charley Jones, whose foul nicked his leg, lay prostrate in the dirt for 10 minutes while his teammates hovered around him solicitously. Later a Saints batter, after being called out on strikes, sprawled on top of home plate and lay there howling in protest for many minutes. Eventually Mr. Fox, the home-plate umpire, had to resort to calling strikes when the batter's box was empty because the Saints players simply refused to stand in and hit.

Milwaukee won the battle, 4–3, but St. Paul won the war. As the slowdown continued into the second game, darkness overtook the combatants, and the game was called in the fourth inning. The Saints thereby edged the Brewers by a percentage point and finished in the first division. Beaumont contributed two bases on balls in his last game. Then he returned home to Rochester to pursue a life of farming.

11

Eight Men In

The darkest chapter in the annals of professional baseball has to be the 1919 World Series. When Arnold Rothstein and his underworld associates "fixed" the Fall Classic in the first year following the War to End All Wars, it cast a pall over the integrity of the national pastime. Iron-fisted federal judge Kenesaw Mountain Landis was appointed baseball's first commissioner with a mandate to remove the stain on the sport's good name. To do it, he banished eight members of the Chicago White Sox for life. Those "eight men out," as author Eliot Asinof called them, acquired the nickname "Black Sox."

The ringleader of the sellout was Charles "Chick" Gandil, a big, rugged, nasty individual who had contact with the gamblers and recruited seven teammates to join the conspiracy. Among the selected plotters was a former Brewers hero, Milwaukee native Oscar "Happy" Felsch. Hap, as he was often called, played on the champion Brewers clubs in 1913 and 1914, then made the jump to the White Sox the next year.

Even after his lifetime ban, Felsch remained popular in Beer City. On May 21, 1933, starting Hap's second season in Milwaukee's sandlot Triple A League, he and his Bucher Brews attracted 15,000 spectators to the Auer Avenue diamond on the north side to watch them defeat the Ziemer Sausage team. The huge crowd ringed the outfield and necessitated ground rules. In four at-bats Felsch slammed four hits, including three doubles. Two of them soared above and beyond the fans in the field and would have been home runs had the ground rules not been in effect.

Easily the most illustrious, and therefore the most tragic, of the Sox fixers was illiterate outfielder Shoeless Joe Jackson. As a rookie with the Cleveland Indians in 1911 Jackson had batted .408 (second behind Ty Cobb). He ended his career, prematurely of course, with the third-highest career average, behind only Cobb and Rogers Hornsby. So great a hitter was Shoeless Joe that Babe Ruth modeled his own batting technique after Jackson's.

Two years before the shameful Black Sox scandal, on September 12, 1917, Comiskey's club gave Milwaukee fans a sort of preview of coming attractions by playing an exhibition game in Athletic Park. Surprisingly, their opponents were not the Brewers. The Brewers were playing a doubleheader that afternoon in Columbus, Ohio, where they were swept by the American Association Senators. In the nightcap Milwaukee was defeated by 41-year-old Mordecai "Three Finger" Brown, the digitally challenged future Hall of Fame pitcher who had completed his big-league career but, like a lot of old ballplayers, didn't know how to quit.

The White Sox arrived in Milwaukee having most recently been awarded a forfeit in a game in Cleveland. With the score tied, 3–3, in the 10th inning, a Cleveland runner was called out on a close play at third. The Indians argued for 10 minutes to no avail. After they failed to score and the visitors came to bat (yes, the Indians chose to bat first), some Indians players threw their gloves in the air or rolled on the ground to demonstrate their displeasure. Dauntless Dave Danforth fanned, and after Cleveland's catcher deliberately threw the ball into center field, umpire Brick Owens got tired of the monkey business and declared a forfeit.

Chicago's opponent in the exhibition game, described as the Milwaukee All-Stars, comprised a motley collection of sandlot players and former minor leaguers. Starting hurler Buster Braun had pitched for the Brewers in their championship years of 1913 and 1914. Catcher Eddie Stumpf had been a Brewer a year earlier. The rest were wannabes and never-wases.

The White Sox, meanwhile, were loaded, the best ball club in baseball. They led the American League standings by seven and a half games. They boasted the most potent lineup and lowest team earned run average in either league, on their way to 100 wins.

The host All-Stars elected to bat first. Chicago's Claude "Lefty" Williams, who would become one of the eight exiled Sox, held them scoreless in the opening frame. The Chicagoans wasted no time, jumping on Buster Braun for a walk, a hit by future Hall of Fame second baseman Eddie Collins, a single by Joe Jackson, and a double by Hap Felsch to pull the Sox up, 3–0. Milwaukee got one back, but in the bottom of the second Collins blasted a three-run homer onto Seventh Street to make it 6–1.

The contest was never really in doubt, but in the fourth inning the visitors removed any pretense with an explosion of eight base hits, scoring six runs to make it a 12–1 game. Milwaukee's only highlight came in the top of the seventh. Left fielder Connie Reik smashed a three-run homer over Eighth Street, probably the peak moment of his entirely sandlot career, off reliever Dave Danforth.

Six of the eight Sox that Judge Landis would ultimately expel played in the game. In addition to starting hurler Lefty Williams, Shoeless Joe contributed a pair of triples and a single. Third sacker Fred McMullin got two hits and scored twice. Happy Felsch hit safely three times, shortstop Swede Risberg contributed two hits, and Chick Gandil chipped in a single.

The only two banned-for-life Black Sox missing from the game were bow-legged infielder Buck Weaver and mound ace Eddie Cicotte. Neither, however, was a total stranger to Milwaukee's ballpark. On October 1, 1914, Weaver and the White Sox had beaten the Brewers, 5–2, in an Athletic Park exhibition. Cicotte, as

After Hap Felsch was banished from Organized Baseball, he returned to his native Milwaukee and kept a tavern. When not at the bar, he could be found barnstorming through the state and playing ball in local recreational leagues.

a member of the Indianapolis Indians on May 6, 1906, had pitched a complete game against Joe Cantillon's Brewers in Athletic Park, losing to Milwaukee, 4–2.

Despite the lopsided score (15–6), the 1917 White Sox exhibition game was a great success. More than 4,000 Milwaukee fans witnessed the finest baseball aggregation of the day. They welcomed back two favorites, native son Happy Felsch (who received a bouquet of flowers the first time he stepped to the plate) and former Brewers catcher and future Hall of Famer Ray "Cracker" Schalk. Local scribe Manning Vaughan declared with tongue in cheek that the White Sox earned "the semi-pro championship of Milwaukee."

This was not, however, the final appearance in Athletic Park for the notorious Black Sox. On April 10 and 11, 1920, six months after the fraudulent World Series of 1919, the White Sox played a pair of exhibition games against the Milwaukee Brewers. The Sox took the first game, 6–2, behind Lefty Williams. The next afternoon the Brewers triumphed, 1–0, in 10 innings, with Buzz McWeeney holding the visitors scoreless. Local hero Joe "Unser Choe" Hauser tallied the game's only run.

By that time the White Sox's suspected fixers were under investigation but had not yet been tried or banished. Of the eight men ultimately exiled by Commissioner Landis, only two were absent from the 1920 Milwaukee contests. One was reserve infielder Fred McMullin, who had been indicted but was not charged or included in the trial. The other was Chick Gandil, the organizer of the Series sellout. He had demanded a $10,000 contract from Charles Comiskey. The tightfisted owner naturally refused, so Gandil, flush with cash after selling the World Series, retired from baseball.

12

Loose Cannon

Ray Cannon never knew his parents, who died when Ray was six months old. He spent his young days in orphanages in Green Bay. It seems likely that his absence of family helped shape his adult life. He always sided with the underdog, and he would take on anybody to protect the downtrodden.

Ray attended Marquette University Law School, waiting tables in local restaurants to defray his educational expenses. He also worked as an assistant to prominent Milwaukee attorney Henry Killilea, one of the five founders of the American League. Eventually Ray became as well known as Killilea, first as a lawyer, then as a three-term congressman (1933–1939) from Milwaukee's Fourth District. In the House of Representatives, Ray demonstrated his willingness to challenge the entrenched power structure in Washington. In 1937 he proposed a constitutional amendment that, if passed, would give the House equal rights with the Senate in confirming presidential nominations. Later he campaigned twice, both times unsuccessfully, for the Democratic Party's nomination for Wisconsin governor. Ray was an indefatigable proponent of progressive political causes and a trial lawyer of wide renown. His true passion, though, was baseball.

A right-handed pitcher, Ray played semipro ball for 15 years but was good enough to compete against the professionals. On the opening day of the 1914 sandlot season, despite a sore arm, Ray was on the mound for the Milwaukee Leaders, a City League team named for the cigar manufacturer that sponsored them. At the time, however, he was the property of the Cleveland team in the American Association. On March 3, 1918, he was the starting hurler for the Philadelphia Phillies in a spring training exhibition against the Boston Braves. In 1919 he traveled south to Evansville, Indiana, with the American Association Milwaukee Brewers and worked out with them through spring training. Whether or not he harbored major league aspirations, Ray could pitch semipro ball in Milwaukee and still carry on his law practice.

Cannon occasionally pitched sandlot ball in Athletic Park. In addition, on August 3, 1918, he took part in a charity game for war relief. He pitched for an aggregation made up mostly of Milwaukee aldermen, using the alias William Coleman. Their opponents were volunteers from the Navy Recruiting Station. The quality of the baseball was about what might be expected, but a few dollars were raised for a good cause.

On the last day of August 1919, Cannon was president of the Milwaukee Amateur Baseball Commission. He and three other baseball leaders, including Henry Killilea, presided over Amateur Day in Athletic Park. Their task was to select the best sandlot player in Milwaukee from among the top ballplayers nominated by their teams and chosen from previous tryouts. The man Cannon and his cohorts picked would have the opportunity to travel with the Brewers on their final road trip of the season, participate in pregame warm-ups and practices, and maybe impress owner/manager Clarence "Pants" Rowland and earn a future spot on the team.

Cannon's committee deemed 19-year-old catcher Fred Klevenow of the Hugin Bakers to be number one. They liked his powerful arm and his batting stroke, although he struggled to hit the curve ball. When the Brewers boarded the train for Toledo,

Klevenow was with them. The young man probably enjoyed the thrill of a lifetime, but alas, his field trip with the professionals did not catapult him to stardom. It took him seven years before he finally made it into Organized Baseball, playing one season for the Waterloo Hawks in the Class D Mississippi Valley League before returning to the sandlots.

Cannon's law practice continued to grow. Among his clients was a promising heavyweight boxer named William Harrison Dempsey, better known as Jack. The young pugilist had gotten into the fight game as a teenager by taking on all comers in the saloons of Colorado mining towns, boxing under the name Kid Blackie. Cannon drew up the contract for Jack's title bout with Jess Willard on July 4, 1919. Cannon, Otto Borchert, and Henry Killilea traveled to Toledo to watch the hard-punching Dempsey inflict a savage beating on the much-larger defending world champ, knocking him down seven times in just the opening round.

Most of the time, though, Cannon's clients were not the aggressors. Three months after Dempsey demolished Willard, the Chicago White Sox took a dive in the World Series. After an investigation, the eight White Sox players stood trial in the summer of 1921, and all of them were found not guilty. Nevertheless, Commissioner Landis disregarded the verdict and suspended the eight ballplayers for life. One of the eight was a former sandlot teammate of Ray Cannon's, Oscar "Happy" Felsch. Hap hired Ray to represent him in trying to get his job back, claiming Charles Comiskey had been part of a conspiracy to force him out of baseball. Over the next three years Cannon also represented others of the Black Sox in similar suits involving back wages: Swede Risberg, Buck Weaver, Eddie Cicotte, and Joe Jackson. Shoeless Joe's trial took place in 1924 in the Milwaukee County Courthouse because Comiskey had incorporated the White Sox in Wisconsin. In the end Jackson settled out of court for a pittance.

The actions of Kenesaw Mountain Landis disturbed Cannon

White-maned Commissioner Kenesaw Mountain Landis sits in the center; behind him, cigar in hand, stands Otto Borchert; to the commissioner's left, in the dark suit, is attorney Ray Cannon. PHOTOGRAPH COURTESY OF THE MILWAUKEE COUNTY HISTORICAL SOCIETY

greatly. The White Sox ballplayers had all been found not guilty, but Landis was able—some would say encouraged—to banish them from baseball forever, to arbitrarily take away their livelihood. With this weighing upon him, Cannon founded the National Baseball Players Association of the United States, a players' union, in 1922. He signed up players from every big-league club. He also received the support of Samuel Gompers, the president of the American Federation of Labor. Even so, the union collapsed, perhaps because of Cannon's ties to the outlawed Chicago players.

Five of the banished Black Sox—Felsch, Cicotte, Weaver, Williams, and Risberg—formed a ball club that barnstormed through Wisconsin in the summer of 1922. Minor league clubs were fearful of sanctions from Landis if they played the outlaws, but the "ex–big leaguers" managed to schedule about 20 games with town teams in places like Marion and Merrill. In many of these contests, their pitcher was Ray Cannon, who was no slouch. He took part in the Chicago Cubs spring training camp on Catalina Island. On June 22 he hurled eight no-hit innings in Marion before Cicotte came in to work the final inning of a 2–0 victory for the visitors.

Cannon had his enemies, and he had his demons. His political rivals accused him of trying to bribe a district attorney with a case of champagne. Ray was indicted, but with the capable legal representation of Henry Killilea he was found not guilty. In 1929 Ray was disbarred by the Wisconsin Supreme Court for "ambulance chasing," soliciting business in an unethical fashion. Two years later the Wisconsin legislature passed a bill to permit him to resume his practice of law. In 1939 Ray was committed to Milwaukee County Hospital as an inebriate. He was released after one month and declared cured, but in 1944 he was arrested for public drunkenness for the 48th time after his car went over the sidewalk outside the Schroeder Hotel.

Ray Cannon made one other contribution to the baseball world: his son, Robert Cannon. Like his father, Robert earned a law degree. He became a circuit court judge in Milwaukee. Judge Cannon was hired in 1959 as legal advisor to the Major League Baseball Players Association, serving in that capacity for six years. The union offered him the position of executive director, but he turned it down.

13

Wet and Wild

On a warm summer evening in Borchert Field, August 4, 1941, before a ballgame with the St. Paul Saints, the Milwaukee Brewers played a five-inning exhibition against an assortment of old-timers, most of whom had some Milwaukee connection. The teams were mismatched, of course. Many of the senior opponents predated the Spanish-American War. Nevertheless, fans arriving early that night had the opportunity to see in the flesh a few of the national pastime's legendary figures. Among these were two master practitioners of the now-outlawed spitball.

Urban "Red" Faber, a 52-year-old ex–White Sox hurler, threw his juicy offerings in the first inning, allowing one hit but no runs. In the third inning 48-year-old Burleigh Grimes took his turn tossing wet ones. Grimes holds the distinction of being the last major league pitcher to throw spitters legally, having been grandfathered when the rule was enacted. Seven years of retirement had taken the edge off his slobber-ball, though. New Brewers manager Charlie Grimm's club cuffed burly Burleigh around for three runs.

Borchert Field was no stranger to pitchers who doctored the baseball with substances both foreign and domestic. In the Brewers' first pennant-winning seasons, 1913 and 1914, one member of their mound staff was Alfred "Buster" Braun. A native of Sheboygan, Buster helped win those championships and later parlayed the spitter into a 28-year career on Wisconsin sandlots, becoming the Chair City's best-known ballplayer. His renown grew from the day in 1910 when, on the afternoon of his mother's death, he was talked into pitching for the local team and hurled a 21-inning complete game, winning 2–1. Mom would have been proud.

About the time the Great War ended, America suddenly became obsessed with legislating dryness. The Eighteenth Amendment to the Constitution was ratified in January 1919, prohibiting the manufacture and sale of alcoholic beverages. This occurred barely one year after baseball's American Association voted to ban the application of saliva, tobacco, slippery elm, or other lubricating agents to the baseball. The reason remains unclear to this day. One of the justifications offered concerned the unsanitary nature of the spitter, but more likely the purpose was to give hitters a better chance at producing hits and runs. In 1920 the major leagues adopted the same rule. Out of sympathy for those pitchers who were at the time relying on the spitball, 17 of them were allowed to continue doctoring the ball throughout the remainder of their careers, including Faber and Grimes.

Like penicillin and the smallpox vaccine, the spitball was essentially discovered by accident. In 1902 a man named George Hildebrand found that applying saliva to a baseball could make it drop noticeably and abruptly. He taught the pitch to his Sacramento Senators teammate Elmer Stricklett. Stricklett showed it to Ed Walsh, his roommate during spring training with the Chicago White Sox in 1904. Stricklett spent that season flinging wet ones with the Brewers in Athletic Park, winning 20 games for Brew City. Walsh, meanwhile, began developing his moistening technique as a Chisox rookie. A headline in the *Milwaukee Journal* on August 18, 1904, proclaimed, "Stricklett's 'Spit Ball' Is Fad of the Year in the Big Leagues." It was Walsh, generally called Big Ed, who perfected the new pitch and made it famous.

Big Ed's success with the spitter was remarkable. His lifetime ERA was 1.82, the best by anyone in history. With the trick pitch he became, according to Frank Chance (of Tinker to Evers fame), the greatest pitcher of his time. Walsh helped lead the Chicago White Sox—the famous Hitless Wonders—to a World Series championship over their crosstown rivals who a few months later acquired their permanent moniker, the Cubs.

In the six seasons from 1907 through 1912, the indefatigable Walsh executed his moist pitches an average of 375 innings per year. His most amazing campaign was 1908, when he worked 464 innings—a third of his team's total innings for the year. He hurled 42 complete games and recorded 40 victories, making him the last pitcher to win that many times in one season. Sure, it was the Deadball Era, but 464 innings is 464 innings. On September 29 he pitched both ends of a doubleheader, winning each one. He also hurled his team's next game, which turned out to be one of the greatest pitching battles of all time.

On October 2, 1908, Walsh squared off with the Indians' star right-hander, Addie Joss, in Cleveland's League Park. Big Ed fired a masterful four-hitter that afternoon, walking just one while striking out 15. He allowed only one run, unearned, that scored on a wild pitch. Joss, however, was even better. He retired 27 consecutive batters, the second perfect game of the 20th century.

After laboring through nearly 400 innings in 1912, the fifth time in six seasons he worked that many, Walsh's once-strong right arm was dead. In 1913 he pitched under 100 innings, and those in great pain. In the next four seasons combined he compiled just 93 innings. World War I found Walsh contributing to the war effort as a laborer in a munitions factory. He never returned to the major leagues.

He did, however, return to playing ball. Sunday, June 1, 1919, found Big Ed toeing the rubber in Athletic Park, wearing a Milwaukee Brewers uniform. He had actually made his Brewers debut on May 23 in St. Paul, defeating the Saints, 6–1, on a five-hitter. In his initial start in his new home city, Walsh received what every pitcher dreams of—a ton of runs from his teammates. They put together a seven-run second inning on their way to crushing the visiting Kansas City Blues, 14–3. Walsh hurled the complete

Master of the spitter, Big Ed Walsh tried to revive his career in Milwaukee after the First World War, but his arm had nothing left. PUBLIC DOMAIN

game, allowing seven hits and two walks while striking out two. He also showed he could handle the bat by contributing a sacrifice fly and a sacrifice bunt.

Walsh knew, however, that he was not the same pitcher he had once been, and not just because he was now 38 years old. While he had been away working in a defense plant, the American Association had taken away his bread and butter. As the major leagues would do the following year, the AA had outlawed the spitball.

Walsh tried a couple more starts, but in the latter he lasted only one inning. Without the wet delivery, he could not make the ball dance. Soon afterward Walsh submitted a letter of resignation to club president Pants Rowland. Big Ed expressed his sincere gratitude for the fairness and kindness with which the Brewers had treated him. Then he complained bitterly, "It is my candid opinion that the anti-spitball regulation is the most ridiculous and the most unfair legislation in the history of baseball as it deprives a man of natural skill and acquired ability." He added, with a severe lack of prescience, "I am sure the majors in their wisdom will never eliminate it."

And so the legal spitball disappeared from the ballparks of the American Association, never to return. Borchert Field, though, did welcome former spitball practitioner Allen Sothoron in 1934 as the Brewers manager. He had been one of the 17 men grandfathered by Major League Baseball when it abolished the spitter. Sothoron was not a total stranger to Borchert Field, having visited in 1923 while a member of the Louisville Colonels. Before joining the Brewers he had replaced Reindeer Bill Killefer, in midseason, as skipper of the St. Louis Browns. After four games Sothoron was quickly succeeded by Rogers Hornsby.

Largely forgotten today, Sothoron was a respectable pitcher in his time. In 1919 he was a 20-game winner with the Browns, posting a 2.20 earned run average. In 1921 he established a post–Deadball Era record by hurling 178 innings without giving up a home run. As Brewers manager, Sothoron led his club to the Junior World Series championship in 1936.

On June 26, 1919, in the oppressive heat and humidity of Sportsman's Park in St. Louis, Sothoron pitched 13 sweat-drenched innings against the Chicago White Sox, finally defeating them, 3–2. If he is destined to be remembered at all, it will be for the lead sentence that syndicated columnist Bugs Baer penned about that event: "Allen S. Sothoron pitched his initials off yesterday."

14

Sweet Science

In the 1954 Academy Award–winning film *On the Waterfront*, Marlon Brando's character, boxer-turned-stevedore Terry Malloy, bitterly laments his brother's making him take a dive to a lesser fighter.

"So what happens?" Malloy asks rhetorically. "He gets the title shot outdoors in the ballpark—and what'd I get? A one-way ticket to Palookaville." Then he adds, "I coulda had class. I coulda been a contender."

A contender. Outdoors in the ballpark. The ballpark Malloy had in mind was probably Yankee Stadium, or maybe the Polo Grounds or Comiskey Park. He certainly was not thinking about Borchert Field. It would not, however, have been out of the question.

On July 4, 1919, Jack Dempsey captured the heavyweight championship of the world by defeating Jess Willard in Toledo. Brewers owner Otto Borchert and future owner Henry Killilea attended the fight. In Athletic Park, meanwhile, thanks to the technology of telegraphy, round-by-round announcements kept the baseball crowd apprised of the progress of the ring event of the year taking place in Ohio.

For several decades Borchert Field served as a venue for the pugilistic art. Amateurs and professionals alike showcased their fistic abilities in a roped rectangle set up in the center of the park's infield. On July 18, 1909, retired undefeated heavyweight champion James J. Jeffries (one year before making a comeback and being TKO'd by Jack Johnson) umpired a baseball game between two local amateur teams. Afterward he was supposed to spar with his partner for three one-minute rounds. Mayor David Rose, however, refused to issue a permit, so Jeffries could only skip rope and do a little shadow boxing.

The ballpark hosted its first prizefight on July 27, 1926, just over a year after Wisconsin governor John J. Blaine signed a bill legalizing outdoor boxing. Joey Sangor, a Russian native who made his home in Milwaukee, outpointed Benny Leonard to earn a 10-round decision in the evening's featured bout. The event was such a success that 16 nights later Athletic Park staged another fight card. Former junior welterweight world champion Pinky Mitchell took on Tommy White, who had defeated him a year previous in a bull ring across the Rio Grande from El Paso, Texas. This time Mitchell emerged victorious with a flurry of 10th-round punches.

Pinky was the younger brother of Richie Mitchell, probably the most popular pugilist Milwaukee ever produced. Richie never won a pro title. He once fought a title match against Benny Leonard in Madison Square Garden in 1921, but he was KO'd. Nevertheless, he was a pillar of the community. He served as a civilian instructor in training young soldiers going off to fight in World War I. Later he taught boxing in physical education classes at Marquette University and became the director of athletics at the Eagles Club. Richie was among the inaugural class of inductees (posthumously) to the Wisconsin Athletic Hall of Fame.

Of all the cauliflower-eared warriors who entered the ring at Eighth and Chambers, none surpassed the athletic stature, foreign and domestic, of Max Schmeling. In the summer of 1929, the ruggedly handsome 23-year-old German heavyweight made a trans-America exhibition tour to earn some Yankee dollars and present himself to the world boxing establishment. His main goal was to achieve a fight for the heavyweight championship, which had become vacant with the announced retirement of ex-champ Gene Tunney. It was Tunney who seized the title from Jack Dempsey in a 10-round unanimous decision in a driving rainstorm in Philadelphia's Sesquicentennial Stadium in front of a throng of more than 120,000 rabid spectators. Tunney defended his title twice, including a rematch with Dempsey, and then retired undefeated as a heavyweight.

On July 23, 1929, Herr Max brought his traveling show to Milwaukee. He arrived by train at the Chicago and North Western depot at the lakefront. Greeted by a gaggle of members of the city's robust German community, he was fêted at an informal reception in the Schroeder Hotel. After lunch he was chauffeured to Washington Park, where he laid a wreath at the base of the statue of Revolutionary War hero Baron Von Steuben.

Lightweight Richie Mitchell was not a world champion, but he was probably Milwaukee's favorite boxer ever. PHOTOGRAPH COURTESY OF THE MILWAUKEE COUNTY HISTORICAL SOCIETY

That night in Borchert Field, the heavyweight hopeful staged a demonstration of his raw power in four two-minute rounds with his pair of sparring partners. As a light drizzle helped cool the warm evening, the future champ used his sledgehammer right hand often enough to floor one of his human punching bags and rattle the headgear of both subordinates. As brief as the show was, the more knowledgeable members of the audience recognized that the man they were watching would soon become a major force in the world heavyweight division. (Less than a year later, on June 12, 1920, Schmeling became the champion. His opponent, Jack Sharkey, appeared to be winning the fight but was disqualified after the fourth round for hitting Max below the belt. On May 20, 1941, Nazi Max Schmeling parachuted into the Greek island of Crete as part of the first mainly airborne invasion in military history.)

Borchert Field never did host an actual world championship fight, but it came close, missing once by just four ounces. Two nights before Schmeling was awarded the heavyweight crown, 4,500 cash customers filed into Borchert expecting to witness a four-bout fight card featuring a title match between world champion junior lightweight Benny Bass and challenger Cowboy Eddie Anderson, the best boxer ever to come out of Wyoming. A larger crowd had been anticipated, but rain that lasted most of the day dampened attendance. Unfortunately, in the afternoon weigh-in the challenger tipped the scale at 130 ¼ pounds, too heavy by a quarter pound, negating the championship implications of the fight. He was fined $500 for the infraction.

Anderson fought aggressively for two rounds while the champ backpedaled. In the third round, everything changed. Bass leaped out of a crouch and landed a left hook squarely on the Cowboy's jaw, knocking him down. He struggled to his feet at the count of nine, only to be floored again. He rose, got decked again, got up, and this time was finished off with a crushing right that he never saw. Ten minutes after the final bell, a wobbly Anderson had to be helped from the ring.

Two of the most accomplished boxers to put on gloves in

Borchert Field were welterweights Tommy Bell and Cecil Hudson. Bell had fought Sugar Ray Robinson, still considered by many to be "pound for pound" the best fighter ever. Robinson carried a 73–1–1 record and had defeated every top-notch man in his weight class. He had for years been denied a title bout because he was reputedly out of favor with the organized crime bosses who controlled the sport. On December 20, 1946, Bell and Sugar Ray met in Madison Square Garden for the vacant welterweight crown.

In front of spectators who included Joe Louis and Jack Dempsey, Robinson and Bell waged a brutal battle. In the second round Bell stunned Sugar Ray with a perfect left hook that landed flush on his jaw. Ray hit the canvas hard but regained his feet by the count of seven. For the next few rounds Robinson tried to stay on his feet and clear his head. In the fifth, Bell rocked him again with a right cross to the jaw. Robinson again went into survival mode. Bell was unable to finish him off.

The battle shifted in round six. Sugar Ray bloodied Bell's nose; it bled for the remainder of the fight. Beginning in the seventh Ray carried out a relentless assault on his opponent's body. Bell lost the ability to breathe freely. In the 11th Robinson knocked him to the canvas. For the rest of the fight, each round belonged to Sugar Ray. At the end of the 15th and final round, Robinson was the champion and Bell looked like his face had been caught in a machine.

Despite the defeat, Bell remained the top contender. On August 4, 1947, Bell was matched with another ranking welterweight, Cecil Hudson, inside Borchert Field. Bell was the clear favorite, but Hudson, who made his home in Milwaukee, was no slouch. He had beaten Bell 15 months earlier in New York. Hudson was known to have great stamina to go with his lightning-quick hands.

Two days before the Hudson fight, away from home with some time to kill, Tommy Bell decided to hit some golf balls at a driving range west of Milwaukee, where the Milwaukee County

Zoo is now located. Accompanying him were Charlie Fuqua, a guitarist and baritone of the Ink Spots, and two other members of the musical group's all-sepia revue who were in town performing at the Riverside Theater.

As it turned out, the four men were not allowed to hit tee shots at the facility because the owner objected to their skin color. They left but returned several hours later, this time in the company of a lawyer (who was also black). Again they were refused. The range operator later explained, "I told them that I had no objection to them personally as Negroes but that if I permitted them to use the range it would ruin my business." The attorney pursued the matter with Milwaukee's district attorney, but nothing came of the complaint.

When fight night arrived, Bell suffered further embarrassment. Perhaps he had been traumatized by his humiliation at the golf range. Maybe Milwaukee's stifling record heat (98 degrees and humid) sapped his energy. Whatever the reason, the leading contender was thoroughly outclassed as Hudson earned a unanimous 10-round decision. Afterward Bell was only too happy to catch the train from Milwaukee back home to Youngstown, Ohio.

15

Frozen Tundra South

Everyone knows that the Green Bay Packers are unique among American sports franchises. Quite simply, they are a throwback to those distant days when athletic teams were loosely organized groups of men representing small cities. They blossomed in places like Pitcairn, Pennsylvania; Decatur, Illinois; Muncie, Indiana; and the Horlick-American Legion Post in Racine, Wisconsin. The athletes played for local pride and physical exercise and little or no money. Over the years, all of these franchises vanished—all except the Green Bay Packers.

One factor in the Packers' survival was the relative proximity of much larger Milwaukee. In a span of 13 years the Packers played in Athletic Park/Borchert Field 10 times, three of them as the home team.

In 1921, one season before the creation of the now-thriving National Football League, the Packers belonged to the American Professional Football Association. On December 4, after their league season was completed, they played a home game in Athletic Park against a semipro outfit from Racine that was not a league affiliate but had aspirations of becoming one. The game proved to be an enormous success for both parties. The stands were packed. All 7,000 seating spaces were sold as general admission at one dollar apiece. The weather was not a hindrance, with

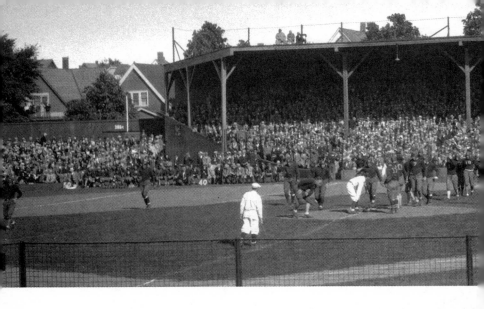

temperatures in the 30s and only a few wafting snowflakes during the contest. Racine arrived with a caravan of 100 decorated automobiles and a 50-piece drum and bugle corps that entertained the crowd before the game and between halves.

The game itself was a dandy, hard-fought and skillfully executed. Green Bay's only score of the day came on a 31-yard field goal in the second quarter by Packers founder, coach, and best player Curly Lambeau. Also excelling for the Packers was former University of Wisconsin Badger Cub Buck, an absolute bulwark on defense. Racine was paced by two players, one of whom was a ringer. Running back Johnny Mohardt had been hired just for this game. Two weeks earlier on this same gridiron, Mohardt had led Knute Rockne's Notre Dame squad to victory over Marquette University. Against the Packers, Mohardt gained more yards than any other player in the game.

The hero of the day, however, was Hank Gillo, Racine's fullback and kicker. A former All-American at Colgate, Gillo tried a long dropkick with less than three minutes remaining. The attempt was wide, but the Packers were offside. Given a second chance and a five-yard assist, Gillo put the ball between the uprights to tie the score. The exciting 3–3 finish felt like a victory to

Two of the NFL's original teams, the Milwaukee Badgers and the Green Bay Packers, went head to head in Athletic Park on November 7, 1926. The Packers are the ones wearing numbered jerseys. Green Bay won the game, 21–0. COURTESY OF THE NEVILLE PUBLIC MUSEUM OF BROWN COUNTY

the faithful folk from Racine. They carried Gillo off the field on their shoulders.

Exactly one year later the same teams met on a sunny day in Athletic Park. This time both were members of the fledgling NFL. The Packers and the Racine Legion had already played each other twice during the season, with Racine winning once and tying once. This third time, the Packers made it an even split for the year by dominating and triumphing, 14–0, in a game that was more one-sided than the score might suggest. The Packers played superb football. Most of the battle was fought in Racine territory. Spectacular punting by Cub Buck and three sensational passes from Curly Lambeau to Charlie Mathys topped the action for Green Bay. Racine's few bright spots featured diminutive quarterback Chuck Dressen, previously a member of the Decatur Staleys, which transformed into the Chicago Bears. In 1924 Dressen would turn to baseball full-time. He managed several big-league teams, including the Milwaukee Braves in 1960 and 1961.

In the first five seasons of the NFL, 1922–1926, the Green

Bay Packers and the Milwaukee Badgers, both charter members, played a home-and-home series that brought Lambeau's men to Athletic Park once each year. In the first of those games, on October 22, 1922, the Green Bay team, most often referred to as the Green Bay Blues, confronted the two most outstanding African Americans in football. Right end Paul Robeson and running back Fritz Pollard were former All-Americans from Rutgers and Brown universities, respectively. Their presence in the lineup made the Badgers heavy favorites in the game. Sadly for Milwaukee fans, both were playing at less than 100 percent. Pollard had been kicked in the face the previous week against Racine. Against Green Bay he did not even enter the game until the third quarter. As soon as he did, the Badgers began to gain yardage. Pollard reinjured himself, though, and had to be helped from the field. Robeson suffered a similar fate. The play of the game was a 45-yard run by Packers reserve Eddie Glick, a Marquette alumnus. His long dash was followed by a pass interception, however, and Green Bay failed to score. So did the Badgers, and the game ended in a 0–0 tie.

That scoreless standoff turned out to be the high point of the Badgers' games against the Packers. On November 18, 1923, the Badgers came close, losing 10–7 in a game that was nearly canceled because the teams couldn't agree on who should be the referee. During the game, a disputed pass-interference call against Green Bay held up play for 15 minutes while the Packers loudly demanded that the umpire be replaced. The most memorable part of the afternoon was probably the appearance of the Green Bay Packers' Lumberjack Band, which marched from the train depot to Athletic Park and performed prior to the kickoff.

Curly Lambeau's team played the Badgers in Milwaukee three more times before the Milwaukee team folded after the 1926 season, never to assemble again. The game of November 16, 1924, was a spirited competition that remained in doubt until the Packers intercepted a pass late in the final quarter to protect a 17–10 victory. The Badgers failed to score a point in the next two years' tussles.

The most interesting aspect of the Packers-Badgers game on November 1, 1925, may have been Green Bay's second look at 21-year-old rookie halfback John McNally. Young McNally and a friend of his had played semipro football under fake names in order to protect their college eligibility. Their inspiration was a theater marquee advertising the Rudolph Valentino film *Blood and Sand*. McNally became Blood; his buddy was Sand. Despite playing on a weak Badgers team, Blood displayed athletic skills that impressed Lambeau. Four years later the Packers signed Blood, who helped lead them to three consecutive NFL championships.

Blood's gridiron talents placed him in the initial induction class of the Pro Football Hall of Fame. What gave him a permanent place in football legend was his flamboyant behavior away from the game. It earned him the moniker the Vagabond Halfback. One often-related story about Blood tells of Lambeau mailing him a contract offering $100 a game, or $110 if he would promise to stop drinking during the four days before every game. Blood responded simply, "I'll take the $100."

The Packers' final game against the Badgers took place on November 7, 1926. Green Bay was heavily favored, but at halftime the score was 0–0. Then in the middle of the third quarter the Packers came to life. They intercepted three passes and turned each one into an aerial touchdown, winning decisively, 21–0. The crowd of about 4,300 was a respectable turnout for an NFL game. To gauge the level of popularity of pro football in 1926, however, consider that the previous afternoon, on the same field, a game between two Milwaukee public high schools, West Division and Washington, was attended by 8,000 spectators.

After the Milwaukee Badgers went out of existence, a team

called the Milwaukee Eagles filled the vacancy in Athletic Park. On October 30, 1927, the Packers paid a visit for a sort of non-conference game with the Eagles. Green Bay won easily, 22–7, with the lone touchdown for the home club occurring on a 55-yard scamper by ex–Marquette star Lester Gerlach after he recovered a fumble. Packers quarterback Pid Purdy, who had just finished the major league baseball season as an outfielder for the Cincinnati Reds, drop-kicked a field goal, and Green Bay added three touchdowns. Marquette alumnus Red Dunn was responsible for two of them, one on a pass to Verne Lewellen and one on a three-yard dive.

On December 12, 1931, Johnny Blood returned to Milwaukee's ballpark, which by then was called Borchert Field. He and his teammates returned as three-time champions of the NFL. Having finished their successful league season, the Packers players decided to make a few extra dollars by barnstorming across Wisconsin, taking on all comers. The NFL and the Packers organization would not permit Blood and his buddies to use the trademarked team name, so the players did what Blood had done before—they adopted a pseudonym, the Green Bay Pros. Seventeen men from the Packers roster took on the champions of the Wisconsin State Professional League, the Ische Radios, who were sponsored by the first store in Milwaukee devoted exclusively to selling and servicing radios. Predictably, the contest was no contest. The professionals from "up north" cruised to a 44–0 victory. There was no drama, but the 3,000 cash customers received their money's worth. They witnessed, in the flesh, eight football heroes who are now enshrined in the Packers Hall of Fame inside Lambeau Field: Blood, halfback Hank Bruder, end Lavvie Dilweg, quarterback Red Dunn, center Jug Earp, end Milt Gantenbein, halfback Verne Lewellen, and guard Iron Mike Michalske. Massive tackle Cal Hubbard was also part of the team but was injured and could not participate.

Two years later the Packers made their last trip to Borchert Field, and this time Hubbard did play. Lambeau had figured out that his franchise needed the larger ticket market of Milwaukee in order to survive, so on October 1, 1933, the Packers played a home game in Borchert Field against the New York Giants. More than 12,000 football fans put up their money and squeezed into the old wooden ballpark.

The game was a strange one. Two years after winning their third title in a row, the Packers were expected to dominate their eastern foe. That didn't happen. The Giants missed two short field goals. They attempted only seven passes, and six of them fell incomplete. Their one pass completion failed to make a first down. In fact, the Giants did not make even one first down in the entire game. Hubbard spent the afternoon overpowering the New York linemen and smashing their running backs. Observers said he played his best game ever. Despite all this, the Packers lost, 10–7. They had two passes intercepted and fumbled seven times, losing three of them. The only Green Bay highlight was a 30-yard touchdown pass reception by Johnny Blood in the fourth quarter.

Almost as unsatisfactory as the bitter loss to the Giants was the stadium's seating configuration. Of necessity the gridiron ran north-south within the park. The grandstand and bleachers were located behind the respective end zones. That layout may have been tolerable for high school games, but for angry fans of a perennial NFL title contender, it was substandard.

Lambeau's financial strategy had proved so successful that beginning the next season, the Packers played at least two games every year in Wisconsin's largest city, a practice they continued for more than 60 years. But they would never again play in Borchert Field. The next year, when the Packers hosted two home games in Milwaukee, they played in State Fair Park.

16

The Rock

College football's greatest coach was Knute Rockne, who won more than 88 percent of his games. Born in Voss, Norway, he immigrated to the United States with his parents at age five. In 1918, at the age of 30, he was named head coach at the University of Notre Dame. One of his players that year was Green Bay Packers legend Curly Lambeau. In 1919 and 1920 Notre Dame went undefeated, earning acclaim as the national champions in both seasons.

Those two powerful Irish elevens featured all-American halfback George Gipp, known to all as the Gipper. He was swift and strong and athletic above all others. Gipp openly defied the recent Volstead Act and supplied himself with illicit booze at a rate that bordered on self-destruction. Nevertheless, on the gridiron he was a genius, and Notre Dame's foes had no answer for him.

Tragically, Gipp contracted a strep infection at his final game and died a few weeks later on December 14, 1920. The moment of his death was described eight years later in a famous inspirational speech that Rockne delivered to his players, telling them that the dying athlete had urged them to "win one for the Gipper." They did, upsetting Army, and the halfback and the speech became immortal. Twenty years after the fact, Ronald Reagan would portray the Gipper in the Hollywood film *Knute Rockne, All American*.

"The Gipper," referred to in Knute Rockne's famous motivational speech at Notre Dame, was played on the silver screen by future president Ronald Reagan. REAGAN LIBRARY/WIKIMEDIA COMMONS

On Saturday, November 19, 1921, Rockne led his young men from South Bend into Athletic Park to clash with the team from Marquette University. Marquette Stadium was still three years in the future, so the Hilltoppers often played their games in Milwaukee's north-side ballpark. The combination of Homecoming and Rockne's glamorous team guaranteed a crowd in excess of 10,000 despite the cold, raw weather. By coincidence, Marquette's third-string quarterback seated along the sideline was Pat O'Brien, destined to become a famous actor and portray Rockne opposite Reagan's Gipper.

Rockne's mighty team was a juggernaut that had no weakness. On October 8 they had stumbled and snapped their 22-game unbeaten streak against Iowa, 10–7, but they remained the powerhouse of the nation. Their lineup included not just strong football players but also skilled all-around athletes. Halfback Paul Castner captained Notre Dame's hockey team and anchored the school's baseball pitching staff. Fullback Chet Wynne was a star hurdler and captain of the track squad. Tackle Art Garvey was a shot put champion. Running back Roger Kiley was the basketball captain and star guard. Rockne's captain, Eddie Anderson, was a three-sport standout, sought after by professional clubs in basketball and baseball as well as football. Tackle Buck Shaw would go on to coach the San Francisco 49ers and the Philadelphia Eagles and in 1960 became the only coach to defeat Vince Lombardi in a championship game.

The contest with Marquette was Notre Dame's third in little more than a week, a murderous schedule that only a supremely confident leader like Rockne would attempt. Rockne had actually skipped the previous game, against the Haskell Indian School in Lawrence, Kansas, leaving his assistants in charge while he went ahead to Milwaukee to scout Marquette in its game against North Dakota. He probably didn't learn a great deal. The Hilltoppers struggled in a 7–3 victory. This was indicative, though, of Rockne's extreme attention to detail. He was the first coach to employ advance scouting. He was also the main force behind the popularization of the forward pass, as well as the "Notre Dame shift," a quick pre-snap movement of all four backs that was eventually ruled illegal.

Notre Dame's football program was no stranger to Milwaukee. From 1908 through 1911 the Fighting Irish played an annual Thanksgiving Day game versus Marquette. Each of those contests, however, was played on the Hilltoppers' campus, near 10th and State Streets. For three years running, 1909 through 1911, the games ended in ties: 0–0, 5–5, and 0–0, respectively. The final Turkey Day match, played on a neutral field in Chicago, occurred in 1912, when Notre Dame walloped their rivals, 69–0.

Many years before Rockne, Notre Dame did compete in Athletic Park. They played the University of Wisconsin Badgers there in 1904 and 1905, presumably to take advantage of its seating capacity in the distant days before Camp Randall Stadium was constructed. Notre Dame in that period did not yet boast a strong program. The Badgers whipped them both times, 58–0 and 21–0.

When Rockne and company arrived at Athletic Park, few observers gave Marquette much of a chance. Coach Jack Ryan's Hilltoppers were respectable but still building. They received the opening kickoff, ran three plays, and punted. Halfback Castner ran one play for the Irish, gaining four yards around left end. On second down he quick-kicked, a popular strategy of the day that seems unexplainable now.

Late in the first quarter Marquette tackle Frank Linnan blocked a Castner punt. Fritz Roessler scooped up the ball and returned it to the five-yard line. Three line plunges advanced the pigskin within a foot of the goal. On fourth down fullback Claude Taugher dove across the line. Taugher had been a Marine during the Great War, earning the Croix de Guerre for bravery in combat in France. He summoned all his strength to push back the Notre Dame linemen and score the game's first touchdown. Future Green Bay Packer Red Dunn added the extra point, and the upstart Hilltoppers owned a 7–0 lead.

It didn't last long. In the second period Notre Dame's finest player, left halfback Johnny Mohardt, brought them back. Mohardt had run interference for and played in the shadow of George Gipp for two seasons. Now he was the star, as dominant as the Gipper had been. After graduation Mohardt would play alongside Red Grange with the Chicago Bears and as a teammate of Ty Cobb with the Detroit Tigers. Against Marquette he swept around end and sprinted 55 yards to pay dirt. Buck Shaw booted the point to tie the game. Before halftime Mohardt tossed a short pass to Eddie Anderson, who ran the rest of the way for a 45-yard TD. Shaw's kick made it 14–7 at the break.

The second half featured tough, physical, sometimes dirty football. Notre Dame earned a number of penalties, capped by guard Hunk Anderson's ejection for throwing punches.

Sportsmanship was not in evidence. At one point the home team requested a fresh football because the cantaloupe-shaped object they were using was waterlogged and mud-smeared. The visitors objected, so the referee refused the clean football.

Mohardt put the game out of reach in the last quarter. He rambled 45 yards around end before being tripped up at the one-yard line. Fullback Chet Wynne took it over from there, and Shaw's placekick made the final score 21–7 for Notre Dame.

The host team and their frozen-toed followers were not pleased with the defeat, but they took pride in a strong showing against a superior foe. Rockne praised Marquette's resilience and spoke most highly of their tackles, Linnan and Larry McGinnis.

"The hospitality which has been accorded us here," Rockne said at a banquet that night at the Wisconsin Hotel, "and the sportsmanship which the city has shown gives us a sincere desire to return here next fall."

It didn't happen. Marquette and Notre Dame never competed again on the gridiron, and after the 1960 season Marquette discontinued its football program.

Knute Rockne died in a plane crash in Kansas on March 31, 1931. He was 43.

17

Up, Up, and Away

In the first three decades of the 20th century, Americans developed a fascination with flying. The Wright Brothers demonstrated that a sustained flight by a powered, controlled aircraft was possible. Soon more and more bold young pilots were taking to the air to expand the limits of air travel. In 1927 young Charles Lindbergh captured the imagination of the world by conquering the Atlantic Ocean. Five years earlier, before his first solo flight, Lucky Lindy entered the aviation business as a barnstorming daredevil wing walker. And just a few days before Lindy walked his first wing, on the last days of May 1922, the nation's aeronautical attention was focused on Otto Borchert's wooden ballpark in Milwaukee. Really.

Over that three-day period, Beer City hosted three notable events: a convention of aeronautical experts, a meeting of the country's top pilots that included a flying exhibition of 30 remarkable airplanes, and the start of the 13th annual National Balloon Race. Much of this activity took place in view of the public, mostly at no charge. The city, of course, got caught up in the excitement of this newfangled flying business.

Tuesday, May 30, Memorial Day, coincidentally was also the day when Milwaukee received its first delivery of mail by airplane—16 bags dropped off at Hamilton Field on Layton Avenue. Postwar sentiment was still strong from the recent war.

The morning saw celebrations and commemorations in all of the city's cemeteries, followed by a parade up Wisconsin and Grand Avenues. After that the air show attracted a huge crowd along Lake Michigan. That evening a special holiday radio broadcast on Gimbel's station, WAAK, was carried to Lapham Park, where a receiving station had been erected. Sponsored by the *Jewish Press*, the program featured two speakers, Mayor Dan Hoan and a Jewish lawyer who spoke entirely in Yiddish. Milwaukee's own Brigadier General William "Billy" Mitchell, the country's most ardent champion of military air power, was to have taken part, but two days earlier he had been thrown from a horse and could not participate.

The afternoon air show was marred by a spectacular but fortunately nonfatal crash. An Army DH-9 piloted by 24-year-old Lieutenant James Eledredge, with *Milwaukee Sentinel* reporter Paul Carpenter aboard, was flying in loose formation with four other planes when its engine started to miss. Faced with a choice of trying to land on railroad tracks near the spectators or the expanse of Milwaukee's harbor, the pilot chose the lake. He tried to pancake but instead somersaulted across the water. Both men escaped the wreckage and swam 200 yards to the inner breakwater. They were subsequently rescued by four men in a rowboat. This crash landing was the fourth one experienced by journalist Carpenter in his 23 years on earth, the first three having occurred in the Great War.

Not everyone in town flocked to the lakeshore to watch the planes. At a cost of 25 cents apiece, thousands of people visited Athletic Park to inspect the huge gas bags that the next afternoon, fully inflated with coal gas, would take off for points unknown in the National Balloon Race. The Aero Club of Wisconsin, which sponsored the event, had already sold thousands of tickets for Wednesday's race-day activities. The plan was for spectators to fill the grandstand and watch as the balloons, each filled to a capacity of 80,000 cubic feet, left the ballpark at five-minute intervals. The day before the race, the gas company decided the liability was too great to allow people to watch from such proximity. A great number of tickets had to be refunded.

The balloons in the race were constructed of small pieces of rubberized silk sewn together to create a large envelope to contain the gas. Suspended below each balloon was a wicker basket, sufficiently large to carry a balloonist and his assistant, sandbags for ballast, and whatever equipment the pilot deemed important or necessary. Each of the 13 entrants in the race had his own ideas about what to take along. Some carried warm clothing and food. All carried more than 200 feet of stout rope in case they landed in tall trees. One flyer carried a collapsible canoe. Another stowed a cage full of homing pigeons in case of being stranded in the wilderness.

The 13 fearless racers seeking the balloon derby's $1,000 first prize included an array of experienced balloonists. The youngest

The huge balloons spread across Athletic Park's playing surface, awaiting an infusion of coal gas. PHOTOGRAPH COURTESY OF THE MILWAUKEE COUNTY HISTORICAL SOCIETY

was 21-year-old Bernard von Hoffman from St. Louis, who nearly won the 1921 International Balloon Race except that he was disqualified for landing in the Irish Sea, a few miles short of the coast.

The oldest entrant, also from St. Louis, was Captain John Berry, a grizzled 73-year-old who made his first balloon flight while he was a drummer boy in the Civil War. Ralph Upson of Detroit was probably the world's most famous balloonist and a four-time champion. Roy Donaldson of Springfield, Illinois, had been ballooning since 1908. In the 1914 race his gas bag fell into a lake in the Cascade Mountains and he and his copilot were missing for 11 days.

The rules of the race were simple. Whichever balloon landed the greatest distance from Athletic Park would be declared the winner. From which direction it arrived or how long it remained in flight made no difference. Each balloon had to show the colors of the Aero Club of Wisconsin. In addition, each pilot had to agree to carry and subsequently drop 100,000 handbills advertising the city of Milwaukee, and all miscellaneous equipment had to be purchased in Milwaukee. Because all balloons were required to inflate with the same kind of gas, Lieutenant Commander J. P. Norfleet was ineligible for prize money. Strictly as an experiment, he flew a US Navy balloon filled with helium.

Shortly before midnight on May 30, the inflation of the balloons began inside the walls of the ballpark. Eighty sailors from Great Lakes Naval Training Center and 45 soldiers from Fort Sheridan assisted in the task. By 4:30 a.m. all the balloons were filled. During the day, minor leaks were discovered and patched. Outside the park, squads of police kept spectators back, especially those who insisted on lighting cigarettes. The smell of coal gas was evident on the baseball grounds. By early afternoon the pilots were ready for takeoff.

As thousands enjoyed balloon parties and watched from nearby porches, rooftops, and streets, the balloons lifted off, one

Once fully inflated, the five-story-high racing balloons were ready to drift into the ether. PHOTOGRAPH COURTESY OF THE MILWAUKEE COUNTY HISTORICAL SOCIETY

after another, drifted southward over the downtown area, then gradually disappeared. The first pilot, Roy Donaldson, knew his craft had a leak; he decided to take off anyway. He barely cleared the roof of the grandstand. His flight ended just 20 minutes later when he brought his balloon down four miles from the starting point, near South Shore Park in Bay View. The other dozen competitors floated away successfully. Ralph Upson gave spectators a thrill by sitting on the rim of his basket, leaning outward, and waving good-bye.

By evening, reports of balloon sightings began to come in from all directions. Muskegon, Michigan, recorded a balloon passing far overhead. So did several cities in Illinois, from Waukegan to Chicago. The first confirmed landing after Donaldson's occurred early the following evening. Upson had touched down at Painesville, Ohio, after crossing Lake Erie. He immediately became the man to beat when a Milwaukee newspaper calculated that his distance aloft measured 390 miles. Upson said he had tried to reach Buffalo but was blown back. Other landings soon followed: one near Cleveland, two in central Missouri, two in Indiana.

One of the landings near Fulton, Missouri, turned out to be the end of a harrowing flight that nearly proved fatal. Pilot J. S. McKibben and his aide floated for 20 hours in a balloon damaged by wind even before they started the race. McKibben intended to make only a short flight without trying to win the race. The air currents, though, propelled them over Lake Michigan. They dropped all their ballast to avoid plunging into the lake. After that they had no food and no warm clothing. They slept in 20-minute shifts and tried to keep from freezing. A northeast wind blew them over Missouri, where they finally were able to set the balloon down.

Upson's lead was overtaken the next day, but not officially. Lieutenant Commander Norfleet's helium-filled balloon touched down at Hancock, Missouri, surpassing Upson by more than 100 miles. The next four pilots to be found all exceeded Upson's mark as well. Ultimately the winner of the 1922 National Balloon Race was declared to be Major Oscar Westover. Piloting a five-story-tall US Army balloon, Westover rode a ferocious 50-mile-per-hour upper air current to a location northeast of the city of Quebec. His winning distance of 911 miles was later recalculated at 865 miles, still more than 300 miles beyond his nearest competitor.

Westover and his assistant reported that the density of the atmosphere was so great and they were driven so fast by the wind at the upper altitude that they could not make out the landscape below them. They threw all their camping equipment and emergency gear overboard in an attempt to make a record flight. Westover said that during the night they maintained an altitude of 10,000 feet, rising to 15,000 feet when the sun was shining. They were able to make a soft landing in the treetops and climb down safely.

One more competitor remained unaccounted for on Friday. The US Navy balloon of Lieutenant W. F. Reed was reported missing. Race officials received reports that he had been variously spotted over Lake Erie, Canada, and Ohio. He turned up later that day in a cornfield in the Ozark Mountains of Missouri. His inability to report was ascribed to a lack of nearby telegraph facilities.

And so the 1922 National Balloon Race entered the record books and the memory banks of thousands of Milwaukeeans. Despite a few harrowing moments, no balloonist suffered injury, and most were already making plans for the next year's race lifting off in Indianapolis.

18

Grid Showdown in Athletic Park

In the 1930s and 1940s Paul Robeson was among the most accomplished and prominent African Americans in the United States, probably the most famous black person in the world. The son of a runaway slave, Robeson had been just the third African American to attend Rutgers College when he enrolled there in 1915. At Rutgers he anchored the debate team, sang in the glee club, achieved Phi Beta Kappa in his junior year, and graduated first in his class. He then moved to Harlem and entered law school at Columbia, where he earned his law degree in 1923.

Having no enthusiasm for legal practice, Robeson turned his attention and talents to performing: singing, legitimate theater, film acting. From the beginning the towering black man with the deep, rumbling voice was a superb actor. What's more, his basso profundo rendition of "Ol' Man River," a song written expressly for Robeson, made his voice instantly recognizable.

From early adulthood, Robeson was a lightning rod. In Greenwich Village in 1924 he starred in Eugene O'Neill's *All God's Chillun Got Wings*, a play about an interracial love affair. Robeson caused a firestorm and received death threats because his character kisses the hand of the white lead actress. Perhaps his crowning stage performance came in 1943 when he played Othello on Broadway, the first of his race to do so in the United States.

Paul Robeson is probably best remembered for his acting and his basso profundo voice singing "Ol' Man River," but he was also a powerful star of the gridiron. WIKIMEDIA COMMONS

For all of Robeson's varied accomplishments, he first gained national acclaim playing football at Rutgers. For four years the six-foot-three, 215-pound Robeson was a virtual colossus of the college game. Famed sportswriter Walter Camp, credited with being the father of American football, named Robeson on his "All-American team" in both 1917 and 1918. It was Camp who had devised the line of scrimmage, the 11-man offensive alignment of seven linemen and four backs, the scoring system, and the four-down, 10-yard standard for a first down. Camp called Robeson "a veritable superman."

Precisely how well Robeson played is impossible to quantify. Statistical records from that era were sketchy and unreliable. Besides that, his stats were expunged from the record books in 1949 because of his outspoken advocacy of civil rights. What outraged many Americans the most were his espousal of socialism, his affiliation with the Communist Party, and the fact that he had lived in Moscow on several occasions.

In the summer of 1915, Robeson worked as a waiter at Narragansett Pier, one of the country's swankiest resort areas, across Rhode Island Sound from Newport. Also waiting tables there was Fritz Pollard, one of two black students at Brown University and the star of the football team there. Pollard was named a first-team All-American running back in his sophomore year. He was a spectacular, elusive open-field runner whose gridiron heroics led Brown to the 1916 Rose Bowl Game. Seven years after waiting tables together, Pollard and Robeson would become teammates.

At the time Robeson and Pollard were playing college football, the reigning Eastern powerhouse of the sport was Harvard, winner of seven national championships. When they kicked off in Harvard Stadium on the afternoon of October 29, 1921, the Crimson had not lost a game in three years, their last defeat coming at the hands of Fritz Pollard and his teammates from Brown. On this afternoon Harvard's overmatched opponents were the Praying Colonels from Centre College, a Presbyterian men's institution in Danville, Kentucky, with an enrollment of 254 students.

In a game still hailed as one of the greatest upsets of all time, Centre defeated the Ivy League juggernaut, 6–0. The only touchdown of the game was scored on a spectacular 33-yard dash in the third quarter by Centre's star quarterback, Alvin Nugent "Bo" McMillin. He was a Texan who had followed his high school coach to Centre College in 1917. McMillin stood just five-foot-nine and weighed 165 pounds on a good day, but he was fast and tough and smart. He was named All-American three times, and at the end of October 1921 he could have been elected to any public office in the state of Kentucky. Instead he accepted a three-year contract as head football coach at Centenary College in Shreveport, Louisiana.

In the year in which the Praying Colonels stunned mighty Hah-vard, a new football enterprise called the American Professional Football Association was struggling along in its second year of existence. The president of the league, hired to lend his prestigious name and provide credibility, was Jim Thorpe. The famous Native American athlete was, as King Gustav V of Sweden proclaimed him at the awards ceremony of the 1912 Olympic Games, "the greatest athlete in the world."

Thorpe was a member of the Sac and Fox tribe, a direct descendant of Black Hawk. He was born in a one-room cabin in the Indian Territory, which became Oklahoma a few years later. At 17 he enrolled in the Carlisle Indian Industrial School in Pennsylvania, where he played football for legendary coach Glenn "Pop" Warner. A fleet-footed ball carrier and a vicious tackler, Thorpe earned first-team All-American honors for the first time in 1911. The following summer Thorpe achieved international celebrity as the outstanding athlete in the Olympic Games in Stockholm. Competing in the pentathlon and decathlon, the two most demanding track-and-field events, Thorpe easily won gold medals in both and established records that lasted for two decades.

Autumn of 1912 found Thorpe back at Carlisle for his final year, helping Pop Warner's gridders win 12 games. The high point of the season for everyone at Carlisle was a November 9 showdown against Army at West Point. Coach Warner did not hesitate to remind his team that it was the grandfathers and fathers of these young Cadets who had slain their ancestors in the Indian Wars.

With the slaughter of Sioux women and children at Wounded Knee only 22 years in the past, the coach had no difficulty motivating his athletes.

The game looked to be a mismatch. Army's players, on average, stood four inches taller and weighed 25 pounds more than their rivals. The starting backfield for the Cadets comprised four future Army generals, including a tough, relentless halfback named Dwight Eisenhower. Army jumped to a 6–0 lead in the first quarter, but after that Thorpe ran wild and led his team to a convincing 27–6 victory. Eisenhower suffered a knee injury while trying to tackle Thorpe and had to leave the game. The injury was serious enough that it nearly kept Ike out of the army.

After three years of failing to learn to hit the curve in major league baseball with the New York Giants, Thorpe was banished to the minor leagues, playing center field for the Milwaukee Brewers in Athletic Park in 1916. He was one of the best players on a bad team, batting a mediocre .274 but leading the American Association in stolen bases.

By 1922 the American Professional Football Association had expanded and taken the name National Football League, which continues today in a larger configuration. The original NFL included several teams of note. One was the Green Bay Packers, now the oldest pro football franchise to remain in the same city. Another was a team in Racine cosponsored by an American Legion post and the president of the Horlick malted milk company. A third was the Milwaukee Badgers. And then there were the Oorang Indians.

The Oorang Indians were the brainchild of Walter Lingo, the owner of a dog kennel in LaRue, Ohio. Lingo was a breeder of Airedales, a relatively rare breed that he claimed was the world's greatest all-around dog. He was also an avid sportsman who hunted with celebrities like Ty Cobb, Gary Cooper, and Jim Thorpe. To advertise his kennel, Lingo purchased a franchise in the incipient National Football League at a cost of $100, less than the selling price of one of his dogs. He hired Thorpe to recruit an entire team of Native Americans and serve as player-coach. Lingo borrowed the Oorang name from a strain of Airedales that he favored.

Because the Oorang Indians were first and foremost a marketing tool, Lingo invented the pregame and halftime shows. Instead of retreating to the dressing room after the second quarter, players with colorful names like Dick Deer Slayer, Big Bear, and Little Twig put on demonstrations of Indian dances and tomahawk throwing. Nikolas Lassa, whose Indian name was Long Time Sleep, sometimes wrestled a bear at midfield between halves. Most important of all for Lingo's purposes, his Airedales were put through their paces by the ballplayers in retrieving exercises and assorted tricks.

On November 19, 1922, the Oorang Indians traveled to Milwaukee to take on the Milwaukee Badgers in Athletic Park. The Badgers had been born during the winter of 1921–22. Two promoters from Chicago, Joe Plunkett and Ambrose McGuirk, approached Fritz Pollard to help form a team in the new NFL. Besides Pollard they hired several other former college All-Americans. In the second week of the season, Paul Robeson joined the team. He needed the money to help pay for law school, so during the week he attended classes at Columbia, and on weekends he took the train and joined his Badgers teammates for the game.

Six days before the big game against the Oorang Indians, the Badgers achieved the pièce de résistance. They received a telegram from Bo McMillin, agreeing to play with them against Thorpe's Indians and then against the Bears in Chicago two weeks later. McMillin's Centenary College team had a game scheduled in Louisville on Saturday, the day before the Badgers' showdown with the Oorangs. McMillin boarded a train at 9:25 that evening and arrived in Milwaukee at 10:00 the next morning, well in advance of the 2:15 kickoff. After the game he caught the flyer back to Louisiana.

The heralded matchup between Jim Thorpe and Bo McMillin—"two of the greatest football players in history," the *Milwaukee Sentinel* needlessly reminded its readers—lured 7,500 fans to Athletic Park's splintery grandstand on a cold November afternoon. The field was dry but somewhat plowed up from two high school contests and Marquette University's homecoming game the previous day. The Badgers had a vocal home crowd to spur them on; the visitors had Long Time Sleep's pet coyote tethered along the sideline for good luck.

The game did not disappoint. In the opening quarter the Oorangs' quarterback and fullback mishandled the handoff. Robeson charged in from his left end position, fought his way to the ball, and rolled into the end zone. Charlie Copley missed the extra point, but Milwaukee led, 6–0. Neither team scored during the rest of the first half, but the game was anything but dull. Thorpe completed several long passes, Pollard "pulled off some neat runs," and McMillin "electrified fans time and again with brilliant open field running."

The second half began with an exchange of punts. After that McMillin and his new teammates took the ball from their own territory to midfield through sheer brute strength, a few fiercely contested yards at a time. The blocking and tackling became increasingly audible as the game went on. Pollard suffered three cracked ribs in a pileup. Milwaukee's player-coach, the poetically named Alfred Tennyson Garrett (called Budge) hobbled to the bench with a shattered ankle. Much of the damage was inflicted by Thorpe, playing every down like a man possessed.

After a short run by McMillin, quarterback Clair Purdy fired the pigskin far downfield. Surrounded by Oorang players, Robeson leaped high to snatch the ball from the defenders, then ran the final 10 yards to the end zone. McMillin tattooed Eagle Feather with a crushing block at the 10-yard line to give Robeson a clear alley for the score. As soon as Robeson crossed the goal line, four or five Oorang players converged on him, intent on bodily harm. Robeson had long ago learned to expect such tactics, and he was ready for them. For the next several seconds, spectators witnessed, as one writer described it, "the amazing sight of this giant black man cuffing and tossing men aside as if they were children." Copley booted the point to make it 13–0.

The rest of the second half was replete with spectacular thrills. Thorpe brought the crowd to its feet with a twisting 35-yard run. Robeson snared another long pass and ran it in for a 40-yard score, but a penalty nullified it. The play that really had people buzzing after the game involved McMillin going into punt formation, then running left instead of kicking. His path was blocked, so he reversed his field and retreated 20 yards behind the line of scrimmage. He stopped and lofted the ball downfield. Robeson outmuscled a defender and caught the ball. He might have scored if his feet hadn't slipped on the loose turf. For all the action, though, neither team scored again. The final score read Badgers 13, Indians 0.

Sportswriters who witnessed the battle described it only in superlatives. "The Thorpe-McMillan [*sic*] three ring circus and an array of Oorang Indians staged the wildest and wooliest and altogether best show of the present professional football season in Athletic Park," raved the *Wisconsin News*. "McMillan [*sic*] was all that had been claimed for him, and then some."

Naturally the man who scored the only two touchdowns in the game also drew praise. The *Milwaukee Journal* said Robeson "was in the thick of every play and stood out head and shoulders over every lineman in the game."

Despite playing in a losing cause, "Jim Thorpe stood out throughout the game," wrote the *Wisconsin News*, explaining that this "specimen of physical perfection played the greatest defensive game seen in Milwaukee in years."

Fritz Pollard simply described it as "the toughest, meanest game I ever played in."

19

Tigers and Bears

On June 12, 1923, the Milwaukee Bears left town and never came back.

Not that anyone in Wisconsin had gotten to know them. The Bears were a new entrant in baseball's Negro National League. They were mostly a bunch of young African American guys with little experience playing on organized teams. They did have a manager, Pete Hill, who had 20 years of professional experience, a future Hall of Famer often mentioned in the same breath with Ty Cobb and Tris Speaker. He sometimes played in the Bears outfield. They also had a couple of other long-in-the-tooth veterans, outfielder Frank Duncan and shortstop Joe Hewitt. Mostly, though, the Bears were a group of relative youngsters, mainly castoffs from other clubs, supplemented by men rounded up in Chicago during tryouts in early April.

The Bears played their home contests, what few they had, in Athletic Park when the Milwaukee Brewers were on the road. They celebrated Opening Day on Saturday, April 28, 1923, taking on the Cuban Stars from Havana. "Local Darkies Win Opener," proclaimed the *Milwaukee Sentinel* without shame the next morning. The final score was 8–5, but the Bears' victory was more one-sided than the score suggests. The Cubans tallied three of their runs as a consolation prize in the ninth inning.

First baseman Percy Wilson led the Bears with a double, a triple, and a home run. His brother Andrew, the center fielder, contributed a single, a double, and a home run. Local sandlotter Sandy Thompson chipped in three singles. Anderson Pryor turned in a spectacular effort at shortstop. Catcher Herman Roth displayed a strong throwing arm. It was an all-around fine display by Milwaukee's newest ball club, one that foretold an exciting season.

One other aspect of the home opener deserves mention. Fans witnessed something never seen before in Milwaukee: two black umpires. The anonymous *Sentinel* reporter wrote, apparently in surprise, that the men in blue "handled the game in faultless fashion," calling it "an innovation that is bound to make a favorable impression along the dusky circuit."

On Saturday, May 5, the Bears played host to the Chicago American Giants, managed and co-owned by the legendary Rube Foster. Formerly a great pitcher, Foster had organized the Negro National League in 1920. He has since been voted into the Hall of Fame in Cooperstown in 1981 and appeared on a US postage stamp in 2010. The Giants defeated the Milwaukee club, breaking a 3–3 tie with five runs in the ninth off Bears hurler George Boggs. Chicago outfielder Jimmie Lyons broke the game open by smashing a triple with the bases loaded. More interesting than the ballgame, though, may have been the Chicago fans and how they got to the game.

The Chicago ballplayers rode the train to Milwaukee. Foster and his white business partner, John Schorling, the son-in-law of White Sox owner Charles Comiskey, rode in motor cars as part of a caravan that gathered in front of the *Chicago Defender* newspaper office and drove together to Athletic Park, making the trip in about three hours. The entourage totaled nearly two dozen vehicles, and each was a showpiece: Cadillac, Packard, Paige Speedster, Oldsmobile, Hudson, Marmon, Stutz Bearcat, and so forth. When the parade of autos parked along the streets

Rube Foster was the founder and ruler of Negro National League baseball in the 1920s. PUBLIC DOMAIN

surrounding Athletic Park, neighbors must have thought that visiting royalty had arrived. And in a way, they had.

Besides Foster and Schorling, the drivers and passengers, most but not all of them black, included some of the most prominent residents of the Windy City. The Reverend M. C. B. Mason was a noted African American educator and a leader in the Methodist Church. Tony Langston was the film and music critic of the *Chicago Defender*. Former lightweight boxer Packey McFarland, the Pride of the Stockyards, was often called the best fighter never to become a world champion. McFarland knew his way around Milwaukee, having fought and won four of his bouts in the Beer City. Edward Jones was one of the kingpins of Chicago's "numbers" gambling racket and a rival of the Capone brothers.

The flamboyant Foster certainly reveled in the attention his flashy motorcade attracted. Beyond that, however, the Chicagoans who made the trip had good reason to travel *en masse*. In 1923 America, black people did not travel freely or without danger. Violence and intimidation were facts of everyday life for dark-skinned citizens. Twenty-six African Americans, including women and teenagers, are known to have been lynched in 1923, although *Time* magazine noted, "There were 61 lynchings in 1922; only 26 last year." *Only 26*, and three of those occurred in states where the Bears competed.

On April 29, while the Bears were losing to the Cuban Stars in Athletic Park, a 35-year-old janitor from the University of Missouri was taken from a jail cell, dragged through the streets by a mob, and hanged from a railroad bridge in Columbia, Missouri, a city the Bears would pass through a few weeks later while going from St. Louis to Kansas City. The janitor was accused of raping a professor's 14-year-old daughter. The *Milwaukee Journal* the next day carried the story on its front page under the headline "Negro Hanged, Coeds Look On."

Attendance for Bears games at Athletic Park was sparse. So was their list of victories. Rain and cold weather prevented the team from practicing throughout most of the spring. After winning the opener they lost nine games in a row and 14 out of 15. On June 11 they were shut out by the Toledo Tigers, 2–0. It was to be their final home game. They hit the road for Detroit with a 7–21 record, never to return. They finished their season with a league-worst 14–32 standing, played a few exhibitions against the independent Dayton Marcos, and then disbanded.

The Bears were not Milwaukee's first talented all-black baseball club. Beginning in 1922 an all-black semipro team, the McCoy-Nolan Colored Giants (named for the plumbing supply business that sponsored them) took on a variety of competitors in Athletic Park when the Brewers were away. On June 17, for example, the McCoys rallied furiously but fell one run short and lost to Rube Foster's Chicago Colored Giants, considered to be the "greatest colored team in the country." A week later Jack McCoy's team broke a ninth-inning tie and defeated the Cuban Stars, 9–8. On Labor Day weekend the McCoys played and beat Universal Cartage, Peterik's Harley-Davidson, and South Side Malleable.

Neither were the Bears Milwaukee's last all-black baseball club. On May 7, 1945, Brooklyn Dodgers general manager Branch Rickey held a press conference at which he announced the formation of the United States League, a new six-team Negro circuit that would include a Brooklyn club called the Brown Dodgers. Rickey said his only direct involvement would be in renting Ebbets Field to the Brooklyn entry for seven or more of their home games. The team would be operated by Joe Hall and managed by former Negro Leagues star Oscar Charleston.

Few people in baseball believed Rickey would not take an active role. Many saw his announcement as a smokescreen to conceal his pursuit of black players for his own Brooklyn club. Those critics were proven correct. Rickey quietly sent out his chief scouts to search the Negro Leagues for talent. Within a year Rickey had signed Roy Campanella and Don Newcombe to minor league contracts. Both men said later they thought they were being recruited to play for the Brown Dodgers.

Before that, however, Rickey had shaken baseball to its very foundation by hiring Jackie Robinson to "break the color line," as people came to describe it. Superscout Clyde Sukeforth introduced Robinson to Rickey on August 28, 1945. That was exactly three months after the fans in Milwaukee made Robinson's acquaintance.

On May 28 the Kansas City Monarchs, with Jackie at shortstop, played the Chicago American Giants in a Negro American League game in Borchert Field. Robinson had earned a considerable reputation at UCLA in football and basketball. He was a baseball rookie, not the headliner of the game or of his team. The marquee player for the Monarchs was probably pitcher Hilton Smith, who had been the announced starter but in fact appeared only as a pinch hitter. Robinson handled six fielding chances, produced no base hits in four tries, and scored one of his team's runs in a 4–2 defeat before an estimated crowd of 2,000.

Two days after Robinson's Wisconsin debut, a team calling themselves the Milwaukee Tigers hosted the Skokie Indians in a doubleheader in Borchert Field. The Tigers were a newly formed black organization that aspired to be accepted into the new United States League in 1946 if they did well enough as an independent club in 1945. The Tigers played a fluid schedule and were constantly on the lookout for games within driving distance. Their roster consisted mainly of talented local sandlot players, among them Shag Johnson, Sanford "Pie" Carter, and Dizzy Adkins.

The Tigers' opening doubleheader on Memorial Day 1945 brought out only a small crowd despite an advertised pregame trick fungo-hitting exhibition by somebody called One Eyed Mike. The Tigers won the opener, 14–9, with three-run homers by Carter and Johnson. They also took the second game as Lefty Martin outpitched former Milwaukee Brewer (and Washington Senator) Ed Linke, 4–3.

For the 1946 season the USL downsized to four ball clubs, only two of which (the Pittsburgh Crawfords and the Boston Blues) displayed professional-level skills. In midseason the Cleveland

Clippers merged with the Brooklyn Brown Dodgers, creating a vacancy. On July 1 two wealthy Chicagoans, H. B. Kinner and Emerson Wynn, purchased a USL franchise for the Milwaukee Tigers.

The Tigers began league competition on the Fourth of July in a tag-team doubleheader in Ebbets Field. In the first game they scored a surprising 6–5 victory over the Boston Blues. In the seven-inning nightcap, the Tigers absorbed a 10–2 shellacking from the Brown Dodgers.

Leaving Brooklyn, the Tigers hopped into their 21-seat team bus and chugged their way home to Milwaukee for their first appearance before home fans on July 7, a doubleheader with the same Brooklyn club. By the end of August the abortive season and the USL had passed into obscurity. The Tigers tried one more season as an itinerant independent team, then disappeared.

20

Papa Bear

George Halas changed the way Americans spend their Sunday afternoons in autumn. He took a brutal renegade sport and helped make it so popular that people across the country schedule their weekends to watch it.

The son of Bohemian immigrants, Halas was born and raised a Cubs fan on the west side of Chicago. After graduating from Crane Technical High School in 1913, he attended the University of Illinois, where he played football, basketball, and baseball. At 160 pounds he was slight even for that era. As a sophomore he got his jaw smashed on the gridiron; in his junior year he suffered a broken leg. His coach, though, the legendary Bob Zuppke, liked the young man's spirit.

Halas narrowly averted death even before his pigskin injuries. In 1915 he had a summer job with Western Electric in Chicago. On July 24, 7,000 company employees were preparing for the firm's annual picnic. Several steamships had been chartered to transport them to Michigan City, Indiana, for the day. Perhaps having overslept, Halas was running late and literally missed the boat. The steamer *Eastland*, on which he should have been a passenger, capsized without warning in the Chicago River, in 20 feet of water, while still tethered to the dock. Of the 2,500 people on

The sinking of the SS *Eastland* in 1915 still ranks as the worst inland marine tragedy in the United States. CHICAGO PUBLIC LIBRARY, SPECIAL COLLECTIONS AND PRESERVATION DIVISION, CCW 6.24

board, 845 were trapped below deck and drowned. It was one of the worst maritime disasters in US history.

When the United States entered the war in Europe, Halas left the university and enlisted in the navy. He was assigned to the Great Lakes Naval Station near Chicago. He joined the base's football team, which played in the Rose Bowl game in Pasadena, California, on New Year's Day 1919. A crowd of 22,000 saw Halas and his sailor teammates overpower the previously undefeated Mare Island Marines, 17–0. Halas caught a 32-yard touchdown pass from Paddy Driscoll and also intercepted a pass and returned it 77 yards to the three-yard line. In addition, he snared another pass in the end zone that the referee ruled had touched the ground. Instant replay might have awarded Halas six points. Despite the nullified score, Halas was voted the game's most valuable player.

Because the war was over, the players on the two military teams were rewarded with military discharges. Halas also was granted a bachelor's degree in civil engineering without having to finish his course work at the university. Instead he took his baseball bat and glove and joined the New York Yankees in spring training in Jacksonville, Florida.

Halas impressed the New Yorkers sufficiently that on May 6, 1919, the football star from the Land of Lincoln started in right field and batted leadoff in Shibe Park against Connie Mack's Philadelphia Athletics. Halas recorded one base hit in four at-bats in a 6–2 loss to the A's.

Five days later Halas started in right field for the third game in a row, this time against the Washington Senators in the Yankees' home park, the Polo Grounds. Halas went hitless in five trips to the plate, hardly surprising since the pitcher for the visitors was fire-balling Walter Johnson, the second-winningest hurler of all time. The game remained scoreless through 12 innings. At that time Colonel Jacob Ruppert, the Yankees president, ordered the umpires to call the game. Ruppert did so because he misunderstood New York's recent Sunday amusement law, believing that it required ballgames to cease at 6:00 p.m.

The following afternoon the two clubs met again, and again they failed to reach a decision. The game lasted 15 innings before darkness halted it. Halas went hitless in four tries. In the ninth inning Yanks manager Miller Huggins sent Lefty O'Doul, a rookie pitcher that he was trying to convert to an outfielder, to pinch-hit for Halas. That essentially marked the end of Halas's Yankees career. He stayed with the club until early July and pinch-hit and pinch-ran a number of times, but he never started another game.

The Yankees farmed Halas to the St. Paul Saints of the American Association. When the Saints came to Athletic Park for a four-game series beginning on July 29, Halas was with them. He took a few swings during the warm-ups and shagged a few flies, but he remained on the bench during the games, still hobbled by a sore hip he had injured while sliding in spring training.

After playing 39 games with the Saints and batting a respectable

.274, Halas decided his future resided in football. On September 17, 1920, he and a group of like-minded individuals convened in the showroom of a Hupmobile dealership in Canton, Ohio, and founded the American Professional Football Conference. In 1922 it was renamed the National Football League.

The team that Halas organized was the Decatur Staleys. They moved to Chicago in 1922 and have been the Chicago Bears ever since. Halas was the owner, coach, and player whose leadership and innovation resulted in the cultural phenomenon that pro football has become. He has often been referred to as "the father of pro football."

On September 19, 1926, Halas returned to Athletic Park, where he and his Bears would face the Milwaukee Badgers, who were in their fifth and, as it turned out, final year in the NFL. The local club, led by player-coach Johnny Bryan, had been practicing every day for two weeks. According to the *Milwaukee Journal*, the Badgers' head man "permitted no sort of loafing." The lineup that Bryan had assembled was huge, with all but one man in excess of 195 pounds. Of special interest was former Marquette University All-American end (and future Green Bay Packer) Lavvie Dilweg.

Halas's Bears were considered the finest professional gridiron team in the land. They boasted future Hall of Famers like Ed Healey, a rugged tackle, and halfback Paddy Driscoll, an outstanding dropkicker, plus a mean 230-pound center named George Trafton. Halas started at right end. The Bears would have been even stronger if sensational running back Red Grange had not quit to form his own team (the New York Yankees) in his own league (the American Football League).

The Bears won the game, 10–7, but the Badgers gave them all they could handle. Driscoll booted a field goal near the end of the first quarter to put Chicago ahead, 3–0. Dilweg partially blocked the kick, but it fluttered between the uprights for the first score. Oscar Krop intercepted his second of two passes, setting up his own touchdown plunge from the one-yard line, giving the visitors a 10–0 halftime advantage.

Feeling comfortable with his lead, Halas substituted for some of his starters, including himself, at the beginning of the third quarter. The Badgers promptly completed a 30-yard pass, Bryan to Stone Hallquist, setting up a first-and-goal situation at the three. Four times Milwaukee tested the Bears defense, but each time the Chicagoans held their ground. On fourth down the Badgers thought they had crossed the goal line, but the official ruled it down one foot short.

Early in the fourth quarter Milwaukee finally scored. Halfback Johnny Heimsch passed to Dilweg at the one-yard line. Heimsch then carried to pay dirt. Don Curtin kicked the extra point to make it 10–7. Taking no chances, Halas sent his first string back into the game to preserve the victory. Despite the Badgers' defeat, fans filing out of Athletic Park had reason to feel hopeful about their football team.

21

Tall Tactician's Team

No major league manager will ever surpass the accomplishments of Connie Mack. He was born Cornelius McGillicuddy in December 1862, 20 months after Abner Doubleday fired the first shots of the Union army in defense of Fort Sumter. Mack was by far the longest-serving field boss in baseball history: 53 years, a total of 7,755 games. He led the Philadelphia Athletics from 1901 through 1950 and earned nine pennants.

After retiring as player-manager of the Pittsburgh Pirates in 1896, Mack accepted the job offer of Matt and Henry Killilea to manage the Milwaukee Brewers in the Western League. Mack directed Milwaukee's club for four seasons, playing home games in the Lloyd Street Grounds. Mack did manage in Athletic Park, though. On September 25, 1922, Mack returned to Milwaukee and brought his Philadelphia A's to the venerable ballyard at Eighth and Chambers for an exhibition game against the Brewers. Despite Philly homers by Heinie Scheer, Frank McGowan, and Jimmy Dykes, the minor leaguers defeated their big-league opponents, 9–8, thanks in large part to a ninth-inning pinch-hit double by an obscure 20-year-old Milwaukee native known as Al Simmons.

The unofficial contest was notable for two reasons. First, it marked the return of former Brewers slugger Unser Choe Hauser, who played for the Brewers the previous season. Adoring fans

Al Simmons (nee Szymanski), the Duke of Mitchell Street, was Milwaukee's greatest hometown ballplayer and one of the finest right-handed hitters ever.
PHOTOGRAPH COURTESY OF THE MILWAUKEE COUNTY HISTORICAL SOCIETY

turned out in force and presented Hauser with gifts: a gold watch plus (this being Milwaukee) a new bowling ball and bowling shoes. Second, this game offered Mack his first glimpse of Al Simmons, about whom Mack would say in 1951, "I have always regarded Al as my greatest ballplayer of all time."

Twenty-two years later a celebration in Philadelphia's Shibe Park commemorated Connie Mack's 50 years as a manager. Organized by sports columnist Ed Pollock, the event featured Abbott and Costello taking batting practice and later performing their famous "Who's on First?" routine. A short film showed highlights of Mack's life in baseball. Afterward the A's and Yankees squared off in their regularly scheduled game, with New York's Hank Borowy outpitching Philadelphia's Bobo Newsom, 1–0.

The fact that the evening's festivities went off without a hitch was near miraculous. An on-going citywide transit strike had sidelined all public buses and subways. The ensuing jam of private vehicles was nightmarish, which made pedestrian traffic the preferred mode of transportation. In addition, because this was 1944, the constant threat of a government-imposed wartime blackout loomed over every night activity, including baseball games. Nevertheless, a crowd of 29,166 made its way to Shibe Park to pay homage to the beloved Tall Tactician.

At the conclusion of the pregame tribute, Mack stood at home plate and announced the members of his all-time all-star team of living ballplayers. Many, of course, were ones he had managed. As Mack read the name of each player, the man would emerge from the Athletics' dugout and line up along the first-base line. Mack's "dream team" selections were first baseman George Sisler, second baseman Eddie Collins, third baseman Frank "Home Run" Baker, shortstop Honus Wagner, catchers Bill Dickey and Mickey Cochrane (Mack obviously could not decide on just one), pitchers Lefty Grove and Walter Johnson, and four outfielders. This last quartet included the Grey Eagle, Tris Speaker; the Georgia Peach,

Ty Cobb; Bucketfoot Al Simmons; and receiving the loudest ova-
tion of all, Babe Ruth. All the ballplayers were present except two:
Mickey Cochrane, because he was on active duty with the Naval
Reserves, and Ty Cobb, because he was Ty Cobb.

Denizens of Milwaukee's Athletic Park were acquainted with
many of Mack's chosen all-stars. Tris Speaker performed in an
exhibition game there as player-manager of the Cleveland Indians
on August 31, 1923. Spoke helped lead the 17–3 onslaught with
four base hits and three runs scored. Also contributing to the
Indians' easy victory were two ex-Brewers, third baseman Rube
Lutzke and catcher Glenn Myatt. The two former Milwaukeeans
attracted a healthy contingent of fans, and each, when stepping
up to bat for the first time, received a gift of a handsome travel bag
presented by the local Owls' Lodge. Myatt rewarded his followers
by blasting a pair of singles, a triple, and a home run.

Speaker's baseball career had another connection to Milwaukee, one far less pleasant. In 1926 he and Cobb were accused by
pitcher Dutch Leonard of fixing and betting on a game played
on September 25, 1919, the same season as the Black Sox scandal. Leonard's shocking accusation against two of baseball's most
revered stars was made in search of revenge, especially against
Cobb, who released him in 1925. Before cutting him loose, Cobb
humiliated Leonard by allowing him to absorb a complete-game
12–4 loss in which he gave up 20 hits.

So what is the Milwaukee connection? The most damning
evidence in the case was a pair of handwritten letters to Leonard,
one from Cobb and one from Speaker's former roommate, Smoky
Joe Wood. During the investigation Milwaukee attorney Henry
Killilea, former and future Brewers owner, who served as counsel
to Ban Johnson and the American League, negotiated the purchase of the incriminating documents from Leonard (reportedly
for $20,000) and presented them to Johnson.

After receiving the letters as evidence, Johnson forced Cobb and Speaker to retire from baseball. In a complicated case muddied by the fierce rivalry and hatred between AL president Johnson and baseball commissioner Landis, the two ballplayers were ultimately reinstated. Each played two more seasons with new ball clubs.

In Milwaukee, most German of America's cities, few visiting diamond stars received more adoring attention than the Flying Dutchman, Honus Wagner, nicknamed Hans. On October 3, 1913, more than 7,000 paying customers, the largest Friday crowd in Athletic Park's 25-year history, watched and cheered Hans's every move in an exhibition game with the Brewers. He was unquestionably the finest shortstop in baseball. Some said he was the finest *ballplayer*. True or not, Wagner cut an imposing figure on the ball field. He was so bow-legged that a first-time observer would marvel that he could run. Nevertheless he had huge hands, long arms, broad shoulders, and a barrel chest. He swung a heavy bat (more than 40 ounces) and could crush even the dead ball of his era. What's more, in 1898 in Louisville he threw a baseball a measured distance of 403 feet.

Wagner was old school, a product of the 19th century, when baseball was played under rough conditions by rugged characters. Hans told the story of his early days playing in Louisville. A New York Giants outfielder walloped his second home run of the day, and as the slugger jogged past him, Wagner cordially said, "Nice hit." The Giant yelled back, "Go to hell!"

"That was the first time any big-league player ever spoke to me on the diamond," Hans recalled.

When Honus and his Pittsburgh club arrived at the train station in Milwaukee, members of the local German community were waiting to escort their famous guest on a tour of the city's breweries. The ballplayer had to beg off—his contract included a temperance clause. For the game Pirates manager Fred Clarke sat in a private box and watched. Wagner managed the team and played the full game at shortstop, going 1-for-3 at the plate. In addition, in the fourth inning, with Max Carey on second, Hans was issued an intentional walk by Brewers southpaw Cy Slapnicka. After the first three balls, Hans tossed away his bat and stood empty-handed in the batter's box and watched ball four. Ultimately Pep Clark's newly crowned American Association champions outscored Wagner's Pirates, 5–4.

When the inaugural class of five Hall of Fame inductees was announced in 1936, one of the five was Honus Wagner. In its first three-quarters of a century, the Hall has also enshrined four Wisconsin natives, one of whom was born and raised in Milwaukee. Al Simmons worked as a messenger boy in a shoe factory before he began his baseball journey on the Milwaukee sandlots. In 1920 he played amateur ball for the Right Laundry team managed by Clarence Dillman. In late 1922 he got his big chance to join the Milwaukee Brewers, and on September 3 in Athletic Park he debuted in left field and banged a home run, a triple, and a single in a 9–5 victory over the Kansas City Blues. Al split the next season between Shreveport and Milwaukee, after which Connie Mack purchased his contract from the Brewers for $35,000 plus two players worth $35,000. Simmons was an immediate success with the A's. He earned recognition as one of the greatest right-handed batters ever, driving in more than 100 runs in each of his first 11 seasons. He played nine seasons for Mack before the cash-strapped owner peddled him to the White Sox in 1933. The record books say that Al batted .334 lifetime, 23rd best all-time. In his nine years with Connie Mack, however, Simmons batted .358, and only Ty Cobb and Rogers Hornsby exceeded that mark.

Bucketfoot Al, so named because he "stepped in the bucket" on his swing, made periodic returns to appear in front of the home folks. In 1923 and 1924 Mack brought Simmons and the rest of the Athletics to Milwaukee for in-season exhibition contests with the Brewers. On October 2, 1932, Simmons and teammates

Connie Mack and Al Simmons's mother attended Simmons's induction to the Wisconsin Athletic Hall of Fame on November 28, 1951. PHOTOGRAPH COUR-TESY OF THE MILWAUKEE COUNTY HISTORICAL SOCIETY

Mickey Cochrane and Jimmie Foxx made a barnstorming stop in Borchert Field as headliners of a so-called all-star game that included Al's brother Walter (also known as Wacky). Al blasted a home run and a pair of singles. Popular Brewers outfielder Tony Kubek, father of the future New York Yankee shortstop, got two hits for the Foxx team.

On June 16, 1933, Simmons came back along with the rest of his new club, the Chicago White Sox, which included guys like Luke Appling and former As teammate Jimmy Dykes. Once again Al rewarded his many local followers by slamming a home run in the 6–2 Chisox win.

Simmons's most memorable exhibition appearance in Borchert Field, though, occurred on Sunday afternoon, October 12, 1930, four days after he and the other Athletics earned their second straight World Series title. Al had been the leading batter of the Series, and he was accompanied by second-leading batter Jimmie Foxx and pitcher George Earnshaw, who earned two victories in the Series.

An estimated 8,500 hero-worshipers contributed some of their precious Depression-era money just to get close to the trio of ballplayers. A cluster of choir boys showed up from St. Hyacinth's Church, where Al had been an altar boy. The youngsters carried a large banner, professionally lettered, that read, "Hello Al! St. Hyacinth's Welcomes You Home."

The afternoon's activities began with a stock of 150 fresh baseballs. Batting practice and autograph seekers quickly depleted the supply. Once the game started, Earnshaw hurled three innings for Foxx's team, then retired for the day. Foxx caught Earnshaw's innings, then moved over and played first base for four frames. He then took the mound and worked the eighth and ninth, allowing no runs.

Following Foxx's example, Simmons also pitched the last inning, also without damage. In the bottom of the ninth, two were out when Al stepped to the plate for his final at-bat. His team was hopelessly behind, 13–6. He swung mightily at one of Foxx's offerings and pulled a mammoth wallop over the left-field wall. The drive cleared the houses along Eighth Street and rolled into Ninth Street. The ball was foul by six feet, but no matter—it was the last available baseball. The game ended, and everyone went home smiling.

22

Galloping Ghost

No individual athlete had a greater effect on the game of football than Harold "Red" Grange. The incomparable running back, nicknamed the Galloping Ghost by Chicago sportswriter Walter Brown, electrified the sports world on the afternoon of October 18, 1924. Against the University of Michigan, on the occasion of the inauguration of Illinois's Memorial Stadium, the elusive redhead returned the opening kickoff 95 yards for a touchdown. He then scored on runs of 67, 56, and 44 yards—all in the first quarter! In the second half he carried for another TD and passed 20 yards for still another. By the end of the game he had earned fame across America.

During his senior season in 1925, Grange only enhanced his reputation. On October 31, on a muddy field in Philadelphia, he ran for three spectacular touchdowns. In his final collegiate game he helped attract a record throng of 84,295 to "the Horseshoe" at Ohio State. Five minutes after the contest ended, the Galloping Ghost scandalized the world of academe by announcing he would leave the University of Illinois immediately and join the professional Chicago Bears, playing for them on Thanksgiving Day, just three days later.

Grange was excoriated for his blatant lust for money. The Cleveland *Plain Dealer*, for example, charged that he had

Halfback Red Grange created a sensation in college football at the University of Illinois, then took professionalism in sports to a new level by founding his own league. MINNESOTA HISTORICAL SOCIETY

"undoubtedly harmed college football and done a disservice to the institution which he has represented on the athletic field." Even his beloved coach, Bob Zuppke, criticized him, saying, "We must have an amateur ideal. If a man plays for himself alone he can't be happy." Zuppke suggested instead that to be "truly a man," an athlete must play "for the spirit of the school."

Grange was a pariah and he knew it. "When I joined the Chicago Bears," he said, "as far as the University of Illinois was concerned, I would have been more popular if I had joined the Capone mob."

But the star halfback saw things differently. Throughout his college days he had been subsisting on the meager financial support his father could provide, supplemented by his own summer earnings delivering ice in his hometown of Wheaton, Illinois. He recognized his value as a newfound celebrity and elected to capitalize. He had previously respected the rules of amateur standing and had rejected numerous lucrative opportunities. In May 1925 he had accepted an invitation to travel to Milwaukee for a Hollywood screen test with actress Virginia Valli. He reportedly was offered a six-figure contract but turned it down.

By joining the Bears, Grange instantly put professional football on the sporting map. His first game, against the crosstown Chicago Cardinals, drew the biggest crowd ever to witness a pro football contest up to that time, more than 36,000. After two NFL games Grange and the Bears embarked on an amazing cross-country barnstorming tour, challenging football clubs of every size and description. In 12 days, between December 2 and December 13, Grange and his teammates did battle in eight games. After a short hiatus, George Halas's Chicago outfit went back on the road for nine more games beginning on Christmas Day. In all they covered more than 15,000 miles, finishing their odyssey on January 31 in Seattle. The team carried only 16 players, all of whom endured a terrible beating. They were so desperate for able-bodied combatants that on occasion they suited up their trainer, Andy Lotshaw.

The tour was brutal, but from it Grange and his business agent, C. C. Pyle, netted a cool half million dollars, an incomprehensible sum in the 1920s. What's more, Grange also became the first football player to endorse products for a fee: ginger ale, sweaters, caps, shoes, even a brand of meat loaf. Ka-ching!

The following season Grange could not come to contract terms with the Bears. Instead he helped organize a new league, the American Professional Football League, with Grange a member of the New York Yankees. In 1927 Grange suffered a serious knee injury against the Bears in Wrigley Field. He was never the same after that, although he did not retire from football until after 1934.

On October 2, 1930, having reunited with the Bears, Grange came to Borchert Field to display his skills and earn some extra dollars with his team. Owner Halas had retired from playing and coaching after a losing season in 1929, so the team was directed by Ralph Jones. The previous Sunday the Bears had lost to their archrival Packers, 7–0, in Green Bay. The next Sunday the Bears were scheduled to play the Minneapolis Redjackets in Minnesota. In between they were taking a detour to play an unofficial game against the Milwaukee Nighthawks.

The Nighthawks were owned by local furniture seller Otto Haderer and coached by NFL veteran Johnny Bryan. The team was described as an "unofficial member" of the National Football League. If they performed acceptably and met their obligations, the understanding was that they would be granted a league franchise in 1931. To accomplish that goal, Haderer had spent $5,000 installing temporary lights to permit evening games—hence the club's name.

The Milwaukee team consisted mainly of recent collegians, supplemented by a few veteran pros like end Tillie Voss and two-sport athlete Gob Buckeye, who had allowed two of Babe Ruth's 60 home runs in 1927. For their effort the Hawks players earned from $25 to $100 per game. They had played together just once, against the Oshkosh All-Stars the previous Sunday. They defeated Oshkosh, 6–0, by recovering a fumble in the last 40 seconds. Oshkosh, however, was not on the same level as the Chicago Bears.

Of course the Bears' biggest crowd-pleaser was Grange, but they brought a lot more. Grange's brother Garland started at right end and showed considerable ability, as did left end Luke Johnsos. At 288 pounds Frank Pauly was a behemoth, easily the largest man on the field. Most of all, the Chicagoans boasted three future Hall of Famers in addition to Grange.

Tackle Link Lyman was an innovative, powerful force on both offense and defense. Center George Trafton, the first to hike the ball with one hand, was simply the best at his position, 245 pounds of muscle. Besides being a dominant lineman, he was an occasional boxer who punched out baseball's Art "Whataman" Shires. Six months earlier Trafton had been knocked out in the first round by future heavyweight champion of the world Primo Carnera. And speaking of heavyweights, the Bears had massive rookie fullback Bronko Nagurski, at 238 pounds the biggest running back of his era. His strength was legendary. His 1932 and 1933 championship rings were size 19 ½. Nagurski would return to Borchert Field as the world's heavyweight wrestling champion on July 18, 1946, one of numerous Milwaukee appearances as a pro grappler. He defeated Fritz Von Schacht in the evening's windup.

The Bears-Nighthawks game proved to be strictly no contest. In the first quarter Red Grange scored on a 20-yard screen pass from quarterback Carl Brumbaugh. Later in the first period Grange ran an option to his right and fired a pass to his brother in the end zone for the Bears' second score. Garland Grange tried to drop-kick the extra points, but he missed them both. With the game firmly in hand, Chicago pulled their starting backfield for the evening. In the second half they also used substitutes along the line. The final score was 26–0 in favor of Chicago. Nevertheless, the 4,500 fans who sat on Borchert's splintered seats on a rainy night felt encouraged because the Nighthawks completed a number of passes and generally performed at a professional level.

Unfortunately for Milwaukee, the Nighthawks soon self-destructed. By mid-October Coach Bryan had been fired and owner Haderer was gone in a flurry of debt, lawsuits, and bounced checks. They never received their NFL franchise.

The Chicago Bears finished their 1930 season on December 15 by defeating the Cardinals, 9–7, in the NFL's first indoor contest, on an 80-yard field inside Chicago Stadium. The charity game raised $10,000 for victims of the Great Depression.

And Red Grange? Until his body gave out, he never stopped chasing the dollars. On January 22 and February 4, 1933, he even played halfback in two charity exhibitions as a member of the Green Bay Packers, in San Francisco and Los Angeles, respectively.

23

Better Than Thorpe

Ernie Nevers may be the greatest football player that hardly anybody remembers. On Thanksgiving Day 1929, while playing for the Chicago Cardinals in the annual city championship game, he scored all of his team's 40 points (six touchdowns, four extra points) against the Chicago Bears, a feat that has never been equaled.

The jersey with a large numeral 1 that Nevers wore as a fullback at Stanford now hangs in the university's Athletic Hall of Fame. In addition to three years of football, Nevers competed in both baseball and track. He once showed up at a track meet wearing his baseball uniform. He scored enough points in the javelin and discus to win the meet for Stanford, then rushed over to the baseball diamond, where he pitched a complete game and defeated archrival Cal.

In 1924 Nevers was a consensus All-American despite playing just three minutes of football all season. That fact demands an explanation. In a preseason practice the so-called Blond Giant (six feet, 205 pounds) cracked his left ankle. He was unable to get into a game until late November against Montana. Three minutes into the game he broke his right ankle.

But that was not the end. Stanford was chosen to oppose Notre Dame in the Rose Bowl in Pasadena on New Year's Day 1925. The Fighting Irish lived up to their reputation and earned a

Ernie Nevers, shown here when he was a member of the Mission (California) Reds in 1928, played professional baseball but excelled in football. NATIONAL BASEBALL HALL OF FAME LIBRARY, COOPERSTOWN, NY

27–10 victory. The hero of the afternoon, though, was Ernie Nevers. With both ankles encased in rubber supports fashioned by his coach, Pop Warner, Nevers played 60 minutes at linebacker and fullback and personally outrushed the fabled Four Horsemen. He carried the ball 35 times for 117 yards and passed for 92 more. In 1925 those were big numbers. Nevers lost 15 pounds during the game. His courageous performance earned a standing ovation as he hobbled off after the game.

Nevers's five-year professional career was limited by injuries. This was no surprise considering the number of barnstorming games that teams played in those times. During 1926 alone, Nevers endured 29 gridiron battles in 112 days. In each of those games except one, he was on the field the entire 60 minutes. Not a man to sit idle, in 1927 he played pro basketball in Jacksonville, Florida, a teammate of Milwaukee Brewers outfielder Cuckoo Christensen. He also pitched three seasons in the American League for the St. Louis Browns, allowing the eighth and 41st home runs of Babe Ruth's record total of 60. He even did a bit of acting, appearing in a film called *The All-American* with Andy Devine and Walter Brennan.

After retiring from the NFL, Nevers continued as a player-coach of all-star games and exhibitions. In San Francisco's Kezar Stadium on January 22, 1933, Nevers's Pacific Coast All-Stars took on the Green Bay Packers, recently returned from a tour of Hawaii, in a charity benefit for the Knights of Columbus. The Packers were fortified by the addition of Bears halfback Red Grange, who played 15 minutes and carried the ball five times for Curly Lambeau's team, but to no avail. Nevers threw the game-winning touchdown pass in a 13–6 All-Stars victory.

Milwaukee's football fans had the opportunity to witness Nevers in his prime. On Halloween night in 1926, his Duluth Eskimos butted heads with the Milwaukee Badgers in an NFL contest in Athletic Park. This was, in fact, a historic day. In Bologna, Italy, Benito Mussolini survived an assassination attempt for the sixth time. In Detroit, escape artist Harry Houdini, who grew up the son of a rabbi in Milwaukee, died, reportedly of a burst appendix. The coincidence of that occurrence is that Nevers, under doctor's orders, was benched to start the game because he was experiencing symptoms of appendicitis.

The conditions in which the teams competed could scarcely have been more unpleasant. An early-season, lake-effect snowfall, followed by a brief warming spell, transformed the gridiron into a slough. The Badgers wore cardinal red jerseys, the Eskimos white, but after a few minutes they were indistinguishable. The ball quickly became hard and slick, and the action had to be halted frequently to towel the mud off the pigskin.

The home club received the opening kickoff and returned it to their 30-yard line. Despite the treacherous playing surface they moved the ball steadily to a series of first downs. When they reached the Eskimos' 20-yard line, Nevers overruled his physician and dashed onto the field, replacing future Green Bay Packers Hall of Famer Johnny Blood. The Badgers advanced the pigskin to a first down at the five-yard line, but there Nevers and his mates stiffened. Four line plunges in succession gained only two yards, so the ball went over on downs to Duluth.

The score remained nothing-nothing until the second quarter. With ankle-deep mud making forward progress difficult, Nevers attempted a long cross-field pass. Duke Slater intercepted and returned it for a Milwaukee touchdown. At the half the Badgers led the favored Eskimos, 6–0.

The third quarter saw lots of plunging and punting and nothing close to a score. Five minutes were left in the fourth quarter when the Eskimos got the ball deep in their own territory. With Nevers carrying the ball on nearly every play, with Milwaukee knowing Nevers would carry the ball on nearly every play, Duluth racked up five straight first downs. From the Badgers 25 the visitors were held for no gain three consecutive times. Facing fourth down and 10 and time running out, Nevers dropped back in punt formation.

He had no intention of kicking. Instead he heaved a high-arching pass to end Joe Rooney at the goal line. Rooney leaped, caught the ball, and tumbled into the end zone with the tying touchdown. In those days an extra point was by no means automatic. Nevers, though, confidently booted the ball between the uprights for a thrilling 7–6 Duluth victory. It was a bitter loss for the Badgers and their followers, but the fans filing out of Athletic Park knew they had seen one of the greatest all-around performances ever by a football player in Milwaukee.

Four years later, on October 29, 1930, Nevers came back to Beertown, this time as the star fullback of the NFL's Chicago Cardinals. The Milwaukee team was now a non-NFL outfit called the Nighthawks. The Nighthawks had upset the Memphis Tigers three days previous, 9–0, in their Tennessee home. On this night, however, it was all Cardinals. Nevers ran the double wing offense to perfection. He rushed for a pair of TDs, passed for two more, blocked, punted, and kicked extra points in a convincing 33–6 Chicago triumph.

On November 28, 1951, Nevers was among the first class of inductees to the Wisconsin Athletic Hall of Fame in the Milwaukee Arena. His eligibility for the honor arose from his having excelled in basketball and football at Central High School in Superior after World War I.

Football legend Glenn "Pop" Warner, who coached both Nevers and Jim Thorpe, called Nevers "the greatest football player of all time." He said, "Nevers could do everything Thorpe could do, and Ernie always tried harder. Ernie gave 60 minutes of himself to every game."

24

Bully in Blue

On September 17, 1940, newspaper readers across the nation were startled to see a photo of a large umpire lying supine in the dirt while being pummeled by a short, pudgy assailant. The story behind the image is as strange as the picture itself—and the man.

The umpire was George Magerkurth, the most vociferous, pugnacious arbiter ever to wear the mask and chest protector. The incident occurred at Ebbets Field in Brooklyn in a game between the Dodgers and the Cincinnati Reds. In the 10th inning a close play at second base caused the umpire working the bases to ask the home-plate ump, Magerkurth, for help making the call. He ruled the runner safe, whereupon Dodgers field boss Leo Durocher went into a tirade. After five minutes of invective, the man in blue sent Leo the Lip to the showers. The runner ultimately scored, and the Reds won, 4–3.

As soon as the game ended, an unemployed truck driver leaped from the stands and attacked the home-plate umpire. From the photograph Magerkurth appeared to be receiving the worst of it, but the bout probably ended in a draw. Several police officers broke it up and hauled away the aggressive intruder, 21-year-old Frank Gernano. It turned out he was not merely an irate Dodgers fan caught up in the heat of the pennant race. He was actually a convicted felon on parole whose objective was to

Umpire George Magerkurth towers over Cincinnati Reds manager Charlie Dressen (left) and general manager/president Warren Giles. NATIONAL BASE-BALL HALL OF FAME LIBRARY, COOPERSTOWN, NY

create a diversion while his confederate in the grandstand picked the pockets of unsuspecting patrons.

The unscheduled fisticuffs were not unusual for the six-foot-three, 235-pound Magerkurth. He had done a little amateur boxing and wrestling in his younger days. After a two-year baseball career with the Kearney Kapitalists in the Nebraska State

League, and in need of a job, the Major (also "Mager") turned to umpiring in the Mississippi Valley League. He earned a reputation for integrity and good judgment. He was, however, born with a short fuse. During a game between Marshalltown and Cedar Rapids in 1922, the Marshalltown catcher, a fellow named Sullivan, made the mistake of "getting huffy" with the umpire. Magerkurth flattened the catcher with one punch, dislocating Sullivan's jaw. Charges were filed, and Big George ultimately paid a $50 fine.

Two years later Magerkurth was umpiring in the International League. Toronto Maple Leafs first baseman Eddie Onslow disagreed with the ump on a close play at the bag. He let loose a string of words that cast aspersions on the relationship between Mager and his mother. The umpire immediately landed a series of blows on the undersized, outmanned ballplayer. Once more the police were summoned. A Baltimore judge levied a fine of $26 plus costs against Magerkurth.

Rather than looking unkindly on the umpire's violent shenanigans, the baseball higher-ups were impressed by them. In particular, Ban Johnson, the American League president, welcomed an umpire who took charge of a game and could not be bullied or intimidated. From the time Magerkurth entered the big leagues, the sport's executives consistently supported him, even when they were suspending him for his more outrageous behaviors.

In the first major league game he worked, Magerkurth ran notorious umpire-baiter John McGraw out of the Polo Grounds. Over the course of 19 tempestuous seasons, Mager's confrontations were numerous: with managers, with ballplayers, and with fans. One of the most famous occurred in those same Polo Grounds on July 15, 1939.

With the Giants leading the Reds, 4–3, in the eighth inning, Cincy outfielder Harry Craft ripped a line drive that hooked toward the left-field foul pole. Home-plate umpire Lee Ballanfant called it a fair ball for a two-run homer. Giants catcher Harry "the

Horse" Danning began hopping around the umpire, berating him in the strongest of terms. After listening to the abuse and after being bumped lightly, Ballanfant thumbed Danning out of the game.

Unable to find a receptive audience in Ballanfant, the Giants immediately swarmed around umpire Ziggy Sears near second base. Sears had not had a good angle on the alleged home run, and he let the Giants know that by tossing out Joe Moore. Then without further provocation the dispute returned toward home plate, toward which first-base umpire Magerkurth had wandered to try to break up the brouhaha. Suddenly the Major was toe-to-toe and nose-to-nose with New York shortstop Billy Jurges.

"This has nothing to do with you," Jurges screamed, according to Arthur Daley of the *New York Times*. "Mind your own business!"

"You little squirt," the Mage yelled back, "this is my business."

As the two men shouted vehemently, a spray of spittle was exchanged between them, giving the episode the inevitable title, again according to Daley and with apologies to Charles Dickens, of "Great Expectorations."

The confrontation quickly escalated. The umpire threw a left hook into Jurges's rib cage. The ballplayer retaliated with a right to the cheek of Magerkurth. More blows were thrown. The next day, league president Ford Frick issued fines of $150 to both fighters. He also suspended each of them for 10 days. This was reportedly the first time a major league umpire was suspended for his actions on the field.

Before hanging up his chest protector, Magerkurth became a living legend. While still in the minor leagues, he was once the target of a bottle thrown from the stands. He picked it up and tossed it back at the person who had hurled it at him. In Cincinnati one time a big-mouthed fan behind home plate rained vulgarities on the Major through both games of a doubleheader. At day's end Magerkurth walked to where the nasty fan was seated and punched him squarely on the snout. The umpire had to pay the man $100 for his medical expenses and give him a signed apology, but assault charges were dropped.

In Forbes Field on June 9, 1946, Magerkurth helped Mel Ott make history by becoming the first manager thrown out of both games of a doubleheader. The list goes on and on. Only a well-respected umpire could have survived all the controversies without being fired. The Major was chosen to officiate two All-Star Games and four World Series. He umpired the 1932 World Series contest immortalized by Babe Ruth's supposed "called shot." The Major claimed that it was true.

Of all his notorious exploits, though, none was more egregious than an incident involving the Milwaukee Brewers and their star first baseman, Ivy Griffin. Magerkurth had begun umpiring in the American Association in July 1926, and he made his first appearance in Milwaukee's Athletic Park on August 10. The local newspapers reported that the big man performed acceptably, although he had two run-ins with Brewers manager Jack Lelivelt. One of these professional differences concerned an apparent balk that was not called. It would have scored Griffin from third base. Magerkurth handled the umpire duties in two consecutive series in Athletic Park.

After the season it was revealed that Magerkurth had been hired to work for the American League in 1927. President Thomas Hickey of the American Association objected, demanding payment of $2,500 for severing his contract. Ban Johnson thought that was excessive, so the deal fell through. Magerkurth was forced to remain a minor-league umpire.

On April 24, 1927, the Brewers absorbed an 11–3 shellacking from the Indians in Indianapolis. In the fifth inning the Major called Griffin out on a bang-bang play at first base. Griffin argued the decision briefly and apparently called the umpire something unkind. Magerkurth was heard to tell Griffin, "I'll get you tonight."

That evening Magerkurth went to the Severin Hotel, where the Brewers stayed. He phoned Griffin's room but got no answer. He waited in the lobby for nearly two hours until Griffin and his wife returned from a show. The umpire gave them a few minutes to get to their room before following them and knocking on their door.

The hulking Magerkurth demanded an apology from Griffin for whatever he had said to him during that afternoon's ballgame. Griffin tried to slam the door. The enraged umpire forced his way into the room. He began beating the smaller man, grabbed him by the throat, and repeatedly bounced his head against the wall. Then he continued to beat him. Mrs. Griffin's screams attracted other hotel guests, and the umpire fled.

Brewers traveling secretary Rudolf Vizny swore out a warrant, and Magerkurth was arrested in his hotel. He was taken to police court and immediately fined $25 plus costs. He also received 30 days in jail, but the sentence was later suspended.

Griffin suffered contusions and abrasions to his face and neck. Worst of all, he dislocated his shoulder, an injury that kept him out of the Brewers lineup for more than six weeks. The shoulder bothered him for the rest of his career. It also may have cost the Brewers the pennant. Milwaukee lost 20 of their 38 games while Griffin was out of the lineup and ended up tied for second place, two games behind the champion Toledo Mud Hens.

The bizarre behavior of George Magerkurth remained a mystery. Many of the people in the Milwaukee organization thought he had attacked Griffin so he would be fired and could then hook on with the American League. The sports editor of the *Milwaukee Sentinel* wrote, "If G. L. Magerkurth is not out of organized baseball for life, then the laws of the game are a joke." Well, cue the laugh track, Professor. Magerkurth soon was working Pacific Coast League games. In 1929 he began his 19-year National League career. The Major never again set foot in a Milwaukee ballpark.

25

Bambino Comes to Beertown

Baseball heroes come and go, but there will never be another Babe Ruth.

The man the newspapers called the Sultan of Swat electrified the sports world in 1921 by slamming 59 home runs, more than twice as many as anyone else had ever hit and more than five of the other American League teams that season.

The Babe and his New York Yankees teammates clinched the World Series championship on October 13, 1921, and Ruth promptly embarked on a barnstorming tour to capitalize on his celebrity. Commissioner Kenesaw Mountain Landis ordered Ruth to desist. The Babe ignored him and set off for Buffalo to start his tour. Landis issued a six-month suspension to Ruth and Ruth's teammate Bob Meusel. Never one to be shown up, the Bambino quickly hired on to a 15-week vaudeville stint, arriving in Milwaukee for a one-week run at the Majestic Theater beginning on February 13, 1922.

Ruth headlined a bill that included a variety of skits, a soft-shoe exhibition, an animal act called Follette's Monkeys, and a one-legged dancing Englishman. (The previous headliner on the same stage had been Helen Keller, "Blind, deaf, and formerly dumb.") The Babe performed with a veteran song-and-dance man named Wellington Cross. The two sang a song together and shared some lighthearted banter. The biggest laugh their act produced followed the delivery on-stage of a telegram:

Ruth: "It's from Judge Landis."
Cross: "Is it serious?"
Ruth: "I'll say. Seventy-five cents, collect."

During his stay in Milwaukee, the great slugger was nearly wined and dined into submission, appearing as the featured guest at a series of banquets that included the Milwaukee Athletic Club, the Milwaukee Press Club, and the Knights of Columbus, of which he was a member. After the show closed on Sunday, Ruth caught a train for St. Petersburg to join the Yankees at spring training (which was exempt from Judge Landis's suspension order).

The Babe's first time competing against the Milwaukee Brewers took place under surprising circumstances. On March 25, 1925, Connie Mack's Philadelphia Athletics played a spring training exhibition in Fort Myers, Florida. The game was a benefit, so to boost attendance, Mack had somehow persuaded the Yankees to lend Babe Ruth to him for the contest. The strategy worked. A large crowd filled the park, including Mina Miller Edison, wife of Thomas Edison, who cheered loudly for the A's. All the stores in town closed for the day so their employees could see baseball's premier slugger. The Athletics' rivals that afternoon were the Milwaukee Brewers. The charity event had been scheduled for March 10, but Ruth was unavailable after chipping a bone in his left hand during infield practice on March 7.

In the game Ruth played left field and batted third, following Bing Miller and preceding Unser Choe Hauser, Al Simmons, and Mickey Cochrane. Ed Rommel was Philadelphia's starting pitcher. He was relieved in the sixth inning by a 25-year-old prospect named Robert "Lefty" Grove, whom the newspapers called "Groves."

The major league club won the game, but the Milwaukeeans gave them a good fight. Frank Luce rapped four base hits for the Brewers and Lance Richbourg added three. Grove retired Bunny Brief on a fly to deep right field with the tying run on second and two out in the ninth to preserve a 5–4 victory. Ruth was 0-for-3 with a walk and a run scored. The star of the game was former Brewer Joe Hauser with a single, a double, and a triple and three runs batted in.

The next time the Babe returned to Milwaukee, barnstorming (the term originated in vaudeville—in the early days shows were sometimes performed in barns) had become permissible through the month of October. On Sunday, October 28, 1928, baseball's two finest home-run hitters—Ruth and his sidekick Lou Gehrig—made their first-ever appearance on a Milwaukee ball diamond. Eight thousand raucous hero-worshipers jammed Borchert Field to cheer as the Bustin' Babes, managed by former Washington Senators shortstop George McBride, faced off against the Larrupin' Lous, skippered by local baseball impresario Eddie Stumpf. The respective lineups were filled out with current and former Milwaukee Brewers and local sandlot players. Most notable among them were Al Simmons and Unser Choe Hauser.

The weather was characteristically cold on this late-October afternoon. After the game the Babe said, "I don't think I ever played on a colder day. Why, my mitts felt as though they would break off every time I hit a ball."

Nevertheless, both Gehrig and Ruth took prolonged batting practice, sending drive after drive into the bleachers and onto properties bordering the stadium. No one had ever smashed a ball over Borchert's scoreboard, but the Babe missed by only a few feet during the pregame hitting.

The exhibition game itself was a brisk 80-minute showcase for the two Yankees standouts. Instead of his customary right-field position, Ruth played the first eight innings at first base, where he

Babe Ruth, flanked by Al Simmons and George McBride, thrilled Borchert Field fans each of the three times he played there. FROM THE AUTHOR'S COLLECTION

was more visible to the folks in the grandstand seats. He batted four times during that stretch, producing just an RBI single in the first inning. In the seventh he batted in Ralph Shinners's spot but lined out to Gehrig. The Iron Horse fared a little better, belting a single and a triple in four tries, scoring twice.

In the ninth inning, with the score tied 4–4, the Bambino gave the crowd what they wanted. He crushed a Dinty Gearin fastball, the horsehide soaring high over Seventh Street and onto the roof of a house across the street. Witnesses agreed it was the most prodigious blast ever in Borchert Field. No one who saw it ever forgot it.

In the bottom of the ninth, Ruth, the erstwhile Boston Red Sox hurler, took the mound. After Ray Thompson flied out to right field, the batting order was waived and Simmons stepped into the batter's box. The popular southside slugger received two chances at a base hit, but the best he could muster was a fly to left. Two out.

The final batter was Gehrig, trying to tie the game against his fellow Bronx Bomber. Lou swung mightily for several minutes but merely produced pop-ups and high fly-ball outs. At last he swung and missed. Ruth retrieved the ball, flung it high into a flock of youngsters, and disappeared under the stands.

Three years later the Sultan of Swat returned to Borchert Field on his announced final barnstorming trip, this time without Gehrig. A special one-inning exhibition before the game showcased two dinosaurs of early Brewers days, catcher Johnny Hughes from the 1913 and 1914 championship teams and 66-year-old hurler Stoney McGlynn, the rubber-armed star of the 1909 club. In the main event, both teams consisted of "all-star" lineups—sandlot and minor league fill-ins like Elmer Klumpp and Fred Baldy. The two pitchers that Ruth faced were 46-year-old Sheboygan (Class D) star Buster Braun, who also tossed three dozen pregame offerings to the Babe, and the redoubtable Humpty Hill.

The world had changed since Ruth's previous appearance in Milwaukee. The stock market had tanked and the country had plunged into the pit of the Great Depression. Ruth was no less popular, but only 2,200 paying customers found their way into the ballpark, plus a thousand newsboys who sat in the bleachers as the Bambino's guests.

The contest was a lackluster affair as Ruth's no-names were overwhelmed by a fame-challenged crew managed by future Hall of Famer Ray Schalk, 6–1. Babe played first base for seven innings and pitched the eighth. He made four plate appearances, singling twice and drawing a base on balls, but the crowd went home disappointed at not seeing a Ruthian blast.

Eight months later Ruth came back to Borchert Field, but this time he brought help. The Yankees, leaders of the American League by seven games, showed up to take on the Brewers. The Bronx Bombers took a day off from their four-game series in Chicago against the White Sox; the Louisville Colonels agreed to postpone their scheduled contest with the Brewers for a couple of days. The reason was simple: money.

The exhibition at Borchert attracted nearly 12,000 customers, drawn by the novelty of seeing baseball's greatest team and most prolific sluggers. The two clubs split the gate. At 75 cents a head, the visitors took home about $4,500, "more than we get for our weekday series with the White Sox," according to Yankees road secretary Mark Roth. The players, of course, received no extra pay.

The stands were filled to overflowing, but there was no such thing as a sellout. The grounds crew roped off a section of left field, people stood on the field and watched the game, and a ball hit into the standing crowd was a ground-rule double.

The ballgame was strictly for fun. The Yanks took a 7–0 lead after two innings, but New York's "official exhibition pitcher," Gordon "Dusty" Rhodes, failed to hold that large advantage, ultimately allowing 18 base hits. Lou Gehrig, who two weeks earlier had become the first batter in the 20th century to slam four home runs in one game, managed only a single and a double. The Babe, despite batting out of turn to get additional chances, could only contribute two singles. Meanwhile, Walter "Cuckoo" Christensen of the Brewers cavorted in left field while smoking a cigar and later donning a fireman's helmet.

The game went to extra innings tied at 9 and lasted two hours and 45 minutes, twice the length of a typical exhibition game. In the 11th inning the Yankees stars had apparently had enough. With a Brewers runner on first, first baseman Ruth allowed an easy grounder to elude him. Right fielder Gehrig let the ball bounce free long enough for the winning run to score. The two legendary sluggers quickly ducked under the stands and made their escape. The Yankees took the train back to Chicago that afternoon.

26

Whataman

Baseball has had its share of characters. It's had self-promoters and egotists and guys who marched to a different drummer. But there has only been one Art Shires.

The man was unquestionably a gifted athlete. No one doubted that he could play baseball with the best of them when the spirit moved him. At the same time, many of his opponents and even his teammates thought he was a blowhard, a loose cannon in the clubhouse and a bully wherever he went. Shires made his debut in the big leagues in Fenway Park on August 20, 1928. Playing first base for the Chicago White Sox, the brash rookie blasted a triple off future Hall of Famer Red Ruffing and followed it up with three singles. Afterward the self-proclaimed "Art the Great" said to a teammate, "So this is the great American League I've heard so much about? I'll hit .400."

Shires didn't hit .400, but in his five-week stint that first season he did bat .341, higher than either Babe Ruth or Ty Cobb that year. He was so pleased with himself that on his trip home to Texas after the final game he hired a private train coach to take him the last 30 miles from Dallas to Waxahachie. He contracted a Dixieland band to join him on the train. To top it off, he staged a parade to welcome himself back to town.

Even before Art the Great made it to the big leagues, he served notice of the dark side of what his life and career would be like. While playing for the Waco Cubs in a game in Shreveport, Louisiana, on May 30, 1928, Shires seemed to be exchanging good-natured wisecracks with the patrons in the "colored" section that every southern ballpark had. Without warning or apparent provocation, Shires fired a baseball into the seating area. It struck Walter Lawson, age 53, on the head and caused a severe spinal cord injury. Seven months later Lawson died. A jury of the ballplayer's peers decided that Shires was not responsible for the man's death. Ida Lawson, Walter's widow, was ultimately awarded $500 for medical expenses.

After just 33 games with the White Sox, Shires somehow persuaded Chisox manager Lena Blackburne to appoint him captain. This was a serious managerial misjudgment. Shires broke curfew in spring training and, when he was benched for it, exchanged punches with the field boss. That was just the beginning. On May 15, 1929, during batting practice before a game with the Red Sox, the Great One was clowning around in a red felt hat. When the manager ordered the buffoonery stopped, Shires replied testily and was summarily suspended. After the game the 195-pound Shires cornered 160-pound Blackburne in the clubhouse and beat him severely, blackening both his eyes and rearranging his nose.

Before becoming a professional punching bag, Blackburne had been the Milwaukee Brewers shortstop on their first pennant winner in 1913. Today he is best remembered, if at all, as the discoverer of Lena Blackburne's Baseball Rubbing Mud. This magical clay, believed to be taken from a secret location on a tributary of the Delaware River, has been used exclusively by ball clubs, major and minor league, to take the shine off baseballs since the 1950s and by the American League starting in 1938. Really, though, Russell "Lena" Blackburne deserves immortality for being the most forgiving man on the planet.

Despite being viciously attacked twice by his renegade first baseman, Blackburne found yet another cheek to turn and allowed Shires to be reinstated. On September 14 the Great One showed his gratitude by punching out his beleaguered field boss once more, this time when the manager tried to intervene in a Philadelphia hotel that was trying to evict the ballplayer for causing a disturbance. At the end of the month both men were gone from the White Sox.

Shires, whom the newspapers enjoyed calling Whataman with more than a hint of sarcasm, decided he could make his fortune as a pugilist. On December 9 in front of a full house in Chicago's White City Arena, Shires made his ring debut against someone using the name Dangerous Dan Daley. Shires entered the ring wearing a multicolored bathrobe with the words "Arthur the Great Shires" embroidered on the back. The Great One triumphed in 21 seconds including the time it took the referee to count up to 10.

One week later Shires fought George Trafton, future Hall of Fame center of the Chicago Bears. The football lineman was no boxer, but he was huge and powerful, outweighing the first baseman by 40 pounds. The fistic display lasted the scheduled five rounds but was never in doubt. "I threw everything but George Halas at him," Trafton later told a writer. "I knocked him down nine times."

Shires peeled himself off the canvas and in the ensuing weeks fought and defeated three stiffs, climaxing with a fourth-round TKO of Boston Braves catcher Al Spohrer. With the fruits of four healthy paydays filling his pockets, the Great One signed up for what promised to be his largest bounty of all: a match with Cubs outfielder Hack Wilson in the Chicago Stadium. Baseball commissioner Kenesaw Mountain Landis disallowed the bout, however, ordering that any ballplayer participating in boxing would be considered retired from baseball.

Arthur the Great quickly became persona non grata on the

south side of Chicago, and on June 16 the Chisox traded him to the Senators. In half a season with Washington he batted a healthy .369. His erratic behavior, however, led owner Clark Griffith to sell Shires's services to the Milwaukee Brewers at the end of November. At the time of the transaction, Griffith told the press Shires was the best ballplayer he had ever sent back to the minor leagues.

The same month the Brewers purchased him, Shires put down his Wisconsin roots by marrying Betty Greenbaum, a teenaged

Art Shires, pictured here with his beautiful wife, had talent galore, but his outsized ego and bombastic personality always seemed to get in his way.
COURTESY OF PAUL F. TENPENNY

University of Wisconsin coed. The wedding was captured by a newsreel camera on the Universal City lot in Hollywood. The Great Shires announced he was embarking on a film career. Word was out that he would appear with Will Rogers in *A Connecticut Yankee*, but if he did, he was uncredited. A month after the nuptials Shires was in a Hollywood jail on a drunk and disorderly rap.

Despite all of Shires's shenanigans, the Brewers were happy to have his bat in their lineup. Even before arriving with the team from spring training, Shires was no stranger to the Beer City. In early 1930 he had performed for a week on the vaudeville stage at the Majestic Theater in downtown Milwaukee. He told a few stories and sang a couple of silly songs. He received surprisingly good notices.

On October 7, 1929, a team of barnstorming Brewers played an all-star team (as they were customarily billed) of major leaguers that included future Hall of Famers Stan Coveleski, Harry Heilmann, and Charlie Gehringer, managed by Connie Mack's son Earle. Despite the array of talent among the visitors, the most ballyhooed of them all was the self-aggrandizing Art Shires. The Great One, a first baseman by trade, displayed his versatility by pitching the last four innings in a 6–3 victory for the all-stars. The crowd loved him.

Shires spent the entire 1931 season as a Brewer. Playing in 157 of the club's 168 games, he led not just the team but the entire American Association with a .385 average. Through the month of May he was batting .443. Consistently good, Art probably had no better game than he produced in Borchert Field on May 14 against Louisville's Colonels.

The 3,071 paying customers certainly got their money's worth. The Brewers lineup boasted colorfully nicknamed outfielders Pickles Gerken and Cuckoo Christensen and pitcher Crip Polli. The game was a slugfest. Each club featured a five-run inning. Milwaukee, however, paced by Art the Great—5-for-5, four runs batted in—prevailed by a 13–8 margin. Shires did something else unique in his career. When Brewers pilot Marty Berghammer was ejected in the fifth inning, Shires was spontaneously appointed the acting manager. He would finish his managerial history a perfect 1–0. Lena Blackburne must have chuckled when he heard about it.

Shires's outstanding performance throughout the 1931 season signaled the end of his abbreviated run with the Brewers. He returned to the majors in 1932, this time with the Boston Braves. His batting average plummeted 147 points, so 1933 found him back in the bush leagues. The Great One made a brief return to Borchert Field, this time as a Columbus Red Bird. Shires led the American Association first sackers in fielding that season, committing just one error. That error occurred in Milwaukee on May 10. With one out in the 11th inning, Shires heaved a throw high above the catcher's reach, letting in two runs to end the game 4–3 in Milwaukee's favor. Never mindful, Shires strutted off the diamond like a proud peacock.

Two weeks after that error, Shires made another one of a different kind. Along with former high school teammate Jimmy Adair, Shires got into a brawl in a house of ill repute in Louisville. Shires got his nose flattened, but the melee culminated with Art the Great picking up a man and throwing him bodily down a flight of stairs and breaking the man's leg. The upshot of the incident was that two women were arrested for "operating a disorderly house" and Shires was sued for $50,000. After the case worked its way through the courts, he paid a $2,500 settlement.

Shires scuffled around in the low minors a couple of years before giving up baseball in 1935, just 28 years old. He tried more boxing and some wrestling (including in the Milwaukee Auditorium on September 29, 1937). After that he nearly disappeared from the public eye. Nearly.

On October 3, 1948, Shires was living in Dallas, where he operated a shrimp restaurant. He went to the dry-cleaning shop of a friend, William "Hi" Erwin, whom he had known since his days in the Texas League. An argument developed. Erwin reportedly struck Shires with a telephone receiver. In response, Art the Great knocked him down, then kicked and stomped on him repeatedly.

When Erwin finally sought medical assistance, he had two black eyes, several teeth knocked out, and severe bruises covering his body. Two months later Erwin died, and Shires was arrested and charged with murder. After a lengthy trial, a jury of six found that Erwin had died from cirrhosis of the liver. Shires the Great was convicted of simple assault and was fined $25.

27

Father and Son

Game Three of the 1957 World Series marked the first appearance of the Milwaukee Braves in a postseason game in County Stadium. The batting star of the day was a Milwaukeean, but he was not a Brave. He was the New York Yankees' jack-of-all-trades rookie, Tony Kubek, a native of Wisconsin's largest city who grew up in Al Simmons's old neighborhood on the south side. The 21-year-old Kubek was no slugger—he had hit only three home runs all season in 127 games—but on this drizzly afternoon he blasted a pair of four-baggers and drove in four runs. Besides Kubek's personal success and the Yankees' 12–3 victory, the day was memorable for Tony because his parents were able to watch him play in person for the first time in the big leagues.

Kubek was a product of the Milwaukee sandlots. As a nine-year-old kid he served as batboy for the Perfex Corporation team in Milwaukee's Industrial League, which his father managed. As a 14-year-old Tony made his Borchert Field debut on August 14, 1950, in the championship game of the Stars of Yesterday league. Tony, the shortstop for Bunny Brief's Stan Galle team, smacked three hits, including a triple, to lead his club to a 17–5 walloping of the Hank Helfs.

Two years later Kubek was back playing shortstop in Borchert Field. On July 25, 1952, he and a few dozen other talented young ballplayers competed in the *Milwaukee Sentinel* All-Star Game. The two outstanding performers were selected to represent Milwaukee in the Hearst All-Star Classic in New York's Polo Grounds. The game's leading hitter was actually center fielder Bob Uecker, who walked, singled, and tripled. He was snubbed, though, in favor of Kubek and catcher Jack Kloza Jr. As a result, Kubek and Kloza traveled to the Big Apple and played on a team made up of two players from each of the 11 cities that had Hearst newspapers. Preliminary to the young stars' game was a two-inning exhibition contest of recent old-timers, including Carl Hubbell, Lefty Gomez, and Joe DiMaggio. The only run was driven home on a single by Rabbit Maranville. In the featured game, Kubek went hitless but got on base by getting hit with a pitch. In the field he was flawless.

The fact that Kubek was a gifted baseball player was not a surprise. His father, also named Tony, had been a ballplayer, and a good one, with the Milwaukee Brewers in the 1930s. Tony the elder made such an impression in his first month in the American Association that the sports editor of the *Milwaukee Sentinel* called him "one of the most spectacular rookies who ever broke into the league." Bob Connery, the owner of the St. Paul Saints, watched Kubek play for the first time and predicted, "He'll be a great hitter if someone doesn't try to change his style. He's a natural hitter."

The elder Kubek began playing team ball as a 12-year-old southpaw pitcher in Milwaukee's Cadet League. He left school after the eighth grade and went to work doing odd jobs in a hardware store. Realizing that the job offered no future, at age 15 he apprenticed himself to a tailor and began pressing pants. That same year he pitched the Riviera Sugar Bowls to the championship of the Midget League. In the next several seasons he moved up through the local amateur leagues, playing for, in successive years, Sunny South Malt and Hops, Otjen Realtors, and Badger Oils. With the semipro Castor Oils in 1930 he tore up the league

For a short time, Tony Kubek Sr. was the hottest-hitting prospect in the American Association. His son, Tony Jr., surpassed him a quarter century later as a New York Yankee. COURTESY OF PAUL F. TENPENNY

with his hitting. Manager Eddie Stumpf thought enough of his star outfielder that he recommended Kubek to the Milwaukee Brewers.

On September 21, the final day of the 1930 American Association season, Brewers manager Marty Berghammer penciled Kubek into the lineup and had him bat leadoff against the Minneapolis Millers. Kubek got one base hit, was robbed of another, and made a fabulous diving, sliding catch in right field. That one-day performance earned him an invitation to spring training and deprived the world of one left-handed tailor.

Kubek's performance in spring training showed promise but failed to excite the manager. Tony probably would not have made the Brewers' roster, but outfielder George "Pickles" Gerken came down with a case of the mumps that lingered into the season and opened a spot on the bench for Kubek. Then in the third game of the season, Milwaukee center fielder Dutch Metzler sprained his ankle. Kubek replaced him in the fourth inning and banged out two hits in three at-bats, including an inside-the-park homer that caromed off the flagpole in deep center. Kubek scored standing up.

On April 20 Kubek proved to his teammates and manager that he had what it takes to play ball in the high minors. In a game in Toledo against Casey Stengel's Mud Hens, the Brewers faced the most intimidating pitcher in all of baseball, Carl Mays, a submarine-ball hurler with a surly disposition and a wicked fastball that was thrown from such a low angle that Mays sometimes scraped his knuckles on the ground as he threw it. It was Mays who, in the Polo Grounds on August 16, 1920, launched a pitch that struck Cleveland Indians shortstop Ray Chapman on the left side of his head. Chapman was helped off the diamond with blood pouring out of his ear. He was rushed to a hospital, where he died the next morning. Mays remained forever unrepentant.

Kubek was down two strikes to Mays in the eighth inning when the nasty right-hander twice aimed beanballs very near his head. Undaunted, the Milwaukee youngster stood his ground. He jumped on the next offering and ripped it into right field, scoring Art Shires from third. By the time the Brewers ended their road trip, Kubek was on fire, the leading hitter in the American Association. At the home opener on April 28, he received a floral bouquet at home plate from his proud hometown fans.

For the next five years Kubek was a popular outfielder for the Brewers, although he spent parts of two seasons, 1932 and 1935, in the lower minor leagues. He played good defense and proved dangerous at the plate, albeit with little power. In a Borchert Field doubleheader with the St. Paul Saints on July 30, 1933, Kubek stroked six hits, including a triple. He never again reached the .357 level of his rookie year, but for his Brewers career he batted a composite .308. Tony Senior never played in the big leagues, but on October 15, 1934, he was a member of the All-Star team assembled by Eddie Stumpf in support of Dizzy and Daffy Dean, recent World Series heroes, who appeared in an exhibition in Borchert Field.

In May 1935 the Brewers needed to release a player to make room for another pitcher. They optioned Kubek to Williamsport, Pennsylvania. He was offered a tryout with the St. Louis Browns, but it would have paid so little that he could not have paid his bills. Instead he was able to find a factory job and later went to work for the Milwaukee post office.

After leaving the Brewers, Kubek returned to where he started in baseball—playing semipro ball for Eddie Stumpf's Milwaukee Red Sox. On June 8, 1936, the Sox played an exhibition game against the House of David, the traveling baseball team of a Michigan religious colony, in Borchert Field. Kubek played center field and contributed a three-run homer in the second inning to please the Depression-era crowd of 900.

Four nights later under the Borchert Field lights, the Red Sox played another exhibition, this one a showcase for the traveling Mexican all-star team called the Aztecas. To spice up the occasion, four representatives of each club staged a pair of running races before the game, a 100-yard dash and a circling of the bases. Kubek took part but did not win either contest.

On August 26, 1952, the Brewers said an early farewell to Borchert Field in a pregame lease-burning ceremony inside their old ramshackle playground. Sportswriter Red Thisted introduced a long list of former ballplayers who had called Borchert Field their home park. Among those receiving the loudest applause was the old pants presser, Tony Kubek.

28

Nowiny Polskie

For many years Milwaukee was known as the most German city in the United States. Beertown even acquired the nickname the Deutsch Athens. By the 1870s, though, Polish immigrants also began arriving in large numbers. The population of the city's Polonia (Polish-American community) reached 30,000 by the late 1880s and nearly 70,000 in 1906.

The Poles who populated Milwaukee expressed their religious zeal by building numerous Catholic churches whose steeples point skyward from the landscape of the city's south side. The crowning achievement was the Basilica of St. Josaphat, just the third basilica in the United States. Constructed of stone salvaged from Chicago's dismantled post office and shipped to Milwaukee by rail, it was completed in 1901. St. Josaphat's still looms large and elegant high above its neighborhood alongside Milwaukee's north-south interstate highway.

Milwaukee's Poles worshiped overwhelmingly within the Roman Catholic faith, but not without some discord. Many of them felt, for example, that Polish members lacked a voice within the church hierarchy. Foremost among the dissidents was Michael Kruszka. In 1888 the aggressive, outspoken Kruszka founded *Kuryer Polski* (Polish Courier), the first successful Polish-language newspaper in America. Kruszka used the *Kuryer* to oppose church leaders and advocate for reform. He supported the teaching of the Polish language in Milwaukee's public schools.

After Milwaukee Archbishop Sebastian Messmer was appointed in 1903, he fought back by ordering the creation of a rival newspaper that promoted the interests and opinions of the church establishment. The paper that the Archbishop approved was named *Nowiny Polskie* (Polish News), originally a weekly but, starting in March of 1908, a six-day-a-week news source sold by subscription at three dollars a year.

Nowiny Polskie never matched its older rival in circulation. It did, however, attract a substantial readership. What's interesting is that many of its customers could not read a word of Polish. The radio listings, most of the comic strips, and some of the advertisements were in English, but it was page six—the sports page, entirely in English and edited by Zygmunt Kaminski—that appealed to Poles and non-Poles alike.

Kaminski began his journalistic career as an office boy, briefly for the *Milwaukee Journal*, then with *Nowiny Polskie*. In 1921 he started writing a bowling column for the latter paper. By the late 1920s he had taken over the complete page six, creating the first sports page in any Polish-language newspaper in America. He presented a comprehensive look at the sports world, but he proudly featured the accomplishments of athletes of Polish extraction. It was no coincidence that on one given day the *Nowiny Polskie* sports page included the names Kowalski, Bieniewski, Skibinski, Piotrowski, Golembiewski, Dzieminski, and Binkowski, to name a few. His daily column—a mixture of sporting information, personal profiles, and opinion—was headed by a drawing of a passenger train and was entitled "Aboard the SPORT SPECIAL with Zyg Kaminski."

Known as Ziggy by people throughout the sports world, Kaminski always sat at the far left (west) in the press coop atop the Borchert Field roof during Brewers games. He would get so nervous about how the home team was doing that he often left his seat and paced around on the roof. Ziggy was a walking encyclopedia of Polish American sports personalities, ever available to share his knowledge with other sportswriters. He was short in stature but always perfectly dressed and groomed, earning the nickname Little Commando from *Milwaukee Journal* baseball scribe Sam Levy. Well respected in baseball circles, Kaminski used his friendships and connections to promote the careers of young ballplayers, especially those of Polish lineage. He helped organize new amateur and semipro leagues like the Milwaukee Lake Shore League, which included the Kosciuszko Reds. He sponsored and coached a team called the Polish All-Stars in the Triple A County League. He also assisted in getting a ballpark built near 19th and Oklahoma on Milwaukee's south side.

Ziggy enjoyed covering the Brewers and rarely missed a game in Borchert Field. He had only one complaint about the contests there: the playing of a recording of "Take Me Out to the Ballgame" during the seventh-inning stretch made no sense to him. He thought the concept was all wrong. The song asks that the singer be taken to the ballpark when in fact he or she is already *in* the ballpark. He thought the song needed to be sung elsewhere.

Perhaps the best example of the influence Kaminski could have on the careers of young ballplayers was the case of Fabian Gaffke. Kaminski first recognized Gaffke's potential when Fabe was a teenager playing ball for the Polish Roman Catholic Union in the Municipal League in the early 1930s. In 1932 he batted over .500 and led the league while playing for the Kosciuszko Reds. "I wanted him to play with the Brewers when he quit the amateurs," Kaminski told a reporter, "but because the Milwaukee franchise belonged to the St. Louis Browns, I steered Fabian away from the hometown club. I didn't want the boy to become a member of a chain baseball outfit, so I took him to the Chicago White Sox."

Gaffke impressed the Chisox. They assigned him to their

Galveston farm team. When he was reassigned to Longview, Texas, however, "The pay there was so small I wired Gaffke to return home," Kaminski explained. Eventually Gaffke joined the Boston Red Sox organization, where he helped lead their American Association affiliate, the Minneapolis Millers, to the Junior World Series championship. He later played in the Millers outfield alongside Ted Williams. A failed elbow surgery ended Gaffke's professional career prematurely in 1943. Two years later he helped Allen-Bradley win the Wisconsin semipro baseball championship.

Besides guiding promising young ballplayers into pro careers, Kaminski took great pride in recognizing successful Milwaukee Brewers of Polish ancestry with special "days" or "nights" in their honor. Ziggy invariably would be the chairman of the organizing committee for a ceremony at home plate in Borchert Field. The honored ballplayer would receive glowing words, gifts, and flowers.

For example, August 27, 1931, was declared Jack Kloza Day. The popular outfielder, known locally as the Buffum Street Bomber, was actually a native of Poland, one of four to reach the major leagues. When he stepped up to bat in the second inning on that August day, the game was stopped. A few jovial remarks were made, after which Kloza received two large floral bouquets and a new Hamilton wristwatch. The man of the hour, several teammates, and the planning committee members posed for a couple quick photographs, and the game resumed.

On August 21, 1936, Kaminski repeated the process, this time for south-side hero Chet Laabs, often called Little Dynamite. A few things were different. Because Borchert Field had acquired lights in June 1935, this was Chet Laabs *Night*. The event had a sponsor: the Catholic Order of Foresters, a fraternal life insurance company. The Detroit Tigers had already contracted Laabs for the following season. And best of all for the Brewers, they were well on their way to clinching their first American Association pennant since 1914.

This confluence of happy circumstances brought a huge crowd to Borchert Field. More than 13,500 enthusiasts jammed every seat and stood many deep around the entire periphery of the outfield. Several thousand latecomers had to be turned away. Local ground rules were invoked declaring that any ball hit among the standing spectators would be ruled a double. Seven of them were. The crowd was the second-largest of the 1936 campaign and easily the largest night gathering the old wooden park had seen.

Before the first pitch, Kaminski's committee and several insurance company executives gathered at home plate and presented Laabs with a matching pen-and-pencil set and a fine leather billfold containing a sum of money. Scarcely 15 minutes later, the recipient sent the overflow crowd into rapturous delight with a long grand slam over the left-field barrier. Two innings later he belted another home run in the same direction. Before the night was over, Laabs had four hits and five runs batted in, and the Brewers had advanced one step closer to their long-awaited title. The next day Kaminski printed in *Nowiny Polskie* a letter of appreciation he had received from the Foresters for his efforts to promote the event.

Of all the ballpark testimonials of which Kaminski was the architect, the best was undoubtedly the first. On August 20, 1928, young Ziggy (not yet 30 and only recently appointed sports editor) and his assistants honored a true minor league legend, a man known throughout the league as Bunny Brief. That was not his birth name, of course. As Zyg would tell his readers, Brief was actually Antonio Bordetzki, or Anthony Grzeszkowski, depending on which family member you spoke to in Traverse City, Michigan. Before World War I he had a few flirtations with major league clubs, but his big-league career was like his professional name—brief. The real story of Bunny Brief is told through his 14 years in the American Association, the last four of these in Milwaukee. In the league's half century of existence, Brief established himself as the all-time leader in hits, doubles, runs scored, RBIs, and home runs.

To honor Brief in Borchert Field, just weeks before the close of the slugger's long career, Kaminski arranged for a 12-piece marching band to emerge through the left-field gates 10 minutes before game time. As they crossed the outfield, they performed a lilting rendition of "East Side, West Side." Behind the musicians followed a shiny Buick sedan to be presented to Mr. Bordetzki/ Grzeszkowski. Zyg and his associates, as well as ballplayers from both teams, surrounded Brief as he stood dumbfounded in the batter's box. Gifts were presented, including the car, a set of matched luggage, a huge floral wreath, an electric heater, and a silver chest presented by the citizens of Brief's hometown in Michigan. While all this took place, visiting manager Casey

On Bunny Brief Day, Bunny (in uniform) received a new 1928 Buick sedan. The short man in the dark suit is Zyg Kaminski. RICHARD LULLOFF COLLECTION

Stengel, who was in the 14th day of a 15-day suspension, circled uninvited around the ceremony in his civilian clothes.

Milwaukee Journal baseball writer Manning Vaughan wrote in his column the next day, "Ziggy Kaminski, who planned this fine tribute to Brief... did a splendid job." Vaughan called it "one of the most remarkable events of its kind in the writer's memory."

Kaminski's journalistic career, unfortunately, was cut short. On July 30, 1944, Zyg collapsed in his home. He was rushed to nearby Johnston Emergency Hospital, but he was dead on entrance.

Several weeks after his death, a benefit wrestling card, including world heavyweight champion Walter Palmer, was presented at South Side Armory, a venue where Zyg had often covered boxing and wrestling matches. A portion of the proceeds was given to his widow, Harriet Kaminski, and her two sons, Conrad and Thomas. Zygmunt Kaminski was just 45 at the time of his death.

29

Nats in Town

In 1933 the United States reached the low point of the Great Depression. One out of four Americans who wanted a job could not find one. Disposable household income had shrunk to a level that precluded many leisure activities, such as watching professional baseball games. The St. Louis Browns' attendance for the entire American League season was just 88,113. In that context the crowd of 1,397 paid admissions at Borchert Field on June 20 does not seem quite so puny.

Nevertheless, the lucky fans who did show up witnessed as amazing an array of ballplayers as you'll ever see when the Brewers and the Washington Senators did battle in an exhibition. Clark Griffith's Nationals had a reputation, inscribed for all time by Charley Dryden, the master baseball writer of the 1900s, who wrote in 1904: "Washington—first in war, first in peace, and last in the American League." In June of 1933 the gag did not apply. The Senators were just a game behind the Yankees en route to the last pennant the nation's capital would ever enjoy. Of greater interest to Milwaukeeans, though, were the fascinating characters the visitors put on the field.

Before the game began, the slapstick baseball tandem of Nick Altrock and Al Schacht performed their popular mimicry and foolishness on the diamond. The pair were listed as coaches, and indeed one or the other did cavort in the third-base coaching box throughout the contest, Schacht unfortunately in a long evening jacket despite the 99-degree heat. Their slow-motion boxing match was, as always, a crowd favorite. Altrock had pitched for the Brewers in 1902, the year the American Association began. In 1933 he was 56 years old but still in good condition. He played the eighth and ninth innings at first base and singled home Washington's last run in the ninth.

The first batter of the afternoon was Senators second baseman Buddy Myer, who at that time happened to be one of the two most-talked-about players in baseball. On April 25, two months previous, in Griffith Stadium, Myer had been the victim of a hard slide by New York Yankees outfielder Ben Chapman. The aggressive Chapman not only spiked Myer but also bombarded him with a string of anti-Semitic epithets. Myer responded by kicking Chapman in the face. Both benches emptied except for two Yankees, who stayed in their dugout: Babe Ruth and Lou Gehrig.

Chapman and Myer both got the heave-ho from umpire George Moriarty, but to get to the visitors' clubhouse, Chapman had to pass through the Senators' dugout. As he did, lefty pitcher Earl Whitehill yelled something disparaging at him, whereby Chapman punched him in the mouth. A free-for-all broke out, and this time the fans joined in, pouring out of the lower deck and onto the field. Before the melee ended, five spectators left in handcuffs, and Myer, Chapman, and Whitehill were banished, ultimately receiving five-day suspensions and $100 fines. To this day, the fracas probably ranks as baseball's most violent brawl. Against the Brewers, Myer belted a pair of singles and scored a run.

The starting Washington shortstop for the Brewers exhibition was first-year player-manager Joe Cronin, who would be the starter in the inaugural All-Star Game the following month. Cronin had been the American League's MVP in 1930. He was one of three future Hall of Fame ballplayers in Washington's lineup.

Another Senator destined for Cooperstown was outfielder Heinie Manush. From 1923 through 1927 with the Detroit Tigers, he had been part of what is sometimes called the best outfield ever, along with Ty Cobb and Harry Heilmann. Manush won the American League batting title when he was 25 years old by getting six hits on the final day. When the Senators arrived in Milwaukee he was sporting an active 23-game hitting streak, soon to expire at 26, and beginning in July he would start another one that reached 33 games. Heinie batted .336 for the year, second in the league, but against Milwaukee right-hander Tot Pressnell he went hitless in three trips.

Also headed for the Hall of Fame (in 1963) was 43-year-old center fielder Sam Rice, in his 19th season as a Washington Senator. Little 150-pound Rice had started out as a southpaw hurler, a teammate of Walter Johnson and George McBride. Rice offered no home-run threat, but he could handle a bat. In 1929, in 689 plate appearances, Sam struck out only nine times.

The baseball exhibition that brought these talented visitors to Borchert Field turned out to be a two-hour version of batting practice. The Senators belted 23 hits off two Brewers pitchers, resulting in a 14–10 Washington victory. On a pennant-bound team featuring three future Hall of Famers, the afternoon's leading batter turned out to be a seldom-used backup catcher named Cliff Bolton. In a substitute role for regular backstop Luke Sewell, Bolton stroked a single, two doubles, and a home run. This was fairly typical for Bolton against minor league hurlers. He often produced gaudy statistics against bush-league pitching but struggled mightily when he got his chance in the bigs.

The final out of the day was made by Milwaukee pinch hitter Benny Bengough. The vertically challenged Bengough (five-foot-seven, maybe) had been to the mountaintop, so to speak, a catcher with the New York Yankees of Murderers' Row fame. He once caught their occasional lefty pitcher named Babe

Ruth and was a friend of the Bambino's away from the ballpark. He never hit a home run in the major leagues, but he was a fine defenseman behind the plate before his arm gave out. On the same day Lou Gehrig took over the first baseman's position from Wally Pipp in 1925, Bengough was given the regular catcher's job for the Yanks. In 1933 he was in his second go-round with the Brewers, a second-stringer on his way down.

Of all the players who paraded their skills in Borchert Field that afternoon, however, perhaps the most interesting—and mysterious—was the man Casey Stengel called "the strangest fella ever to play baseball."

His name was Moe Berg. Born in Harlem to Russian Jewish immigrant parents, Moe may have been the most erudite athlete ever to play baseball. Fluent in many languages, he pursued an Ivy

Moe Berg's eccentric behavior and secretive life continue to baffle researchers just as they did his teammates. NATIONAL BASEBALL HALL OF FAME LIBRARY, COOPERSTOWN, NY

League education at Princeton, where he studied Latin, Greek, Spanish, Italian, German, French, and Sanskrit and graduated magna cum laude in 1923. He later studied experimental phonetics at the Sorbonne in Paris. One of his teammates, when told that Berg spoke seven languages, said, "Yeah, and he can't hit in any of them." Berg also earned a law degree from Columbia in 1930.

Berg played baseball well enough at Princeton to impress the Brooklyn Robins, as the Dodgers were sometimes known in the World War I era. They signed him in June 1923. The next day he was in their starting lineup at the start of a 15-year professional career. For five years he was a versatile infielder; after that he became exclusively a catcher. In 1924 Moe visited Milwaukee's Athletic Park a number of times as a member of the Minneapolis Millers. In August of that year the Toledo Mud Hens experienced a rash of injuries that left them short-handed. In a rare act of sporting courtesy, the Millers sent Berg to them on loan. In late September Moe played four games in Athletic Park as a Mud Hen.

When Berg was first evaluated by a big-league scout named Mike Gonzalez, the report the talent hunter turned in was blunt and succinct, so much so that, although it originally was applied to Moe, it became a dreaded catchphrase: "Good field, no hit." Of course a capable defensive catcher is always in demand, and Moe was, especially with his arm. With the White Sox in 1929 he caught 106 games and allowed only five stolen bases. When the Senators arrived at Borchert Field for their exhibition, Moe was in the midst of a string of 117 games behind the plate without committing an error.

Despite his long baseball career, Moe Berg will be remembered most for his clandestine life away from the ballpark. Simply put, he was a spy. As early as 1932, on a baseball tour of Japan, he was taking photos of Tokyo and its infrastructure. In 1934 he returned with Babe Ruth and Lefty O'Doul and this time wore a kimono, went to the roof of a tall hospital, and shot reels of

home-movie footage of the skyline, harbor, and munitions facilities. Berg later claimed that his films were used to prepare
Jimmy Doolittle's Raiders for their attacks on Tokyo, but that
seems highly unlikely.

What is not unlikely—in fact, it has been documented—is
that Moe worked for the OSS, the forerunner of the CIA, during
World War II. He parachuted into Yugoslavia in 1943 to report
on local resistance groups. The following year the spy agency
had Berg pose as a student and attend a lecture in Switzerland by
German nuclear scientist Werner Heisenberg, considered the
greatest theoretical physicist in the world. Armed with a pistol
and a cyanide capsule, Berg was instructed to find out if the Nazis
were close to perfecting an atomic bomb. If so, Berg was ordered
to assassinate Heisenberg and use the cyanide to take his own life.
Fortunately for Moe that did not prove necessary.

During his baseball career, Berg was primarily known as an
eccentric. Every day he purchased many newspapers, some in
foreign languages, and he was known to read them even in the
dugout. He never allowed anyone to touch the papers before he
read them. If someone did touch one, he became enraged, considered that paper "dead," and bought a replacement.

Sometimes when the Senators had an off-day while at home,
Moe visited the burial place of Edgar Allan Poe in Baltimore. Moe
would stand over the grave and recite verses he had memorized.

In the Senators' game against the Milwaukee Brewers, Berg
replaced his manager, Joe Cronin, at shortstop in the fifth inning.
Moe had been a catcher for the past six years, but this was an exhibition game. He played an adequate shortstop and batted three
times, singling twice and scoring two runs.

Moe Berg's ashes are believed to be buried in an unmarked
grave outside Jerusalem.

30

Hot Enough for Ya?

Beginning at two thirty in the afternoon on July 10, 1936, the league-leading Milwaukee Brewers hosted the third annual American Association All-Star Game in Borchert Field. The Minneapolis Millers had won the two previous summer classics. This all-star lineup looked to be the best ever, though, so the outcome seemed more likely to favor the aggregation of the league's best players.

The backdrop of the All-Star exhibition revealed a portrait of an American nation far different from our modern 21st-century edition. The world's political scene was ominous. Less than two decades after the horror of the War to End All Wars, Adolf Hitler and his Nazi followers had seized power in Germany and had begun burning books and boycotting Jewish-owned businesses. Hitler, officially Der Führer, had announced that Germany would pay no heed to the Treaty of Versailles. Another war was becoming inevitable. In three weeks the Berlin Olympic Games would commence, giving Hitler a world stage for his hatred of Jews and blacks.

The United States, and the city of Milwaukee, had their own social problems surrounding ethnicity. Not one of the participants in the All-Star Game in Borchert Field had dark skin. The country had a harsh view of justice. Within the 24-hour period preceding the game, 13 convicted murderers were legally executed in nine different states, using four different methods—gas chamber, electric chair, firing squad, and hanging. At Coushatta, Louisiana, three men described as "colored" were punished by hanging for an ax murder allegedly committed during a robbery. Huntsville, Texas, in a rare spirit of biracial equity, dispatched three men, one after the other, with its trusty electric chair—one white man, two black. Of the 13 recipients of capital punishment that day, eight were black.

The Great Depression continued to squeeze the nation. One out of six adults could not find a job. Any job. Every day in the Dust Bowl the hot wind stripped away the once-fertile soil from the farmland of mid-America's struggling rural residents. Closer to Milwaukee, farmers in south and central counties of the state endured biblical-style plagues of army worms, chinch bugs, and grasshoppers. Yet despite the ills of society, each of the ticket-holders who traveled to Borchert Field to see the All-Star Game had one thought in mind: man, it was hot.

In fact, it was the hottest July 10 on record, the third day in a row of stifling 100-degree misery, part of a deadly heat wave that in one week claimed 119 lives in Wisconsin, hundreds nationwide. The accompanying drought motivated Archbishop Samuel Stritch to send a letter to local priests instructing each parish to pray for rain every day at Mass. Eighteen women employed by the Works Progress Administration, repairing toys and sewing clothing items, collapsed on the job and had to be hospitalized. Thirty others walked off the job even though doing so cost them their much-needed wages. In Juneau Park near Lake Michigan, hundreds of families slept overnight under the stars. Police patrolmen walking the beat received permission to unbutton their coats.

In spite of the withering temperature, the exhibition involving the finest ballplayers in baseball's top minor league attracted attention from some of the sport's elites. American League president Will Harridge was there, and so were a couple of team owners, a handful of big-league scouts, and a few managers. Baseball commissioner Kenesaw Mountain Landis and National League president Ford Frick had been expected but may have succumbed to the heat. Because of their exalted status, the executives all wore jackets and ties and presumably perspired freely.

Also in the stands in suit and tie sat Brooklyn Dodgers manager Casey Stengel, eight years before his season as Milwaukee Brewers skipper. Stengel's presence was notable because the Dodgers played the Cubs in Wrigley Field that afternoon. Casey left his ball club in the hands of his coaches while he took the train to Milwaukee to assess the available talent for Brooklyn's future. After the game Casey huddled with Brewers manager Allan Sothoron near the dugout. Later Casey identified half a dozen players who he thought could help his club. Among them were two Brewers, slugger Rudy York and smooth-fielding shortstop Wimpy Wilburn. Because the Brewers were a Detroit Tigers affiliate at that time, York went to Detroit in 1937 where he blasted 35 home runs despite starting fewer than 100 games.

Another ballplayer on Stengel's wish list was a Columbus outfielder named John "Long Tom" Winsett. Long Tom was a longtime minor leaguer in the midst of his career year. For the season he would bat .354 and belt 50 home runs. In seven partial big-league seasons, most of short duration, Winsett never approached that level of power. In fact, he never hit more than five home runs in a major league season. In the American Association All-Star Game, however, he was the Sultan of Swat. Long Tom belted a homer in the first inning, added another one in the seventh, drove in four runs in all, and paced the All-Stars in their 9–5 victory over the league leaders.

The Brewers did have their moments, including two-run home runs by Chet Laabs and Lin Storti. The blast by Laabs occurred in the fourth inning off Toledo hurler Alta Cohen, one of the league's best. The fact that Cohen was pitching in the All-Star Game was

Casey Stengel skipped out on a league game to scout the talent in the 1936
American Association All-Star Game. RICHARD LULLOFF COLLECTION

surprising. For the previous seven seasons he had been an outfielder, in both the minor and major leagues. His major league
debut was on April 15, 1931, the only game in which he appeared
that year as a Brooklyn Dodger. In Braves Field in Boston, Cohen
entered as a defensive replacement. He was so excited about being
in the big leagues that he batted out of turn and stroked a single.
The Braves failed to notice Cohen's mistake and did not protest.
Cohen then batted again in the correct slot, in the same inning,
and banged another base hit.

The Brewers generated nine safeties against the All-Star
pitchers, but they were no match for the avalanche of 17 hits of
their opponents. All-Star starting pitcher Lou Fette shut out the
Milwaukee team in the first three innings and received credit for
the victory. Deservedly so. Fette, the pride of the St. Paul Saints,
was the league's best pitcher. At season's end he led association
moundsmen in innings pitched, games started, and winning percentage with a record of 25–8. After nine years in the American
Association, he was more than ready for the big show. He proved
it by winning 20 games the following season for the fifth-place
Boston Bees. And by the way, the correct pronunciation of Fette's
last name could easily be discerned by the fact that his nickname
was Con.

By the end of the game the temperature had mercifully
dropped into the mid-90s. No cases of heat prostration were reported to mar the festivities at Borchert Field. The 4,715 paying
customers filed out of the sweltering ballpark and made their way
to their sweltering homes. The next afternoon the Brewers hosted
Fred Haney's Toledo Mud Hens, and once again the Fahrenheit
reading reached 100 degrees. The local ball club won, 8–7, in 10
innings, but only about 400 fans were on hand to enjoy it. It was
just too hot.

31

Deans Cause a Riot

In autumn of 1934, no ballplayer was more celebrated than Dizzy Dean. At age 23 the hard-throwing right-handed mound star of the St. Louis Cardinals' Gas House Gang had conquered the baseball world. In just his third big-league season, young Diz had won 30 games, lost only seven, and earned the National League's Most Valuable Player Award. More important, he had led his wacky team to the National League pennant, overtaking the New York Giants in the final week. Dean started and won three of the Cardinals' final six games, including two of the last three, both shutouts.

To make the story even better, Dizzy's little brother Paul, a.k.a. Daffy, a lean 21-year-old rookie right-hander, had won 19 games for the Cardinals, most notably a no-hitter against the Dodgers on September 21. These two uneducated "hillbillies" from the Ozarks had led their club past Bill Terry's defending world champions from the big city.

Against the Detroit Tigers in the World Series, the Deans did nothing to diminish their fast-growing legend. Dizzy started three games, winning two; Daffy started two games and won both. Two of the Series games featured incidents that became part of baseball lore. In the deciding seventh game, St. Louis slugger Ducky Medwick slid hard into third baseman Marv Owen. When Medwick returned to his position in left field, Detroit fans pelted him with fruit, lunch boxes, and whatever debris they could get their hands on. Commissioner Kenesaw Mountain Landis quelled the disturbance by ordering Medwick removed from the game, a move that had no impact on the outcome because the Cardinals, and Dizzy Dean, were leading 9–0 at the time.

What could have been a more serious incident occurred in Game Four. In the fourth inning of a close contest, Cardinals manager Frankie Frisch sent his star hurler, Dizzy Dean, who was not pitching that day, into the game as a pinch runner. That decision seems foolhardy today and nearly proved so at the time. Trying to break up a double play, Dean went into second base standing up and was struck square in the forehead by shortstop Billy Rogell's relay.

Dizzy was knocked unconscious and carried from the field. To Frisch's great relief, Dean suffered no serious injury and in fact pitched the next afternoon. The most enduring memory of that near-tragedy, though, is the statement that Diz gave to reporters the next day: "The doctors x-rayed my head and found nothing."

All of this is to establish the fact that, in October of 1934, the Dean brothers were baseball's hottest property. One can only imagine the excitement in Milwaukee when it was announced that on October 15, six days after the Cardinals won the World Series, Dizzy and Daffy Dean, supported by a team of local all-stars, would play an exhibition game in Borchert Field against a barnstorming Negro Leagues team, the renowned Kansas City Monarchs, with Satchel Paige on the mound.

Promoters of the event announced that the Brothers Dean would split the pitching chores, five innings for one, four for the other. What fans did not know was that, before the game, the Deans had received a long-distance phone call from Sam Breadon, president of the St. Louis Cardinals. He warned Daffy, who had experienced pain in his throwing arm late in the season, not to risk further injury in the exhibition.

Daffy (left) and Dizzy Dean were the heroes of the 1934 World Series, but a week later they shortchanged Milwaukee fans and caused a riot at Borchert Field. NATIONAL BASEBALL HALL OF FAME LIBRARY, COOPERSTOWN, NY

Dizzy started the game for the "home" team and pitched two innings, allowing one run on two walks and a base hit. Daffy took a position in right field. In the third inning Dizzy moved out to left field while Daffy stayed in right. The crowd of 3,300 began to grow restless, realizing they may have been hoodwinked out of their 75-cent admission fee. (Not everyone had to pay, though. The Green Bay Packers, including legendary figures like Arnie Herber, Iron Mike Michalske, and Buckets Goldenberg, were in town for an exhibition game with the Chicago Bears, and they attended the Deans' appearance as guests of the promoter.)

In the bottom of the third, Dizzy provided the only highlight of the brothers' performance by lining a home run over the left-field wall and onto Eighth Street. After that the Dean men quietly continued to occupy their outfield locations until the bottom of the sixth. Then both abruptly left the premises.

They were not the only ones. Hundreds of fans began leaving their seats and heading for the stadium box office to demand a refund. Some in the crowd drew up and circulated petitions demanding that justice be served. Fearing violence, promoter Eddie Stumpf summoned the riot police. Captain Arthur Luehman and 10 members of his doughnut squad soon arrived and restored relative calm.

Inside the ballpark, the Monarchs scored four times in the top of the ninth to take an 8–5 lead. The Deans' former club rallied, however, with three runs in the last of the ninth to tie the game. No one cared to continue, and most of the crowd had left, so the game was declared a draw. By that time Dizzy and Daffy, richer by $1,700 minus expenses, were on their way to the airport to catch an overnight plane for Philadelphia.

After the game, promoter Stumpf, who had rented Borchert Field and hired the World Series heroes for the occasion, lamented, "If they had only stayed around until the finish to satisfy autograph hunters, it wouldn't have been so bad."

32

Stars of the Negro Leagues

Until the 1970s the Baseball Hall of Fame in Cooperstown managed to ignore the prickly subject of inducting former Negro Leagues ballplayers. One of the leading proponents of including black players was Teddy Ballgame himself, the great Ted Williams. Eventually the Hall could no longer pretend these diamond heroes had never existed. In 1971 a special selection committee chose nine former stars of the Negro Leagues, one at each defensive position. In subsequent years more were added, and the total now exceeds 30.

The first man honored for his exploits in the Negro Leagues was Satchel Paige, and rightly so. Old Satch pitched in five decades with countless teams in numerous countries throughout the Western Hemisphere. He was probably the best-known player in the history of the Negro Leagues. His blend of rare athletic talent with a humorous personality kept the fans coming to the ballpark even in the depths of the Great Depression. Throughout the 1930s and 1940s he barnstormed with teams that regularly played and often defeated all-white all-star teams headed by major league standouts like Bob Feller. Master showman Bill Veeck signed Paige to a contract with the Cleveland Indians in 1948, making him the oldest rookie ever in the major leagues. In August of that year, Satch attracted record crowds when he pitched in

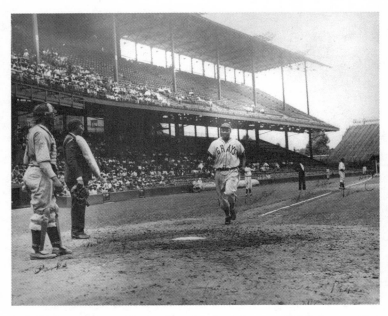

Josh Gibson trots toward home plate after slamming one of his home runs that his Hall of Fame plaque says totaled nearly 800. NATIONAL BASEBALL HALL OF FAME LIBRARY, COOPERSTOWN, NY

Municipal Stadium, twice breaking the night game attendance mark, as he helped Veeck's club capture both the pennant and the World Series.

The second Negro Leagues alumnus to be enshrined in Cooperstown may have been the greatest. Catcher Josh Gibson was often called "the black Babe Ruth," but even that superlative may not have done him justice. "Josh was the greatest hitter I ever pitched to," Satchel Paige said flatly, "and I pitched to everybody." Gibson became the first slugger to hit a fair ball out of Griffith Stadium. Negro Leagues statistics are suspect at best, but Gibson is believed to have slammed more than 900 career home runs. In 1936 alone he reportedly belted 84 of them while batting .517.

The best-fielding third baseman in the Negro Leagues, by acclamation, was William Julius "Judy" Johnson. His Hall of Fame plaque, dedicated in 1975, describes him this way: "Considered best third baseman of his day in Negro Leagues." He was a contact hitter who consistently put up a high average and was considered the ultimate clutch hitter. Connie Mack told Johnson, "If you were a white boy you could name your own price." Johnson served as captain of the legendary Pittsburgh Crawfords teams from 1935 through 1938.

Oscar Charleston, inducted to the Hall of Fame one year after Johnson, earned a reputation among his contemporaries as the best all-around ballplayer in the Negro Leagues. A barrel-chested, fearless brawler with a short temper, Charleston fought with opposing players, umpires, even teammates, and earned the nickname "the black Ty Cobb." He was a five-tool player who routinely led the league in batting, home runs, and stolen bases. Because of his speed he was able to play a shallow center field and prevent many base hits. He was a native of Indianapolis, so the black press referred to him as "the Hoosier Comet."

The 1974 Hall of Fame plaque of James "Cool Papa" Bell says, "Contemporaries rated him the fastest man on the base paths." Originally a pitcher, Bell soon became a center fielder to capitalize on his gift as the fastest man ever to play baseball. His swiftness afoot spawned numerous tall tales and legends. For example, one story says Cool Papa hit a grounder past the pitcher and as he slid into second base, the ball struck him on the back. Most famous of all is Satchel Paige's assertion that Bell could flip off the light switch and get into bed before the room turned dark.

One oft-remembered Cool Papa Bell story is absolutely true. When he was 45 years old, he scored from first base on a sacrifice bunt. In an exhibition game on October 24, 1948, in Wrigley Field in Los Angeles, Bell was on first base with none out. The next batter was Satchel Paige, who laid down a perfect sacrifice bunt to the third baseman. Bell had been running with the pitch, so as Don Lang threw to first to retire Paige, Bell sprinted around second without breaking stride. No one was covering third because Lang had moved in to field the bunt. Seeing the base unattended, catcher Roy Partee moved up the line to cover third base. As he got half way, Cool Papa ran full tilt past him in the opposite direction. Because startled pitcher Gene Beardon had neglected to cover home plate, Bell scored without a throw.

From 1932 through 1936, these five black superstars—Paige, Gibson, Bell, Charleston, and Johnson—played for a team that historians believe was the finest Negro Leagues club ever assembled. They were the Pittsburgh Crawfords, owned and operated by an underworld figure named Gus Greenlee. The notorious Greenlee sold illegal whiskey during Prohibition and ran the numbers racket in Pittsburgh. He was thereby able to hire and support the best ballplayers in the Negro Leagues.

On the evening of August 28, 1935, the Crawfords took on the Chicago American Giants in a Negro National League game in Borchert Field. Four of the Crawfords' Hall-of-Fame-bound stars were in the lineup. The only one missing was Old Satch, who had jumped the team early in the season in a salary dispute. Satch did appear in Borchert Field multiple times, though. On August 13, 1941, he started and hurled four shutout innings for the Kansas City Monarchs in a 1–0 loss to the Birmingham Barons. On June 28, 1942, Paige worked the first four innings against the Chicago American Giants in a game that KC won in 13 innings. Satch's final appearance in Borchert Field came on July 21, 1952, when he pitched one scoreless inning for the St. Louis Browns in an exhibition game against the Brewers.

The Crawfords' opponents, the Giants, boasted a formidable lineup of their own, featuring three future Hall of Famers. Shortstop Willie Wells was considered black baseball's finest at his position. Turkey Stearnes was a fleet-footed power hitter and an excellent outfielder with a strong arm. Mule Suttles swung at the ball viciously, and many observers believed he had the most raw power of any hitter of his time, having slammed several home runs of more than 500 feet.

The same two teams had played each other the previous evening in a Ladies' Night game in Borchert. Stearnes and Suttles had been nursing injuries and could not take part. The result was a 17–2 whomping administered by Pittsburgh. With the two absentees returned to the lineup the following night, the contest was closer. But not much.

The Chicagoans scored once in the first inning but never led after that. A base hit by third baseman Alex Radcliff and a passed ball by Josh Gibson permitted the run. After that, Crawfords hurler Sam Streeter did not allow another base hit through the first eight innings.

Meanwhile, Pittsburgh used Giants pitcher Ted "Long Boy" Trent for batting practice, rapping out 15 hits. Cool Papa Bell banged a pair of doubles and scored twice. Oscar Charleston doubled and scored. Josh Gibson and shortstop Sam Bankhead each had two hits. One of Gibson's was a home run that sailed across Eighth Street and landed on somebody's house. Pittsburgh second baseman Andrew Patterson led all hitters with three singles and a home run.

The Crawfords carried an 8–1 lead into the last of the ninth before solo home runs by pinch hitter Larry Brown and then Willie Wells offered consolation and made the final score 8–3 in favor of Gus Greenlee's guys.

The Pittsburgh victories in Milwaukee were not flukes. The powerful Crawfords went on to defeat the New York Cubans in the postseason playoff series, four games to three, and win the Negro National League championship.

One other Hall of Fame athlete merits attention here. He was inducted not to the Baseball Hall of Fame but to basketball's Naismith Memorial Hall of Fame in 2011. Reece "Goose" Tatum, most famous of all Harlem Globetrotters and the original "Clown

Prince" of the hard court, was a two-sport standout. He played seven seasons in baseball's Negro Leagues and in 1947 was selected to play in the East-West All-Star Game. In Borchert Field on the evening of August 20, 1942, Goose played first base for the traveling Lincoln Giants of New York in a doubleheader against the Birmingham Black Barons. Tatum showed the 2,000 patrons his batting skills by recording five base hits in nine at-bats. The teams split the twin bill. He returned to Borchert on September 2, 1947, as a member of the Indianapolis Clowns. He could not play in the game because of an injury suffered in Detroit. He did, however, entertain the crowd by putting on his popular comedy act before the game.

33

No Runs, No Hits

There's something magical about a no-hitter. Any pitcher who retires 27 batters without allowing even one base hit earns a little slice of baseball immortality. Some years no one in either major league accomplishes the feat. From August 9, 1931, through September 20, 1934, only one big-league hurler tossed a no-hitter. Minor league no-hitters are just as scarce and equally prized. In the Milwaukee Brewers' half century in the American Association, 1902 through 1952, their total number of these hitless masterpieces could be counted on the fingers of one hand, without using the thumb. Among those who achieved what the players call a no-no was right-hander Crip Polli.

Polli had been born in Baveno in the Italian Alps, one of six major leaguers born in Italy. Sportswriters almost invariably referred to his ethnicity when they mentioned him, calling him "the spaghetti king," among other terms. A newspaper photo of Polli, George Detore, and Lin Storti once showed them eating long strands of pasta, and the caption said simply, "Three Wops." Polli's given name was Louis Americo Polli, but since prep school in Vermont, when a football injury "crippled" him and put him on crutches for a short time, he had answered to Crip.

At Goddard Seminary on June 3, 1921, Polli earned a place in *Ripley's Believe It or Not* by striking out 28 batters in a 10-inning game. Crip enjoyed two slurps of coffee in the big leagues, with the St. Louis Browns in 1932 and the New York Giants in 1944, but between 1922 and 1945 he was one of minor league baseball's top hurlers, winning 263 games in 21 seasons.

In 1934 Polli was in his fourth year as a Milwaukee Brewer. On Saturday, May 26, in Borchert Field, the Brewers were taking on the Indianapolis Indians in the second game of a three-game series. The contest offered an unusual incentive—club owner Henry Bendinger told his ballplayers that if they took the series from the Indians, he would buy each of them a new straw hat. Polli was not pitching that afternoon, so he occupied the first-base coach's box and began to barrage Indy pitcher Jim Turner with a stream of insults and invective. Crip was an acknowledged master of "riding" his opponents. By consensus of 1932 American Association managers, he was the champion of bench jockeys.

By the third inning Turner had heard enough. He started toward Polli but was intercepted by the umpire and first baseman Fred Bedore. A moment later, catcher Johnny Riddle (a Milwaukee Braves coach in the 1950s) sucker-punched Polli from behind. Crip returned the blow. The two combatants wrestled each other to the ground. Eventually their teammates and a trio of Milwaukee's finest separated them, and the game continued with no ejections. The Brewers won easily, 10–2, and were rewarded with handsome new lids.

Eleven days later Polli tossed the best game he ever pitched in the ballpark at Eighth and Chambers. Against the St. Paul Saints he allowed just one hit, a sharp single to right in the sixth inning by rival pitcher Lou Fette. Brewers catcher Tony Rensa produced the game's only run with a smash over the left-field fence in the fifth. The 1–0 contest was briskly played in one hour and 18 minutes, mercifully so for the 503 paying customers who shivered (yes, this was June 6 in Milwaukee) in temperatures more appropriate to late October. "I almost froze in left field waiting for someone to hit a fly ball to me," Jack Kloza proclaimed after the game.

Polli failed in his no-hit attempt, but all things come to those who wait. Thirteen months later, on September 7, 1935, Crip fired a 10-inning no-hitter at the same St. Paul club, not at home but in Lexington Park, home of the Saints. The Brewers won, 2–0, and coincidentally defeated Lou Fette, whose single had broken up Crip's previous near-masterpiece.

Speaking of near-masterpieces, an earlier Brewer had also experienced an almost-no-hit gem. On April 14, 1913, in Athletic Park, in the third contest of Milwaukee's first championship season, New Hampshire dairy farmer Ralph Cutting hurled a sort-of no-hitter in beating Louisville, 2–0. The diminutive Cutting was a pitcher of considerable skill, but he was probably better known for being the owner of Fatima, a small goat that roamed the ballpark during off-hours and kept the grass closely cropped. Nevertheless on this afternoon, relying heavily on a breaking pitch he called his "codfish ball," Cutting allowed just three bases on balls and no safe hits, with one possible exception. The second batter of the game, Ovid Nicholson, smacked a roller to third baseman/manager Harry "Pep" Clark. The throw to first was in the dirt and slightly late. Every scribe on press row agreed that it was a base hit—except one. That one, however, was significant.

Tom Andrews, the sports editor of Milwaukee's afternoon newspaper, was the official scorer in Athletic Park for the first half of the season. Andrews did not attend this game, though. In his place he dispatched a young apprentice who thought the play should be ruled an error on the throw. The young man's decision was passed on to his boss, Andrews, and Cutting was officially if not justly credited with a no-hitter. Controversy quietly raged. Fifteen years later Cutting still appeared in the league's listing of no-hitters. By the time of Polli's no-hitter, though, Cutting's name had been expunged.

Dainty Dinty Gearin made all of his teammates, like Bob Trentman here, look like giants. RICHARD LULLOFF COLLECTION

Nine seasons before Crip Polli hurled his no-hitter in St. Paul, another popular Milwaukee moundsman tossed a hitless performance at the Columbus Senators. The pitcher was Dennis John Gearin, commonly known as Denny or Dainty Dinty or, because he stood five-foot-four and weighed scarcely 145 pounds, Kewpie. He, like Cutting, was referred to as a midget and a mighty mite and a squatty southpaw and a hatful of other condescending monikers. But the man could pitch, and the locals loved him.

Gearin had thrown balls and strikes a little in 1923 and 1924 for John McGraw and the New York Giants, who paid Otto Borchert $25,000 for his services. Besides being a reliable pitcher, Dinty also excelled as an outfielder and pinch hitter. In 1920 he appeared in the Brewers' outfield in 88 games, batting .276. In both 1921 and 1922, in fewer opportunities at the plate, he batted above .300.

Brewers manager Jack Egan sometimes used Gearin's versatility in an unusual fashion. If Dinty was pitching and a feared right-handed hitter came to bat, Egan would shift Gearin to right field, bring in a right-handed hurler to face that one batter, then bring Dinty back to the mound. The first time that owner Otto Borchert saw Egan make this exchange, he was livid, reportedly yelling down from his perch atop the grandstand, telling Egan not to make a mockery of the game. When the switch worked successfully, Borchert became an instant convert to the strategy.

Gearin became just the second Milwaukee Brewers hurler to throw a no-hitter in Athletic Park. Czechoslovakia native Joe Hovlik had accomplished the feat on August 20, 1912, in the first game of a doubleheader with Louisville. Fourteen years and one day later, Gearin "stalked into the heaven of baseball's immortals," as Manning Vaughan described it in the *Milwaukee Journal*. Two men were issued walks and one batter was safe on an error, but no Columbus runner reached third base in a 10–0 shellacking. In an odd display of what used to be considered sportsmanship, the final two Columbus batters of the game each signaled surrender by taking a called third strike.

It took a 25-year wait after Gearin's dazzler, but the Milwaukee Brewers pitching staff produced one more home no-hitter. This one was an abbreviated seven-inning affair, the customary short leg of a doubleheader in Borchert Field against the Toledo Mud Hens on August 16, 1951. Charlie Grimm's pennant-bound Brewers trounced the visiting Hens, 5–0, in the opener with the help of a double and a home run by big George Crowe. Right-hander

Bert Thiel, who had pitched a similar seven-inning no-hitter for the Hartford Chiefs in the Eastern League a year earlier, was in total command throughout the contest. He allowed two base runners, one on a walk in the second inning and one in the sixth when massive shortstop Buzz Clarkson dropped an easy pop-up. Despite the muff, Thiel remained unflappable. He eventually struck out Don Lund for the game's final out.

"Yes," Thiel said afterward, "I knew I had a no-hitter all along."

34

Out of Darkness

Night baseball came to the major leagues on May 24, 1935, in Cincinnati's Crosley Field. President Franklin D. Roosevelt flipped a switch in Washington, DC, and illuminated 632 arc lights 500 miles away, brightening the Reds and Phillies and the future of baseball.

Thirteen days later, Borchert Field followed suit. Barbara Bendinger, youngest daughter of Brewers owner Henry Bendinger, pulled a string and lit up the old wooden ballyard with banks of arc lights mounted on 90-foot poles. The estimated cost of the electricity was an astronomical $18 per hour. A crowd in excess of 10,000 had been expected, but an unseasonably chilly temperature and a threat of rain held attendance to 4,747 paying customers.

The ballgame they witnessed was not close but neither was it without interest. The league-leading St. Paul Saints swamped the host team, 7–3, behind the pitching of towering Monty Stratton. The tall right-hander, on loan from the Chicago White Sox, was destined for fame in a way he never imagined or sought. His life would become the subject of an eponymous Hollywood film with Jimmy Stewart in the title role.

Following a 15–9 season for the Chisox in 1938, Stratton suffered a self-inflicted gunshot wound when he fell while hunting

The addition of lights in 1935 made Borchert Field games accessible to fans who worked during the afternoon. PHOTOGRAPH COURTESY OF THE MILWAUKEE COUNTY HISTORICAL SOCIETY

rabbits three days after Thanksgiving. A damaged artery required the amputation of his right leg. Even with a wooden prosthesis, he vowed to return to the major leagues. He failed, but until 1953 he continued to pitch in the minor leagues.

On the home side, fans had the opportunity to see two Brewers of more than passing interest, each of whom recorded two hits. Shortstop Eddie "Doc" Marshall singled and homered onto Eighth Street, thereby extending his hitting streak to 36 games. The consecutive-game total would ultimately reach 43, which at the time placed him sixth on the minor league list. Marshall was a former New York Giants teammate of Carl Hubbell, Bill Terry, and Mel Ott.

Also getting two hits for Milwaukee was catcher Earl Webb. Predictably, both of his hits were doubles—predictably because four years earlier with the Boston Red Sox, Webb had established the major league record of 67 doubles in one season, a mark that still stands.

Despite the disappointingly small crowd, the Brewers management recognized that night baseball would attract new fans. They hastily rescheduled their series-ending ballgame the following day as another evening affair. They had actually been considering the addition of lights since July 1932, when American Association president Tom Hickey suggested it to them. Only the estimated installation cost of $25,000 discouraged them.

Milwaukee's morning newspaper called the Stratton game "the first night game in Milwaukee's history," but that was not correct. It was the first American Association contest played under the newly installed stadium lighting system. There had been, however, a number of exhibitions played beneath the portable lamps of the traveling House of David teams.

The Israelite House of David was a religious colony founded in 1903 by an itinerant preacher named Benjamin Purnell, along with his wife, Mary, on donated land in Benton Harbor, Michigan.

Within a few years nearly 500 members were living in the society's commune near Lake Michigan. By 1920 the colony had spawned a baseball team that barnstormed across the United States, raising money and proselytizing new colony members. Each ballplayer was required to grow a full beard. In 1928 the Daves (as newspapers liked to call them) visited Borchert Field for the first time to play an exhibition against the Brewers.

On April 17, 1930, the traveling Davids added a new wrinkle—electric floodlights on telescoping poles—in an exhibition in Independence, Kansas. The novelty of artificial sunshine attracted crowds and increased the availability of ballparks for the Daves. On the evening of June 5, 1931, the bearded nine brought their $20,000 lamps and their hirsute ball club to a curious crowd in Borchert Field for a contest with the Milwaukee Red Sox of the Wisconsin State League. In the afternoon the Brewers had entertained the St. Paul Saints, losing 10–3. Immediately after the game, workmen began erecting 20 light standards to illuminate the nightcap.

The game, of course, was strictly for fun. The 6,000 patrons who shelled out 50 cents apiece were treated to a comedy featuring a pair of Milwaukee Brewers, first baseman Art "Whataman" Shires as umpire of the bases and left fielder Cuckoo Christensen as the Red Sox's third-base coach. Cuckoo clowned in a flowing fake beard, and the Great Shires cavorted with smoked glasses, a cane, and a large stogie. Between the fourth and fifth innings the Davids amazed the fans with their game of pepper, a sort of baseball equivalent of the basketball warm-up wizardry for which the Harlem Globetrotters became famous.

The final score of the show, in case anyone cared, was 9–4 in favor of the Michigan cult. While the result mattered little to the fans, many of them had made their way to the park to see one particular House of David ballplayer: Grover Cleveland Alexander.

Alexander had been one of baseball's all-time greats. No

pitcher in National League history won more games in his career than Old Pete did—373, tied with Christy Mathewson. Three times with the Philadelphia Phillies Pete won the pitcher's Triple Crown, leading the league in victories, earned run average, and strikeouts.

Named for the US president at the time of his birth, Alexander later had the distinction of being portrayed in a Hollywood motion picture (*The Winning Team*) by a future president, Ronald Reagan. Alexander was the league's best hurler before he was drafted and shipped overseas to fight in the Great War. He returned from the bloodshed shell-shocked and suffering frequent seizures. He continued to pitch in the big leagues for a decade and, almost miraculously, became the hero of the 1926 World Series by helping the St. Louis Cardinals beat Babe Ruth's Yankees. But he was never the same pitcher he had been before the war.

In 1930, at age 43, Pete finally played his last big-league game. He had no money, though, and all he knew was baseball, so he signed on to travel with the House of David ball club and pitch a few innings in their exhibitions. When the Davids came to Milwaukee, Pete still carried enough reputation to attract a crowd of 8,000 to Borchert Field.

Against the local semipros, the bearded visitors were simply too talented. By the time Alexander took the mound in the eighth to work the final two innings, his club had built a 9–3 lead. Alex appeared thinner than he had in recent years. The *Milwaukee Sentinel* described him as being "without the German goiter he used to carry around in front of him." He was easy to recognize, though. He was the only clean-shaven face on the House of David ball club.

The experiment in moonlight baseball was a new experience for most of the fans, but it was not actually Borchert Field's first. Borchert's initiation to baseball under the arc lights occurred on Wednesday evening, September 3, 1930. Barely 10 months after the stock market crash, the defending Negro Leagues champions, the Kansas City Monarchs, came to Milwaukee to show off their brand of diamond entertainment and $30,000 worth of portable lighting equipment.

As was typically the case, the Monarchs' opposition was a so-called all-star team of semipros and former major and minor leaguers, put together by local impresario Eddie Stumpf. Former Cleveland Indians third baseman (and Milwaukee native) Rube Lutzke anchored the lineup, and three former play-for-pay pitchers hurled three innings each for the Milwaukeeans.

One-time Milwaukee Brewer Eddie Schaack was an easy pigeon for Kansas City, giving up four runs in the first inning and another in the third. Sheboygan's ancient spitball artist Buster Braun worked three innings unscathed, and portly Gob Buckeye, who a few years earlier had given up home runs to Babe Ruth, escaped after allowing just one marker while his team fought back to tie the score at six-all.

In the bottom of the ninth the Beertown all-stars loaded the bases for cleanup hitter Lutzke. He belted a fly ball to medium center field that L. D. Livingston either misjudged or lost in the lights. The winning run scored, and the crowd went home happy with a 7–6 victory over the best of the Negro Leagues. A few fans complained about their eyes smarting from the glare of the lights, but it was a small price to pay for the advent of incandescence.

35

Added Attractions

Like musicians and jugglers and other entertainers, baseball players have traditionally had to take to the road to show off their talents and earn a living. Among the notable "barnstorming" ball clubs of the 1930s through the 1950s were Negro Leagues teams like the Ethiopian Clowns and the bearded House of David nine.

Visitors to Milwaukee's ballpark never knew what they would see—in this case, a group of American Indians from Glacier National Park. PHOTOGRAPH COURTESY OF THE MILWAUKEE COUNTY HISTORICAL SOCIETY

These barnstormers used whatever gimmicks they could dream up to attract customers to the ballpark: donkey baseball, shadow infield practice, portable light systems, and in those distant days before the Phillie Phanatic, clowns like Nick Altrock and Max Patkin.

In the end, though, nothing proved more successful than celebrities at drawing a crowd. In a baseball environment, famous athletes always held an appeal. For example, the House of David came up with the idea of adding a woman to pitch for them for an inning or two each game, but not just any woman. They hired 1932 Olympic star Babe Didrikson (who later married the Weeping Greek from Cripple Creek, wrestler George Zaharias), the nation's first female stud athlete. In those Olympic Games women were restricted to three events. The Babe won gold medals in the javelin throw and the 80-meter hurdles and would have won gold in the high jump except she was disqualified in the finals because her head cleared the bar before her body did. This arcane rule had never before been enforced, nor would it be again, but it cost her a third gold medal.

The 1931 House of David baseball team in all their hirsute glory. NATIONAL BASEBALL HALL OF FAME LIBRARY, COOPERSTOWN, NY

The Babe appeared in Borchert Field with the Davids on August 30, 1934. In a nine-inning game under portable arc lights, the bearded ones lost to the Milwaukee Brewers, 6–2. Tony Kubek, Tedd Gullic, Billy Sullivan, and George Detore all contributed extra-base hits for the winners. The Babe pitched only the first inning, giving up one base hit and no runs and ending her stint by striking out second baseman Lin Storti. Many observers felt the strikeout was bogus, just part of the show. After the game, in case the fans had not received their money's worth, the two teams staged a two-inning version of baseball while riding on donkeys. Jack Kloza reportedly slammed a home run, but the bewhiskered bunch won the battle.

Didrikson was not the first female celebrity to pitch against the Brewers. On August 28, 1933, the House of David had arrived with their portable illumination setup and a teenaged girl southpaw for an exhibition. It was the first game under arc lights at Borchert Field for Milwaukee's American Association club. The young hurler was Jackie Mitchell, one day before her birthday (19th or 20th, depending on whom you believe). She had burst onto the national scene in 1931, becoming the first female in Organized Baseball. Pitching for the Chattanooga Lookouts in a preseason contest with the New York Yankees, Mitchell fanned Babe Ruth and Lou Gehrig back-to-back, each on three pitches.

The diamond duel between the Davids and the Brewers was unusual because typically the bearded team would oppose a picked nine of semipros and old-timers. Perhaps the level of the Davids' performance was elevated by stronger-than-normal competition, but the local newspaper the next morning called the game "as exciting baseball as has been offered American Association fans here in several years." The Brewers won, 7–6, but it took them 16 innings and nearly three and a half hours to do it.

Jackie Mitchell's portion of the game was limited by a sore arm. She worked the fourth inning, with her team leading 2–1, and held the home favorites scoreless. She dispatched first baseman Buck Stanton and right fielder Jack Kloza on ground balls. Cuckoo Christensen and Bud Connolly both singled, and Mitchell walked catcher Benny Bengough, loading the bases. She retired starting pitcher (and future Brooklyn Dodger) Tot Presnell to conclude her evening without damage.

Mostly forgotten today but prominent in her time was another female athlete, sprint champion Helen Stephens, who also toured with the House of David. Stephens, however, did not play in the ballgames. Instead she gave exhibitions of her running prowess before the game or sometimes between the middle innings. She would challenge all comers in a 100-yard dash, and she claimed never to have been defeated. On occasion she would race against a horse or a motorcycle, generally adjusted by an appropriate head start. On July 16, 1939, in Borchert Field, she presented a 20-minute show, running the 50- and 100-yard sprints and racing the fastest runners from the Ethiopian Clowns and House of David clubs around the bases. On Sunday, June 9, 1940, Stephens again demonstrated her speed in Borchert Field between innings of a House of David exhibition game against the West Indian Royals from the British West Indies, making their first tour of the American circuit. As usual, Stephens finished first.

Helen Stephens first caught the public's attention as a high school speedster in Missouri, but she achieved her greatest acclaim in the 1936 Olympic Games in Berlin, Germany. Those were the Hitler Olympics, forever remembered as an intended showcase for Der Führer's supposedly superior Aryan athletes. Stephens captured the gold medal in the 100-meter dash and also apparently captured the Nazi leader's heart. Stephens was the only American competitor who had a private meeting with Hitler, and by her account, he seemed intent on fondling the tall, thin runner. She also reportedly received a kiss on the hand from Hitler's henchman, Hermann Goering.

The 1936 Olympics had numerous interesting moments and achievements, among them the first men's basketball competition sanctioned as a medal event. Basketball was not commonly played in Europe. As a consequence, the German hosts scheduled the basketball games outdoors on former grass-surface tennis courts. On the day of the medal games, torrential rain transformed the basketball court into a quagmire. Dribbling became impossible; only passing could advance the ball upcourt. The sodden American team defeated its Canadian counterpart to win the gold in a 19–8 slosher, low-scoring even for that era.

Of all the brilliant performers in the Games of the XI Olympiad, none shone more brightly than US sprint champion Jesse Owens. While belying the Nazi myth of white supremacy, Owens captured gold medals in four events: the 100-meter dash, the 200-meter dash, the broad jump (as it was called then), and the first leg of the victorious 4x100 relay team.

Owens returned to the States aboard the Queen Mary, to great adulation. He discovered, however, that his fame did not translate into dollars, especially for a black man. Needing to earn a living, he tried opening a dry-cleaning business. It quickly failed. Desperate, he took tap-dancing lessons from Bill "Bojangles" Robinson in hopes of finding work as a nightclub performer. That too failed.

In the end he turned, as Helen Stephens did, to traveling with itinerant ball clubs and displaying his track-and-field talents in ballparks. Also like Stephens, Owens raced against anything that moved. Against other men, he often gave a 10-yard head start. When he challenged a horse, he took a 10-yard advantage. "People say that it was degrading for an Olympic champion to race against a horse," Owens said years later, "but what was I supposed to do? I had four gold medals, but you can't eat four gold medals."

For years Owens barnstormed with Negro Leagues teams like the Crawfords of Toledo and then Pittsburgh. His name, like his medals, was gold. Thousands of fans flocked to Borchert Field on June 30, 1940, to watch the Ethiopian Clowns sweep a doubleheader from the Toledo Crawfords. The real attraction, though, came between games as Owens hurdled, broad jumped, and flashed his Olympic speed and style across the uneven surface of the Borchert outfield, easily defeating several challengers.

Four years later, on August 29, 1944, the great Olympian returned to Borchert. Between the fifth and sixth innings of a contest matching the Pittsburgh Crawfords and the Chicago Brown Bombers, the nearly 31-year-old sprinter ran three races. First he ran against a relay quartet of the fastest ballplayers. Then he gave a group of players a head start. Finally he ran the low hurdles while his opponents ran a flat race. He also gave a 10-minute talk over the barely audible public address system. The novelty had worn off, and much of the potential audience was gone to the war. Only about 600 curious souls bothered to attend.

Owens was not finished, though. He returned to Borchert on May 26, 1946, accompanying the Cincinnati Crescents and the Havana La Palomas. He outran a clutch of inferior sprinters. Less than three months later he was back in Borchert. On August 12 Havana lost its game, 12–11, to the Seattle Steelheads. Owens lost his race across the ball field to a younger, better-conditioned horse.

36

Strike Up the Band

"Hi-dee-hi-dee-hi-dee-hi, (Hi-dee-hi-dee-hi-dee-hi), Ho-dee-ho-dee-ho-dee-ho ... He-dee-he-dee-he-dee-he ..." It's the most famous scat singing ever employed by any vocalist. These non-sense syllables became the trademark of one of the best-known song-and-dance men in Harlem and ultimately throughout the world. Cab Calloway was his name. In 1931 during a live radio broadcast he was performing "Minnie the Moocher," a tune he had recently written, when he forgot the lyrics. To stall for time while he groped for the words, he improvised his "Hi-dee-ho" and in the process created a best-selling number that earned him fame and fortune. That same year he began a three-year stint as bandleader in the Cotton Club, Harlem's famous mob-controlled night spot where only white patrons and only black staff members were permitted. The director he replaced was Duke Ellington.

The son of a lawyer in Rochester, New York, Calloway had been an exceptional athlete in high school. He played basketball for the Baltimore Athenians of the Negro Professional League while he was in the 12th grade. Two years later he was offered but refused a chance to join the Harlem Globetrotters. He attended Crane College in Chicago but dropped out of law school to pursue a life in show business.

On May 28, 1937, Calloway brought his World Famous All

New Orchestra and Stage Revue to Milwaukee's Palace Theater. With them were the Harlem Tramp Band and two dazzling singers, Avis Andrews and Evelyn Keyes. As part of the vaudeville circuit, Calloway's troupe did four shows a day, beginning at 1:20 in the afternoon and continuing well into the night, with tickets ranging from 35 cents to a dollar. The shows drew record crowds throughout their weeklong run, with reviewers hailing the King of Swing for his "sizzling" performance. Calloway's marquee status would increase even more a few months later with the release of the Hollywood picture *Manhattan Merry-Go-Round*, in which Calloway appeared along with Joe DiMaggio and Gene Autry.

Despite their grueling schedule, Cab and his musicians often found time to play morning baseball exhibitions against local amateur teams. On June 1, Calloway and his entourage traveled to Borchert Field to take on the Variety Club nine in a charity contest. The umpire, it was announced, would be none other than Joe Louis, one of the most revered African Americans in the country. Louis was training in nearby Kenosha for an upcoming title fight with reigning heavyweight champion James J. Braddock, to be held in Chicago three weeks hence. (As it turned out, the Brown Bomber KO'd the champ in the eighth round and ascended to the heavyweight throne.)

The Variety Club team comprised mostly theater and film folks from southeast Wisconsin, plus newspaper entertainment columnist Buck Herzog, who did as well as a 31-year-old journalist could as a second baseman. The Calloway contingent, meanwhile, offered talents both musical and athletic. Sometimes Calloway pitched in these exhibitions; on this day he anchored the infield at the shortstop position. He was fit and slender and, at age 29, still a formidable specimen. He proved it by pounding out three base hits and stealing—although the statistics from the game were suspect at best—about nine bases. He circled the bases numerous times with impunity.

Calloway's supporting cast was stellar. In the outfield he featured Slop Wright and Doc Cheatham, both trumpet virtuosos, and trombonist Deedlo Wheeler. The right side of the infield boasted a pair of tenor sax players, Flat Brown and Foots Thomas. Drummer Cash Maxey guarded the hot corner. The battery consisted of two alto saxophonists, Bunky Harris on the mound and Rip Barefield behind the plate. All up and down the lineup, these cats could *play*.

And play they did. The music men walloped the men of the footlights, 15–3. A good crowd enjoyed seeing the celebs. About 300 children from St. Benedict the Moor elementary school attended as guests of the bandleader and the future heavyweight champ. And Louis, who had been delayed in transit, arrived in the middle innings and spent the rest of the morning cavorting in the dugout, shaking hands, and greeting the Borchert Field faithful.

The Cab Calloway Orchestra was not the first musical ensemble to attract a large audience by playing ball in Borchert Field. In 1933, at the depth of the Great Depression, when money for entertainment was scarce and every penny mattered, a huge mass of Milwaukeeans descended on the old wooden ballyard bent on seeing their idols play a game of softball. The stadium seated only about 10,000, but that capacity was often exceeded by allowing spectators to stand in a 10-person-deep semicircle around the perimeter of the outfield. A ball landing among these standees would be judged a ground-rule double and play would continue. Lots of ballparks permitted this ad hoc regulation.

This eager throng, however, exceeded all others. The event was scheduled to begin at 3:00 p.m. on September 1. By 2:15 the park's gates were barred and further entrance was prevented. More than 17,000 people had wedged their way in. An estimated 4,000 additional hopefuls had to be turned away.

So what form of entertainment could evoke such an outpouring, this three-decades-early precursor of Beatlemania? It was

A sensation on Milwaukee's airwaves, Heinie and the Grenadiers also proved popular in their appearance at Borchert Field. PHOTOGRAPH COURTESY OF THE MILWAUKEE COUNTY HISTORICAL SOCIETY

an inseam softball match between members of two aggregations of music makers. One was Seymour Simons's orchestra. They were well-known musicians of the airwaves, and Simons was the co-writer of the recent smash hit "All of Me." In truth, though, they were not the main attraction. The people really had come out to see and perhaps hear Wisconsin's most popular radio entertainers: Heinie and His Grenadiers.

In America's most German city, the Grenadiers were *wunderbar*. They called themselves the Band of a Million Friends, which was only a small exaggeration. They played folk music from Deutschland, wore lederhosen, and clowned around in faux-German accents. They were known individually by monikers like Villie and Valter and, of course, Heinie.

In real life Heinie was Jack Bundy, a former vaudevillian actor who, before hiring on as an announcer with WTMJ in March 1932, had directed a similar band called Heinie and His Hinky Dinks on WJBK in Detroit. With the Grenadiers Heinie caught on at once. Within a short time all of Milwaukee seemed to pause daily at noon to listen to the hokey humor and oom-pah-pah stylings of these dozen Dutchmen.

So it was that on a warm first day of September, 1933, Milwaukee's favorite tunesters brought more customers to Borchert Field than any sporting personality or team ever had. For folks unable to attend, the game was broadcast over WTMJ. At the microphone was Johnny Olson, just a youngster then, a sometime vocalist of the Grenadiers. Much later in his life he became television's preeminent game-show announcer on daytime stalwarts like *Name That Tune, The Match Game,* and *To Tell the Truth.* His most enduring contribution to the medium was the catchphrase he created on *The Price Is Right* with Bob Barker: "Come on down!"

The ballgame that ensued was predictably silly and lacking in athletic grace. In the pregame the Grenadiers paraded onto the diamond, wearing old Brewers uniforms and carrying their instruments. After circling the infield they gathered around home plate and played a snappy medley. Then the Seymour Simons outfit emerged from their dugout, the bandleader in a wheelchair and his band members heavily bandaged and on crutches. The players were introduced individually to the crowd, and then "Play ball!" was called.

Each home run earned a reward. Heinie slammed one and received a bouquet of vegetables. One of Simons's sluggers won a belt, buckle, and tie clasp. And every so often, all the action stopped while both ball clubs quaffed generous amounts of beer (well, near beer, the 3.2 variety, because Prohibition still had three more months to run its course). Meanwhile, the voracious music lovers in the audience emptied the refreshment stands of their bounty—soda, chips, ice cream, and candy.

A German band and plenty of snacks—could life in Milwaukee get any better?

37

Goober Zuber Beans Splinter

Ted Williams's oft-repeated goal in life was simple: to have people say, "There goes Ted Williams, the greatest hitter who ever lived." He may have achieved it. On August 3, 1938, however, inside Borchert Field, the Splendid Splinter's baseball career nearly ended before he even reached the big leagues.

Everyone who saw young Ted Williams swing a bat knew he was destined for stardom. As a sophomore at Herbert Hoover High School in San Diego he had batted almost .600. His prowess as both a pitcher and an outfielder attracted attention from the New York Yankees and the St. Louis Cardinals. Reportedly the Yanks would have signed him immediately after graduation if not for his mother's insistence on a $1,000 bonus. The Yankees' scout thought that figure was exorbitant.

To stay near home, Williams accepted a contract with the San Diego Padres. After a year and a half in the Pacific Coast League, Williams was invited to spring training by the Boston Red Sox. He impressed the Bosox, but his young age (19) and cocky attitude led them to farm him out to the Minneapolis Millers for the 1938 season, to gain a little seasoning.

Williams quickly demonstrated that he was the finest hitter in the American Association. On his first trip to Milwaukee in late May, though, he was less than spectacular. In a three-game series

In 1938 young Ted Williams was the toast of Minneapolis and the batting star of the American Association. HENNEPIN COUNTY LIBRARY SPECIAL COLLECTIONS

he was just 2-for-8, with a home run in game one and a two-run double in game three. A month later the Millers returned and Williams fared even worse, producing only two harmless singles in three games.

On Wednesday night, August 3, the Millers arrived at Borchert Field for their third Milwaukee series. The Minneapolis starting hurler was a guy with the unlikely name of Beveric Benton Bean, better known as Belve Bean. Brewers manager Al Sothoron's mound choice to oppose him was Wild Bill Zuber.

A tall right-hander with a wicked fastball, Zuber had pitched for Milwaukee throughout the 1937 season, winning 15 games despite allowing 146 walks in 250 innings. "Bill Zuber and the strike zone have never been formally introduced," observed Toledo Mud Hens manager Casey Stengel. That erratic control partially accounted for Zuber's "Wild Bill" moniker. The other contributing factor was his active, aggressive lifestyle. As a child he had experienced five separate accidents in which he broke at least one limb.

Zuber had been born and raised in the Amana colonies of

Iowa, a communal society of strict conservative Christian immigrants from Germany. It was a five-hour drive and a century away from Milwaukee. As a boy he spoke only German; as an adult he spoke English with a thick accent. Playing ball, he also acquired the inevitable rhyming nickname of Goober.

Wild Bill had been pitching for Cleveland, but when the Indians recalled Ken Jungels from Milwaukee, Zuber was sent down to make room for him. This was his first appearance since his return.

Zuber's first inning back with the Brewers was not an auspicious one. Leadoff batter Andy Cohen bounced to third base, but Oscar Grimes fumbled the ball and Cohen was safe. After Coaker Triplett grounded out, Zuber walked Stanley Spence. Williams batted next, and he made Zuber pay with a double in the gap in left-center. Williams's smash gave him 100 runs batted in for the season, by far the league's highest total, and put the Millers in the lead, 2–0.

The home team tied the score in the bottom of the first with a walk, a bloop double, another base on balls, and a single by Fritz Schulte. The Minnesotans jumped ahead again in the top of the third. Cohen was again safe on an error by Grimes. Spence doubled with one out to put men on second and third. With first base open, Brewers manager Sothoron elected not to walk Williams. The strategy backfired. The Millers' lean batting machine ripped a base hit up the middle, scoring two more runs. Catcher Earl Grace singled home Williams to make it 5–2 for the visitors.

That was the score in the top of the fifth inning when Zuber walked leadoff batter Spence for the second time. That brought up Williams. Zuber fired a fastball up and in that caromed off the back of the slugger's head and dropped him as though he had been shot. Ted lay unconscious in the dirt for several minutes before gradually reviving and slowly sitting up. He was helped to the visitors' clubhouse, where he received treatment from Dr. William J. Murphy. Pitcher Alta Cohen pinch-ran for Williams, then finished the game as the right fielder.

Apparently shaken by the incident, Zuber proceeded to walk Roy Pfleger to load the bases with nobody out. Zuber escaped with just one run scoring thanks to a double play, but the Millers held a 6–2 advantage. Brewers first baseman Mickey Heath slammed a solo home run across Seventh Street in the bottom of the fifth, then blasted a three-run shot to the same area in the last of the seventh. The game was tied, 6–6, and remained that way through the ninth inning and into the bottom of the tenth.

Right fielder Roy Johnson lofted a soft single to left to start the Brewers' tenth. Then slugging center fielder Tedd Gullic did something that power hitters today cannot do: he successfully laid down a sacrifice bunt. Schulte received an intentional pass. Tommy Irwin bounced into a fielder's choice, forcing Schulte for the second out. Catcher William Hankins was purposely walked to load the bases and get at the pitcher. Finally, on a 2-2 pitch, Wild Bill bounced the game-winning single through the box into center field and Milwaukee won, 7–6.

Williams was fortunate. After the game he had a booming headache and a knot on his head, but the damage turned out to be superficial. The next night he took batting practice before the Brewers-Millers game. As a precaution, though, manager Donie Bush held him out of the game. In Ted's place, rookie pitcher Bill Lefebvre played right field and batted cleanup. Friday was a travel day. On Saturday in Kansas City, Williams was back in the lineup. He smacked a double and a home run and drove in four runs.

In Borchert Field's tiny visitors' locker room, an hour after he was beaned, Williams told a reporter, probably in jest, "I never want to hit against Zuber again." Alas, he did not get his wish. On the penultimate day of the season, in Nicollet Park in Minneapolis, the Millers faced Goober Zuber one last time. No blood was shed, but Teddy Ballgame, on his way to leading the American Association with a .366 average, 43 home runs, and 142 runs batted in, managed just a single in four times at bat against Wild Bill.

38

Men in Pinstripes

In the New York Yankees' first 18 years in the American League, they never won a pennant. In their next 44 seasons, they earned their way into the World Series 29 times, winning 20 of those Fall Classics. A generation of baseball fans grew up believing that the World Series was played each October between the Yankees and whoever won the National League pennant.

Collectively and individually, the Bronx Bombers always attracted interest wherever they went, including Borchert Field. On June 17, 1932, the New Yorkers played an exhibition game in the Brewers' park. The big stars—Ruth and Gehrig—played the full game. Both famous sluggers had been to Borchert before on postseason barnstorming tours. Some of their teammates were visiting for the first time, including outfielder Myril Hoag. Never a Yankees regular, Hoag is perhaps best remembered for his tiny feet. He stood five-foot-eleven and weighed 180 pounds, but his custom-made (and differently dimensioned) shoes were size 4 ½ for the left and 4 for the right.

Of course some Yankees played in Borchert on their way to the big leagues, before they wore the New York pinstripes. Phil Rizzuto, the diminutive (five-foot-six) shortstop known affectionately as Scooter, played for the Kansas City Blues in 1939 and

1940. Consequently he appeared in many games in Milwaukee against the Brewers. He was easily the league's best at his position besides being among the American Association's top hitters.

On July 1, 1940, in Borchert Field, Brewers left-hander Paul Sullivan singled in the bottom of the third inning. Next batter Claude Corbitt bounced one to second sacker Jerry Priddy. He tossed to Rizzuto covering second. Scooter fired toward first to complete the double play, but the ball struck the sliding Sullivan squarely on the bridge of the nose. Sully collapsed as if he had been shot. Seeing what had happened, Rizzuto burst into tears. Sullivan was placed on a stretcher, carried to an ambulance, and transported to Misericordia Hospital.

Although deeply affected, the little shortstop still managed two singles and a double, drove in a run, and scored a run in a 3–2 Kansas City victory.

Rizzuto visited Sullivan in the hospital the following morning. The burly pitcher had suffered a fracture of the nasal bone and a concussion. His entire face was swollen and discolored. He remained hospitalized for more than a week and away from baseball for more than a month. In spring training nine months later, he still experienced pain near his eardrums.

Meanwhile Rizzuto completed an MVP season and was named *The Sporting News* 1940 Minor League Player of the Year. That achievement helped earn him a one-way ticket to the big leagues. On May 19, 1942, Scooter and his league-leading Yankees mates brought their big bats to Borchert Field to show the Brewers how the game should be played. More than 10,000 fans paid their way into the ballpark on a Tuesday afternoon to see the defending world champions and their big-name ballplayers. Red Rolfe, Tommy Henrich, Buddy Hassett, Twinkletoes Selkirk, and Charlie "King Kong" Keller each drew his share of attention. Rizzuto took part in three of New York's snappy double plays.

Third baseman Red Rolfe (in circle) and his New York Yankees teammates did their warm-ups before taking on the Brewers on May 19, 1942, in Borchert Field. RICHARD LULLOFF COLLECTION

All-Star second baseman Joe Gordon slammed a pair of massive home runs. Without question, though, most people were there to see one particular player: the great Joe DiMaggio.

Before the game Joltin' Joe was besieged by scorecard-bearing autograph seekers of all ages. The Yankee Clipper scribbled his name for many of them, while others had to be content with seeing the famous slugger at close range or maybe taking a snapshot of him. He was, after all, the reigning American League Most Valuable Player and the most glamorous athlete in the nation. Joe was less than one year removed from his much-ballyhooed 56-game hitting streak. Hundreds, maybe thousands of hero-worshipers had skipped school or work just to see him in the flesh.

When he strode to the plate in the first inning swinging two bats, proudly displaying his famed numeral 5 on the back of his jersey, the stands erupted in applause and whistles. Joe did not disappoint. With the crowd rhythmically chanting his name, he ripped a base hit to drive home a runner from second and give the Yanks a lead they never relinquished.

Joe went to bat three more times. He popped out to the second baseman in the third, flied out to left in the fourth, and walked in the sixth. After that he retired for the afternoon. The crowd had been rooting for a home run, but even so, no one left the stadium unhappy. For the record, the Yankees won by a score of 8–2.

Lots of future Yankees played in Borchert Field as members of New York's American Association affiliate, the Kansas City Blues. Among these was center fielder Cliff Mapes. On May 31, 1947, in an 18–10 slaughter inflicted by KC, Mapes accomplished a feat that no one else had done in the 59-year history of the ballpark. He crushed a home run that cleared the distant scoreboard in right-center field. Stadium announcer Art Truss went into the bleacher seats and interviewed witnesses to the historic blast. He learned that the ball had cleared the fence on the northern perimeter of the park and landed in Burleigh Street, nearly 500 feet from home plate.

In fairness to half a century of sluggers, Mapes owed a debt of gratitude to Brewers owner Lou Perini for the mammoth clout. Perini had purchased the Brewers the previous summer. In the off-season he had ordered that home plate be moved 20 feet to the north to improve the sight lines from the grandstand. Without the 20-foot boost, Mapes would likely have settled for an extra-base hit high off the scoreboard. Either way, it was a tremendous wallop.

Another future Yankee who played for the Blues in Borchert Field was classy southpaw Ed "Whitey" Ford, who had recorded a 1.61 earned run average at Binghamton in 1949, best in all of baseball. On a frosty Monday night, May 1, 1950, Ford faced the Brewers and held them scoreless for six innings. In the seventh Johnny Logan led off by drawing a base on balls, eventually scoring and tying the game at 1–1. In the eighth, with two out and nobody on base, Ford nicked Howie Moss on the elbow with a curve ball. He walked the next batter. Then Logan bounced a single up the middle that the shortstop couldn't reach, driving home the winning run for Milwaukee. Ford earned the loss despite striking out 10, four of them belonging to Pete Whisenant.

One other Yankees farmhand worth noting is Lew Burdette. The crafty right-hander paired up with Warren Spahn to win more games than any other mound tandem in the past hundred years. Before being traded to the Boston Braves, though, he pitched for Kansas City for two seasons and visited Milwaukee numerous times. On June 23, 1950, the Blues had a doubleheader scheduled at Borchert Field. The Brewers had just returned from a disastrous road trip having lost 12 of 15 games, including the last six in a row. Burdette was the KC starting pitcher. Hank Workman staked him to a 3–0 lead with a first-inning three-run homer.

But this was not Burdette's night. The Brewers roughed him up for eight hits in five innings, combined with three walks. The Blues had a 4–3 lead when Johnny Logan touched his future teammate for a game-tying home run to start the sixth. That was the last batter Burdette faced in the game. He did not lose the game, but the Blues did. In the first extra inning, Logan walked and eventually scored on a single by Bob Montag.

In October 1957 Burdette and Logan and their Milwaukee Braves teammates celebrated together after defeating Whitey Ford's Yankees in the World Series, one year after Phil Rizzuto played his final season as a Yankee.

39

Jack and Bunny

Any boy fortunate enough to play baseball in Milwaukee between 1937 and 1961 probably learned the basics of the game from Bunny Brief or Jack Kloza. Those two men, both former American Association stars who played in Borchert Field for the Brewers, directed the baseball program of Milwaukee's Municipal Recreation Department throughout those years, Brief on the south side and Kloza on the north. The department hired Brief in 1937. The following spring he left town to manage Wausau in the Northern League, so Kloza replaced him. In 1939 Brief returned and they commenced working in tandem.

Brief was born Antonio Bordetzki in the village of Remus, Michigan, on July 3, 1892. He changed his surname after a sportswriter balked at having to spell out such a mouthful. Reportedly the scribe suggested that whatever name he chose he should "make it brief." The ballplayer took the idea literally. As for his first name, it began as a childhood nickname—Bunty—and evolved into Bunny as he entered Organized Baseball. Later in his career he was often referred to as Old Bunions because he was such a slow runner.

After three seasons with the Traverse City Resorters in the Michigan State League, Brief earned a trial with the St. Louis Browns. Over the next several years he also played for the

Chicago White Sox and the Pittsburgh Pirates. In 1916 with Salt Lake City of the Pacific Coast League, the young slugger set a league home-run record with 33 circuit blasts. Following a final shot at the big leagues with the Pirates in 1917, Brief moved to the American Association, where he made history.

In seven years with the Kansas City Blues he rewrote the record book, including 42 home runs (later broken by Milwaukee native Joe Hauser) and 191 RBIs in 1921. In six seasons between 1919 and 1924, he drove in 831 runs. By the time he quit playing he held league career records for home runs, RBIs, hits, runs, and doubles.

Apparently the Blues thought Brief was getting old after the 1924 season, so they let him go to Milwaukee. When Brewers owner Otto Borchert signed the former KC muscleman the day after New Year's, he had no inkling of how much the outfielder had left in the tank. Brief led the association with 37 homers and 175 runs batted in while batting a hefty .358. He played three more strong campaigns as a Brewer, then hung up his spikes and returned to Traverse City and ran a filling station.

Jack Kloza arrived at his professional baseball career in an unusual way. In spring of 1925 he answered a classified ad in the *Milwaukee Sentinel.* He had been strictly an amateur and semi-pro ballplayer around Wisconsin, but the ad seeking prospective minor leaguers intrigued him. Although leery at first, he heard that Red Smith, a Notre Dame all-around athlete who later played for and coached both the Packers and the Brewers, planned to join up. Besides, Kloza needed a job. He packed his bag and, along with a bunch of other ballplayers of fortune, lit out for the wilds of Arkansas in two beat-up 1912 automobiles.

The man who placed the advertisement in the *Sentinel* was a former sandlot catcher from northern Wisconsin named George Kromer but known to everyone as Stormy. The eccentric Stormy had been an engineer on the North Western railroad line between

Stormy Kromer was a man of vision who brought his unique style to designing railroad engineers' caps as well as organizing baseball teams. STORMY KROMER COMPANY

Kaukauna and Antigo. One of the difficulties his train job presented was that, when he stuck his head out the side of the engine compartment, his hat blew off. He solved the problem by having his wife modify an old baseball cap, sewing on a flexible visor and side flaps that not only kept his head warm but also held the hat in place.

Stormy received so many inquiries about his headgear that in 1914 he bought a vacant factory building in Milwaukee and founded the Kromer Cap Company, manufacturing and selling his product in either red or black, cotton or wool. The firm thrived and remained his livelihood for half a century until, nearing age 89, he sold out to a local businessman in 1965. In 2001 that company was bought out, but the venerable cap survives today. It is available at more than 800 stores throughout the United States.

In 1925 Stormy assembled and managed a low-minors baseball club in the Tri-State League, the Blytheville Tigers. His primary means of recruitment was classified ads in newspapers. And that was how young Jack Kloza entered Organized Baseball.

"I went to Blytheville," Stormy explained years later, "with the intention of trying to win with a bunch of boys just off the corner lots."

Stormy was nothing if not an innovator. He taught his young hitters always to take two strikes before swinging at a pitch. This, he told them, would train each man's batting eye and also make the pitcher throw something good to hit. Stormy later claimed that the "take two" rule helped make Kloza "the Babe Ruth of the minors." Although Kloza was the only one of Stormy's pupils to reach the big leagues, at least half a dozen of them rose to at least the Class B level. On the other hand, Stormy's Tigers rarely experienced the thrill of victory. They established a dubious record by losing 35 consecutive games, and in the second half of their season they tasted defeat 44 times in 48 games.

Kloza, though, had a great year. He batted .373 and began to make the slow climb up the minor-league ladder. After the 1927 season his contract was purchased by the Washington Senators. The following spring he contracted malaria at the club's training camp in Tampa. He lost 40 pounds and his major league job.

"I have spent 10 years in professional baseball," he said sadly in spring of 1936, "and I have never got one good break out of the game."

He was right. In 1934 with Milwaukee he enjoyed his best year, slamming 26 homers and batting .326. In 1935 he was hitting above .300 when, on August 4, he ran into a light standard in Borchert Field while catching a fly ball and injured his arm. His season ended that day. Two weeks later the club physician operated to remove a growth that developed on Kloza's throwing elbow. Despite the surgery, except for a few pathetic attempts to come back the next spring, his career was over. "The Buffum Street Bomber," as the Milwaukee newspapers liked to call him, was finished at age 32.

Beginning in 1939 Kloza and Brief together taught baseball classes to boys under 15 and supervised the Stars of Yesterday leagues, with each team named for a famous local diamond hero. Every year Kloza and Brief each selected and managed a 15-player all-star team. The two squads then competed in Borchert Field in the Hearst Diamond Pennant Series game. The game was sponsored, in Milwaukee and other cities, by the local Hearst newspaper. Two outstanding players were picked from each city to travel to New York and play in the national championship game in the Polo Grounds.

On July 25, 1952, Brief and Kloza coached their final game in Borchert Field. (The old ballpark was demolished in March 1953, and the game was moved to shiny new County Stadium.) Brief's group won the game, 5–2, but Kloza's players earned individual honors and the trip to the Big Apple. Actually the hitting star of the evening was center fielder Bob Uecker, the only participant to get more than one hit. The future broadcaster/comedian/actor singled, walked, and tripled. The two players selected by the judges, however, were both sons of former Milwaukee Brewers outfielders: Tony Kubek, 16-year-old shortstop for Al's Custard, and John Kloza Jr., 17-year-old catcher for Bay View Linoleum. Neither boy selected had recorded a base hit in the game. The judges who chose them included Brewers manager Bucky Walters, Brewers general manager Red Smith, and Brewers radio announcer Earl Gillespie.

Jack Kloza and Bunny Brief died in Milwaukee in 1962 and 1963, respectively. Their philosophy of teaching boys to play baseball was simple, and they stated it often: "We excuse errors and strikeouts, but there is no excuse for not hustling."

40

No Tie

June 23, 1941, was among the most important days in Milwaukee's sports history. The baseball world at large, however, probably had its attention focused elsewhere. Lou Gehrig had died just three weeks before. In the third month of the season, Ted Williams was batting over .400. Joltin' Joe DiMaggio had gotten at least one hit in 35 straight games. Considering these events, the change of ownership of a minor league franchise in mid-America could easily go unnoticed. In retrospect, it deserved more recognition.

On that day a syndicate of Chicago and Milwaukee businessmen headed by Bill Veeck completed the purchase of the Milwaukee Brewers from Henry J. Bendinger and his minority partners, Walter Hofer and Gene Tiefenthaler, for $100,000. The numerous new owners included Doc Jones, former boss of football's Chicago Cardinals; F. W. Magin, president of the Square D Company; Chester Baird of the Van Dyke Baird Box Company; Armin Schlesinger, a Milwaukee socialite; manager Charlie Grimm, who received a 25 percent share; and 28-year-old Veeck, the nation's youngest owner.

American Association president George Trautman had power of attorney and helped broker the deal. Baseball's equivalent of a garage sale had become necessary at the start of the month when Bendinger could not meet his payroll and the league had

It's pretty easy to pick out Bill Veeck among this group of American Association team owners: he's the one with his trademark open collar. COURTESY OF PAUL F. TENPENNY

to assume financial responsibility. The youthful Veeck had been seeking a ball club to operate, a neat trick when you have almost no money. While his partners had the wherewithal to allow the purchase, the leadership and vision of the outfit clearly belonged to Sport Shirt Bill, as the sportswriters liked to call him because he shunned neckties. Veeck and manager Grimm immediately became the faces of the franchise.

Veeck had been employed as assistant treasurer of Philip Wrigley's Chicago Cubs, a club that Veeck's father had served for 14 years as president. Bill Junior had worked his way up the Cubs' corporate ladder, beginning as a teenaged popcorn sales-man. In 1937 Wrigley did an extensive makeover of his ballpark, adding outfield bleachers and the huge manual scoreboard that still stands beyond the center-field wall. At that same time the younger Veeck (his father had died in 1933) was allowed to carry out a fantasy he had harbored since age 13: he planted 350 Japanese bittersweet plants (which were eventually crowded out) and 200 Boston ivy plants along the entire outfield wall. It was this stroke of botanical inspiration that established Wrigley Field's most distinctive feature and provided Veeck's earliest reputation as an innovator.

Before putting his group together and buying the woebegone last-place Brewers, Veeck consulted with his most-trusted friend, Harry Grabiner, a baseball lifer and close associate of Charles Comiskey, founder of the Chicago White Sox. "Harry is the smartest man I ever met in baseball," Veeck explained, calling him "the brains of the White Sox." Grabiner gave his nod of approval, and the transaction went forward.

Grimm had resigned as the Cubs' first-base coach to take the reins in Milwaukee, replacing Reindeer Bill Killefer. He proved to be a perfect partner in crime for the outlandish Veeck. He willingly played the foil to Veeck's practical jokes and harebrained promotional schemes. The gregarious Grimm joined Veeck in making the rounds of civic groups to drum up interest in their stumbling ball club. They performed like a vaudeville team, telling stories and endearing themselves throughout the community. Frequently in public appearances both inside and outside Borchert Field the pair enlisted a few ballplayers to form musical combos, generally featuring Grimm as a left-handed banjo player, Veeck playing some kind of slide whistle, general manager Rudie Schaffer thumping an improvised bull fiddle, and the others playing who knows what else. Grimm was a musician of long standing. In 1921 with the Pittsburgh Pirates he had sung baritone in a quartet along with Rabbit Maranville, Cotton Tierney, and Possum Whitted. Their specialty was "The Band Played On."

The Brewers ball club and ballpark that Veeck and Grimm took over were both awful. The wooden grandstand and stadium walls that greeted the relative handful of loyal fans offered splinters, peeling paint, dirt, and a dismal atmosphere well suited to eighth place. Veeck immediately hired a crew of painters to give the outside wooden surfaces a fresh battleship-gray coat and a battalion of cleaning ladies (sorry, it was the custom) to spruce up the shabby innards of the old structure. Head groundskeeper Eddie Kretlow, who had resigned two weeks previous, was rehired to get the playing surface into playing condition.

To signal the new era in Milwaukee baseball, Veeck staged another Opening Day, proclaimed as such by Mayor Carl Zeidler, who also threw out the first pitch. The cellar-dwelling Brewers sported a pathetic 19–43 record as they took the field against the first-place Minneapolis Millers. Nevertheless, an enthusiastic crowd of 4,417, the largest since the other opening day, greeted the guys in the home uniforms.

Veeck had pulled some strings with his Chicago connections to establish a working relationship with the Cubbies and receive the use of five new ballplayers, among them outfielder Lou "the Mad Russian" Novikoff and shortstop Billy Myers, captain of the 1940 World Series champion Cincinnati Reds. Novikoff had briefly been a Brewer in 1939. In 1941 Cubs GM Jim Gallagher sent the Russian to help out Veeck and Grimm, and did he ever! In the final 90 games he batted .370 and led the American Association. Novikoff was happy to leave Wrigley Field because he thought the foliage on the outfield wall was poison ivy.

Despite the Russian's batting prowess, he did have his short-comings. In one notable inning as a left fielder, he allowed two base hits to roll between his legs and all the way to the wall for inside-the-park home runs. After that Veeck instructed the grounds crew to keep the grass long in left field. Novikoff's lack of facility with the glove was emblematic of Milwaukee's 1941 season. They finished dead last, 40 games out of first place. Even so, the excitement was back inside Borchert Field, and the good times were only beginning.

The good times required money. Veeck and his general manager found it in an unlikely place. With the cooperation of Abe Saperstein, impresario and founder of the Harlem Globetrotters, Veeck and Schaffer became the promoters of a basketball doubleheader in the Milwaukee Auditorium involving four of the contemporaneous powers of the hoops world: the Oshkosh All Stars versus the Globetrotters, and the New York Renaissance (a.k.a. Rens) versus the Sheboygan Redskins. The two Wisconsin teams were members of the National Basketball League, an all-white aggregation of professional status. The other two were touring all-black teams and were no match for their light-skinned opponents. More than 3,400 paying customers supported the event, and Veeck said later, perhaps with just a hint of hyperbole, the profit saved the Brewers franchise.

Nineteen forty-two witnessed the rebirth of the competitive Milwaukee Brewers. Attendance tripled as the ball club played exciting, winning baseball. Veeck continued his wheeling and dealing for new and better players. He worked the phones and constantly had players coming and going, frequently at a profit. The Cubs sent another contribution, a catcher-outfielder named Greek George. From the Texas League Veeck swiped outfielder Bill Norman, who batted .301 for Grimm's team, and first sacker Heinz Becker, who hit .340.

Only one batter in the league surpassed Becker's average, and that was feisty Brewers second baseman Eddie Stanky, who batted .342. The five-foot eight-inch Stanky, formerly of the Macon Peaches in the Sally League, earned the hearts of Milwaukee fans and the American Association MVP Award with his gutsy, all-out, anything-to-beat-you style of play. Grimm kept his guys in contention all season, entering September in a three-team fight for the top spot. On Labor Day the Brewers hosted the Kansas City Blues in a season-ending doubleheader, needing a sweep to claim the pennant. Leading 2–1, they lost the opener when a seventh-inning error by Stanky opened the floodgate. The Brewers finished as runners-up, three innings short of being champions.

The outcome might have been different if not for a strange accident that occurred on September 3. Outfielder Hal Peck, possessor of the league's third-highest batting average, was shooting rats near the henhouse behind his home when he tripped over a vine and shot himself in the foot. The mishap cost him the second and third toes of his left foot and the remainder of the Brewers' season.

The Brewers subsequently captured American Association pennants in each of the next three seasons. They played great baseball and attracted large, raucous crowds. Their on-field success, though, was often overshadowed by the zany promotional stunts for which Veeck will always be remembered. Many of these came later when he was the owner of teams in the American League. The midget Eddie Gaedel comes first to mind. But it was in Milwaukee that Sport Shirt Bill cut his promotional teeth, so to speak. He tried to make one-armed outfielder Pete Gray a Brewer, but the Memphis Chicks would not agree to the deal. (Gray did appear in Borchert Field on June 6, 1946, as a member of the Toledo Mud Hens. Playing despite nagging injuries, Gray led off the first inning with a single up the middle against Brewers pitcher Buck Ross. On the next play Gray was forced at second. As he slid into the bag he aggravated his injured knee and had to leave the game for the night.)

One of Veeck's favorite tricks was the "lucky fan" lottery. He would draw a ticket stub at random and select an unwitting recipient of, for example, a 50-pound block of ice. The flustered fan would be left holding his prize and wondering how to dispose of it while the crowd howled in laughter. Veeck never ran out of prizes to give away—a stepladder, a basket of fruit, a live turkey or pig, or maybe a pair of nervous pigeons. Fans never knew what to expect in Borchert Field, which was of course the genius of Veeck's marketing.

On August 28, 1943, Charlie Grimm celebrated his 45th birthday. Naturally Veeck used the occasion for his patented form of merriment. In a pregame ceremony at home plate, he had a 15-foot birthday cake wheeled onto the field. In answer to Veeck's prior question, Grimm had said that what he most wanted for his birthday was another left-handed pitcher. Lo and behold, the top of the cake popped open and out jumped a gaggle of dancing girls. Right behind them came a six-foot-tall left-hander named Julio Acosta, whom Veeck had quietly obtained from the Richmond Colts of the Piedmont League. Acosta pitched for the Brewers that day and acquitted himself well before losing in extra innings. He remained a Milwaukee Brewer as long as Veeck owned the club.

Another of Veeck's brainstorms was only partly successful, through no fault of his own. He scheduled a game at ten o'clock in the morning to accommodate night-shift workers who could

Charlie Grimm (right) got what he wanted for his birthday: a left-handed pitcher, Julio Acosta (left), who emerged from this enormous birthday cake.
RICHARD LULLOFF COLLECTION

not attend at regular hours. He offered a seven-piece swing band dressed in nightgowns and stocking caps to serenade the fans before the game, and he personally helped serve corn flakes and milk to early arrivals. Unfortunately the game could not start on time because the rival St. Paul Saints were not able to catch an early enough train to make the trip from Kansas City to Milwaukee. Undaunted, Veeck cheerfully refunded ticket money to about 2,000 fans unable to stay for the whole game. Then he rescheduled his "breakfast at Borchert" for a future date.

Of course 1943 was not all fun and games. World War II was robbing baseball, and the United States, of many of its young men. In November Bill Veeck, married with three small children, enlisted in the Marine Corps. He left for boot camp in San Diego a week later. Two months after that he was serving with an artillery squad on Bougainville in the South Pacific. An anti-aircraft gun recoiled and smashed his right leg, leading to a long period of hospitalization, dozens of surgeries, and ultimately amputation.

Returned from the war in August 1945, Veeck was eager to get back into baseball. His sights were set above the Triple A level, though. At the end of October, Veeck and his partners sold the Brewers to Chicago attorney Oscar Salenger. Eight months later Veeck led a group of investors who purchased the Cleveland Indians. True to the example he had set in Milwaukee, Veeck and his Indians set major league attendance records and won the World Series in 1948.

41

Ladies Days

The whole thing was Phil Wrigley's idea.

Beginning in 1943, women ballplayers competed against one another in their professional version of America's pastime. At first their organization was called the All-American Girls' Softball League, but that did not sound compelling. It was quickly renamed the All-American Girls' Professional Baseball League, which also does not exactly roll off the tongue. The 1992 Hollywood film *A League of Their Own*, starring Geena Davis and Madonna, portrayed a fictionalized version of this female offshoot of major league baseball.

Wrigley said he created (and bankrolled) the ladies' league to keep the spirit of the game of baseball alive during World War II, while 60 percent of the big-league ballplayers were engaged in the military. Certainly ample evidence exists that the level of talent in both the American and National Leagues had sunk to a historic low. Athletes compromised by physical infirmities and age, both young and old, filled out most big-league rosters during the war years.

For example, one-armed Pete Gray played courageously, if not well, in the outfield of the St. Louis Browns. Fifteen-year-old hurler (he was big for his age) Joe Nuxhall took the mound against the defending National League champion St. Louis

Cardinals, with the predictable result. Nuxhall was only a few months younger than Philadelphia A's right-hander Carl Scheib and Brooklyn Dodgers shortstop Tommy Brown. Forty-year-old Pepper Martin had been away from the majors for four years, but he came back and rejoined the team calling itself the Cardinals. Roy Schalk had been in the minor leagues for 12 years following a big-league sojourn of three games, but he became the everyday second baseman of the Chicago White Sox. Baseball continued throughout the war, but it was certainly not the same. Even the Milwaukee Brewers felt the effects. Instead of training in Florida, for three years running they held their spring camp in balmy Frame Park in Waukesha, Wisconsin, to save fuel.

To help fill the talent void the war caused, chewing-gum magnate Wrigley held tryouts for female ballplayers and divided the 60 best ones into four teams, each representing a midsized city near Chicago: Racine, Kenosha, South Bend, and Rockford. Spring training took place in—where else?—Wrigley Field. Concerned about image, Wrigley required that each team employ a full-time chaperone, all players wear makeup and lipstick, and every young lady attend charm school. The girls wore tunics with short skirts and knee-high socks. The league even had an official song, with hard-hitting lyrics that included "Our chaperones are not too soft, They're not too tough."

The league rules approximated baseball's regulations with a few notable exceptions. The ball was a 12-inch inseam softball, the pitchers threw fast-pitch underhand, the bases stood only 65 feet apart and the pitching rubber 40 feet from home plate, and base runners could lead off after the ball left the pitcher's hand. With each succeeding season the ball grew smaller, the base paths grew longer, and by 1948 the pitchers delivered the ball overhand.

In 1943 the playoff champs were the Racine Belles. Despite spotty attendance the league expanded the following year, adding teams in Minneapolis and Milwaukee. For some reason the league administration took a long time in naming the new Milwaukee club. Eventually they were officially dubbed the Chicks, but by that time the local papers had grown tired of waiting and had already christened them the Schnitts (German for "short beers," i.e., little Brewers). The name stuck.

The AAGPBL was breaking new ground, but in 1944 all six teams were managed by men. Five of the six had played major league baseball; the other, Russian-born Johnny Gottselig, had been a star left winger for hockey's Chicago Blackhawks. Two were former Milwaukee Brewers, Jack Kloza and Claude Jonnard. The best known and most accomplished of the group was Milwaukee's manager Maximilian Carnarius, who played for the Pittsburgh Pirates and the Brooklyn Dodgers under the name Max Carey. After a 20-year big-league career, Carey retired as the third-leading base stealer in history, and second only to Ty Cobb in steals of home. Little wonder that his Chicks ball club played an aggressive style and led the ladies' circuit in stolen bases. Carey was voted into Cooperstown in 1961.

The general manager of the Chicks was Milwaukee's sports impresario Eddie Stumpf, who the previous year had been the field boss of the Rockford Peaches. Stumpf had been the skipper of one of the two teams in the league's first all-star game, on July 1, 1943. That contest was held in Chicago's Wrigley Field and is best remembered (if at all) for being Wrigley's first night game. It was played under the scant illumination of a temporary lighting system installed just for that event.

The Milwaukee Chicks made their initial bow in Borchert Field on May 27, 1944. The world situation at the time was unsettled to say the least. The Allied D-Day invasion of Normandy was just 10 days away, for example. Nevertheless, the paltry turnout for the opener, estimated at 700 (couldn't someone just go around and count them?), did not bode well for the home team. The game began as a pitchers' duel, but the mound efforts of Milwaukee's Connie Wisniewski were seriously undermined by her team's nine errors, including her own pair of wild pickoff attempts. Each allowed a run to score. The Chicks scored in the bottom of the ninth to tie the game and would have won it except for some shoddy base running. The visiting South Bend Blue Sox won the contest with a run-scoring single in the 10th.

The games scheduled for June 6 were postponed, along with all the others throughout baseball, in deference to the massive amphibious landing taking place on the beaches of France. That was just fine with the Chicks, who had four injured players at the time. Rosters of 15 did not provide many replacements. To fill the vacancies, because the ball clubs had no individual ownership, the league simply took players from other teams and transferred them to Milwaukee. Vickie Panos was shifted from South Bend. Gladys Davis, the 1943 batting champ, was transplanted from the Rockford Peaches. In some cases rookies who had not made the initial cut were brought in. During the season, the Chicks acquired Doris Tetzlaff, Merle "the Blonde Bombshell" Keagle, and Milwaukee-native pitcher Sylvia Wronski, who came within one out of throwing a no-hitter.

After a bad start to the season, including losing their first three tilts, the Chicks struggled to reach the .500 mark and finally surpassed it on July 2. Win or lose, they seemed to shoot themselves in the foot, so to speak. On May 29 Thelma "Tiby" Eisen blasted a home run but was declared out for failing to touch second base. On the Fourth of July they swept a doubleheader from Minneapolis despite committing 12 errors.

The Schnitts finished the first half of the season with a 30–26 record. In August, though, the Chicks started to click. Beginning on August 13 they put together an 11-game winning streak that gave them a commanding lead and ultimately carried them to the title. They had to finish their scheduled home games in Oshkosh because the Brewers were occupying Borchert Field. Then the

Discussing strategy in front of their Borchert Field dugout are four of the Chicks' stars in 1944: from left, catcher Dorothy "Mickey" Maguire, left fielder Thelma "Tiby" Eisen, catcher Emily Stevenson, and shortstop Gladys "Terrie" Davis. COURTESY OF JIM NITZ

Chicks were forced to play all of the playoff games in the Kenosha Comets' home park for the same reason. They were able to overcome the home-field disadvantage and defeat the Comets in seven games. Chicks hurler Wisniewski earned all four of the Milwaukee victories, two of them on three-hitters and two of them on shutouts.

Despite their championship season, the ladies from Milwaukee did not achieve financial success. The club tried a variety of promotions: a pregame track-and-field meet staged by the ballplayers, concerts by the Milwaukee Symphony Orchestra, women's amateur softball contests. The only promotion that attracted a sizable crowd (more than 4,000) was a free game admission given to people who donated blood to the Red Cross on D-Day plus six.

Several factors held down the attendance at Chicks games. Brewers owner Bill Veeck preferred night games for his club, forcing the Schnitts to play during a time when more potential fans were at work. Also, the Brewers were pennant-bound and pulled fans away. Some Milwaukeeans thought the 95-cent ticket price was exorbitant during hard times. To top it off, a polio outbreak in late summer that closed elementary schools throughout the county probably discouraged people from venturing into the mass of strangers inside Borchert Field.

And so that was it. One and done. Despite a championship, the next season Max Carey was the new president of the AAG-PBL, and the Chicks were roosting in Grand Rapids, Michigan, never to return.

42

The Mighty Casey

Charlie Stengel hailed from Kansas City, so naturally he picked up the nickname of KC (Casey). On the last four days of the 1910 season, the 20-year-old Stengel played in the American Association for the first time, filling an outfield spot for his hometown Blues. Their opponents for those games were the Milwaukee Brewers. Two years later, on September 17, 1912, Casey rapped four singles in his major league debut in Washington Park, Brooklyn's old wooden stadium. He was left-handed all the way, but in his fifth at-bat that day, he turned around and batted right-handed and drew a base on balls.

Casey played 14 years in the big leagues, a solid but not spectacular ballplayer. As he told the Kefauver committee in the US Senate antitrust hearings on July 8, 1958, "I had many years that I was not so successful as a ballplayer, as it is a game of skill." He played two full seasons in New York under the legendary John McGraw. Although not generally a power hitter, Stengel slammed two game-winning home runs in the 1923 World Series, both in Yankee Stadium. The first one was a ninth-inning, inside-the-park blast, the first Series homer in the House That Ruth Built. The second one, in Game Three, scored the only run in the 1–0 contest.

From his earliest days in baseball, Stengel developed a reputation as a clown. He was quick with a quip and a master of mimicry.

Nothing in his career as a funnyman, however, surpassed what he did in Ebbets Field on May 25, 1919. Teammate Leon Cadore had captured a sparrow in the bullpen. Casey put the winged intruder under his cap. When he stepped up to bat, the fans booed him lustily for misplaying a fly ball in the previous half-inning. Stengel turned toward the grandstand, lifted his cap, and bowed. The bird flew off his head and into baseball legend while the fans, and even the umpire, roared with laughter.

After ending his big-league career as a Boston Brave, Stengel became the player-manager of the Toledo Mud Hens in 1926. In that capacity he made regular visits to Borchert Field over the next six seasons. On June 15, 1926, he brought the Hens to Milwaukee at a historic moment. The Brewers had won 20 consecutive games and had their sights set on the New York Giants' record streak of 26, established 10 years previous. Stengel penciled himself into the lineup in the number six slot, playing center field, and recorded a pair of base hits. However, the Milwaukee center fielder, Fritz Schulte, keyed a six-run burst in the first that put the game out of reach before it was barely begun. The Brewers cruised to a 9–1 win over Stengel's club, their 21st in a row.

The following afternoon Stengel took himself out of the lineup. His club responded by pounding 12 hits and ending the Brewers' streak, 9–6. A couple of months later, on August 22, Casey brought his team back to Athletic Park. Milwaukee fans were jacked up. The previous afternoon, diminutive Brewers southpaw Dinty Gearin had hurled a no-hitter against Columbus, helping the Brews sweep a doubleheader and take a game-and-a-half lead in the standings. With pennant fever rampant in the city, nearly 16,000 people showed up to watch the Brewers try to increase their advantage in a twin bill with the Stengels. It was the largest turnout the ballpark had ever accommodated. The local cranks packed every corner of the park—atop the scoreboard, on the fences, and standing 10 deep on the outfield surface from foul line to foul line.

In the opener the Mud Hens trailed, 3–1, in the ninth inning. With a runner on second and two out, Stengel pinch-hit for catcher Johnnie Heving. Old Casey still had some pop in his swing—he drove the ball deep to left-center. Schulte ran full-throttle into the mass of spectators, made a leaping grab, and tumbled into the sea of bodies. Stengel argued long and loudly that the catch was fraudulent. He followed the umpires all around the diamond while presenting his case, but the men in blue simply gathered up their equipment and headed for their dressing room. The game was over.

Casey had more than his share of run-ins with umpires, but one time he helped save one's neck. In Borchert Field on May 2, 1931, while Stengel was managing Toledo, the Brewers were losing to the Mud Hens, 6–4, with two out and two on in the ninth inning. Milwaukee pinch hitter Jack Kloza was at bat. With the scoreboard showing a count of 1-and-1, Kloza took a pitch over the heart of the plate. Umpire Bill Clayton called "strike three," and the game was over. Thinking that Kloza had been called out with only two strikes, the angry partisan crowd stormed the field.

As one irate fan pulled back his arm to punch the offending ump, Stengel grabbed the attacker by the collar and tossed him out of the way, then quickly escorted the umps to the shed where the arbiters changed clothes. Eventually police arrived to clear the field and protect the boys in blue from mayhem. Stengel knew what the mass of spectators did not and would not learn until the next day's newspapers came out: the scoreboard operator had mistakenly entered the first pitch to Kloza as a ball. It was really strike one.

From 1938 through 1943 Stengel served as skipper of the Boston Bees, formerly and subsequently known as the Braves. In '38 the club finished in fifth place, slightly above .500. The next four years saw them in seventh place, though, and the final season was only marginally better. Shortly before the start of the season, Stengel was struck by a cab while crossing the street near his Boston hotel. His leg was fractured, and he missed two months of the season. Not everyone mourned his absence. Vitriolic sports columnist Dave Egan of the *Daily Record* wrote, "The man who did the most for baseball in Boston in 1943 was the motorist who ran Stengel down two days before the opening game." (It should be noted that Egan is the same guy who wrote that Ted Williams was not worthy of a tribute from fans as he went off to fight in the Korean War.)

One of Stengel's peers found humor in the accidental injury. Pittsburgh Pirates manager Frankie Frisch sent Casey a telegram that said, "Your attempt at suicide fully understood. Deepest sympathy you didn't succeed."

After the season Stengel, a man of considerable wealth, tried to buy a controlling interest in the Boston club. When his offer was rejected, he submitted his resignation. He thought his managerial days might be over. Then fate and the Chicago Cubs intervened. Eleven games into the 1944 campaign, the Cubbies were 1–10 and looking for a new manager. They hired former Cub Charlie Grimm away from the Milwaukee club of the American Association. Brewers president Bill Veeck was off in the South Pacific fighting World War II. In his absence his compatriot Grimm recommended Stengel for his replacement.

Stengel knew that Veeck disliked him, but he accepted the job anyway. The jovial, fun-loving Grimm was a tough act to follow "for a man with a game leg who doesn't play the banjo," as Stengel said of himself. As soon as rumors of Chicago stealing Grimm began to circulate, fans registered protests with the newspapers and circulated petitions, demanding that Jolly Cholly stay in Milwaukee. Nevertheless, on May 7 Stengel took the reins, leading his new club to a doubleheader sweep of the Columbus Red Birds in Borchert Field. Under Casey, the Brewers stretched their winning

Casey Stengel was no favorite of owner Bill Veeck, but Ol' Case led the Brewers to the championship in 1944.
COURTESY OF PAUL F. TENPENNY

streak to 12 games, running their record to 20–2. They held first place for the duration of the season.

Nineteen forty-four was a momentous year, in the world and in the season of Stengel's Brewers. Hundreds of professional ball-players, both major and minor leaguers, were in faraway lands fighting the war. A reminder of this occurred on May 13 when, in the sixth inning of a game with Indianapolis, Lieutenant Fred Tolle, son of Borchert Field's guardian of the press gate, led a low flyover of fighter planes above the ballpark. Lieutenant Tolle waved to his dad as he passed over.

The athletes still in the homeland were a mixture of veterans and unproven youngsters, so anything was possible in any given ballgame. Case in point, the Brewers game in Toledo's Swayne Field on the afternoon of May 23. Stengel's former club acted as congenial hosts. Milwaukee thumped the Hens 28–0, the highest score ever in the American Association. The winning hurler was 39-year-old side-armer Earl Caldwell. The visitors pasted 27 hits off four Toledo pitchers, with every Brewer getting at least one hit and five men, including Caldwell, belting three or more.

Two weeks later the Brewers had a home game postponed for an unusual reason: all scheduled contests in the American Association, along with the major leagues, were called off because of the D-Day Allied invasion of Europe. Milwaukee's planned game with Louisville turned into a twilight doubleheader the next evening.

The following week, on June 15 to be exact, Mother Nature took a swing at Stengel and his charges. At the end of the warmest day of the year, Borchert Field hosted the Columbus Red Birds. In the fifth inning Columbus third baseman John Antonelli sliced a ball down the right-field line. It bounced into the corner, Antonelli legged a triple, and two runs scored to tie the game, 5–5. Stengel bolted out of the dugout and confronted umpire Peters, arguing vehemently that the ball had landed foul. Casey's strong objection earned him his first ejection as field boss of the Brewers.

Shortly before 10 o'clock, following the seventh-inning stretch and the crowd's singing of "Take Me Out to the Ballgame," the atmosphere changed. The dark sky turned darker, the temperature dropped noticeably, and the towering light poles around the periphery of the field began swaying. After two quick outs the Brewers put runners on second and third for Jack Norman. The Milwaukee left fielder had a count of one ball and two strikes on him when suddenly the field lights dimmed twice, then went completely out. The only illumination came from the lights under the grandstand.

At once rain pelted the park. Thunder and lightning erupted. A huge gust of wind picked up a 100-foot section of the east grandstand and dropped it violently on the front porches of houses across Seventh Street. A large wooden beam that formerly supported the roof fell onto the seating area, striking and injuring 30 spectators. Four patrons sustained serious though nonfatal injuries, including two with skull fractures. Those people most grievously wounded were conveyed to the Brewers clubhouse, where trainer Doc Feron administered first aid until ambulances arrived.

Some screaming occurred during the commotion, but for the most part the fans remained calm. Many fled to the playing field, where they stood drenched but unharmed. Transit workers restored downed trolley wires above Eighth Street. Firemen extinguished small blazes caused by sparking wires. They also used their axes to cut the damaged roof into pieces small enough to be removed.

As luck would have it, the Brewers were scheduled to go on the road the next day. The ballgame was rescheduled for the Red Birds' next visit in July. The ballpark, the oldest in the American Association, was quickly restored with one major exception: the roof section was not replaced. The building was a nonconforming structure in a neighborhood zoned for residences. By city ordinance the amount spent on repairs could not exceed one-half the original cost of construction. The ballpark had been assembled in 1888 at minimal cost, so substantial rehabilitation was not permissible. For the final eight years of its existence, Borchert Field stood partially uncapped.

The rest of the season for Stengel's club provided less drama and more success. The only real low point was the American Association All-Star Game in Borchert Field on July 26. The All-Stars possessed a potent lineup and were expected to win for the fifth straight time. Stengel's league-leading Brewers, however, didn't just lose—they were humiliated in front of a home crowd of 12,000. They hit into a triple play. They failed to score. Milwaukee starting pitcher Julio Acosta struck out the side in the opening inning but surrendered eight runs in the second. The All-Stars led by 16 runs after five innings, and the Brewers finished the evening's embarrassment on the wrong end of an 18–0 shellacking. Even clowning Casey could not find any humor in the result. In retrospect, maybe it was humorous that each player in the game received no pay, only a $25 war bond.

The Brewers clinched the American Association flag on September 7. Their final record was 102–51, seven games ahead of the pack. On September 11 Stengel announced that he would not return as Brewers manager in 1945.

43

Life and Limb

Many athletes live for the rush of adrenaline that their sport affords them. Rodeo, for example, clearly has the element of danger as its major selling point. It's likely that no other competitive sport offers greater risks and less security than professional rodeo.

In the 21st century certain organizations—notably PETA (People for the Ethical Treatment of Animals)—oppose rodeos for putting animals in harm's way. They may have a point. In one day at Canada's famous Calgary Stampede, six animals lost their lives. Even apart from the deaths, PETA claims that normally docile creatures are abused with electric prods and bucking straps to make them act wild, thereby enhancing the obvious courage of the cowboys and cowgirls who perform with them.

In the mid-1940s, before farm animals had their own lobbyists, Borchert Field hosted several rodeos and thrill shows. These spectacular productions mixed the ranching skills of the American frontier, circus feats at death-defying heights, and loud, fast motor vehicles crashing into each other. Every evening from August 2 to August 7, 1945, with matinees on weekends, the Wild West Rodeo and Thrill Circus, operating as the Circle-A Rodeo, delivered a world of entertainment priced at 90 cents for general admission, 30 cents for children, rain or shine. Folks unable to attend could hear a live broadcast of the activities every night at nine o'clock on WEMP radio.

The day before the show hit town, a local reporter interviewed Pop Staples, one of the featured performers. Staples was a genuine cowboy from El Reno, Oklahoma, who had spent the past 10 years in the rodeo. He told the writer, "They tell me that this is the first time in its existence that this ballpark is going to hold a rodeo. Boy, is this place in for a shock."

Like any good circus, the show opened with a parade. After a blare of trumpets, the procession began with ruggedly handsome Lyle Van Patter leading the way on his glorious silver-white stallion. Van Patter was well known to Milwaukee, having appeared at the State Fair in 1943 and at an indoor circus in the Milwaukee Auditorium the following year. Van Patter was half of the Lone Ranger—half because he did the public appearances around the country. Meanwhile the radio voice of the "daring and resourceful masked rider of the plains" emanated from a sound studio, first from Earle Graser, then after his death in a car crash, from Brace Beemer. Both men had virile pipes, but neither of the two looked the part of the Masked Man.

Pop Staples was right. The opening performance was only a few minutes old when a bronc-riding cowboy from Kissimmee, Florida, demonstrated why rodeo is not for the faint of heart. The angry horse he was trying to hold onto succeeded in bucking him loose and tossing him violently against a protective barrier. The animal became disoriented and leaped over and through the low outfield fence into an empty bleacher section. It crashed against the seats before managing to return to the relative safety of the outfield grass, where it was finally corralled. Officials announced that the horse was uninjured, but the thrown rider fared somewhat worse. An ambulance drove onto the field, collected the dazed cowpuncher, and transported him to Johnston Emergency Hospital.

The ambulance had no sooner returned to the ballpark than it was needed again. One of the rodeo clowns, the fearless jesters who risk their necks distracting bulls and broncs from trampling downed riders, had been one step too slow. A wildly flailing Brahma steer knocked the clown to the dirt and stomped on him for good measure. The medical transport team took the clown away. They later made two more runs for a couple of unsuccessful bull riders.

One of the night's memorable events involved Staples. For almost a decade he had been the sport's bull-dogging champ. As he got up in years, his specialty changed. His new act was hardly less daring, though. Pop drove a stock car at high speed up a ramp, became airborne, hurtled over a large transcontinental bus, and pancaked atop five parked automobiles. The crowd loved it, and Pop was unharmed.

The Rodeo and Thrill Circus was such a big success that it returned to Borchert Field on June 14, 1946, for a four-day run featuring mostly different acts. A young lady named Jackie Reinhart, who had been a trick rider the year before, showed off her rope-spinning skill by lassoing several horses. A dancing donkey amused the audience with its fancy footwork. Costumed Indians riding bareback showcased their equestrian skills. There was even a stagecoach holdup.

Courageous (or foolhardy) spectators were offered the opportunity to ride Big Syd, an aptly named Brahma bull with a rotten disposition. Anyone holding on to the big fella for 10 seconds could win $100 (adjusted for inflation, that would be about $1,200 today). Few tried, and no one lasted even three seconds.

After the cowboys finished their portion, the auto thrill guys took over. A barrel-chested Hollywood stuntman calling himself Iron Man Decker set the tone by letting a car drive over his outstretched body. Then Walter "King" Kovaz and his Auto Daredevils put spectators on edge with some tricky driving as cars drove over and around each other at lightning speed. They made a loud racket and kicked up plenty of dust. No crashes occurred, though.

The collision segment of the show belonged to Lucky Teter's Hell Drivers. Earl "Lucky" Teter had been a gas station attendant in his native Indiana. In 1932 he began doing auto and motorcycle stunts, basically inventing the thrill show and earning the title "World's Greatest Daredevil." He was credited as the first person to turn over an automobile intentionally. Teter performed twice at the Wisconsin State Fair Grounds, once achieving a four-time rollover in a sedan.

On July 5, 1942, at the Indiana State Fair Grounds, Teter was the final act in an Army Relief benefit show. He announced that it would be his last performance for the duration of the war. It was. While he was speeding up a ramp for his routine jump, his car's engine failed. Teter died while attempting the stunt. Four years

Lucky Teter practically invented the art of automobile stunt driving. He and his Hell Drivers performed in venues like the Wisconsin State Fair (seen here) and Borchert Field. PHOTOGRAPH COURTESY OF THE MILWAUKEE COUNTY HISTORICAL SOCIETY

later his partners and understudies, still using Teter's name, put on their exhibition in Milwaukee's ballpark.

After a one-year absence, the rodeo and thrill show returned to Borchert Field beginning on June 24, 1948, the same day the Republican Party nominated presidential candidate Thomas E. Dewey and his running mate, Earl Warren, at their convention in Philadelphia. This show had a different flavor than previous ones. It was sponsored as a fund-raiser for three police benevolent organizations, in place of their annual band concert. Instead of crashing vehicles, the show offered a troupe of performing dogs. The rodeo events were about the same as before, with bucking broncs and bulls. At one point several steers escaped from their enclosure and charged into the box seat area of the grandstand. The spectators scampered to higher seating areas and avoided injury. The bulls were quickly rounded up by rodeo personnel and returned to their pen.

These were not the only critters bent on entering the seating area. A cowpoke named Coyote Perry, from the Indian Territory of Oklahoma, was astride a bucking bronco that made a sudden dash toward the stands, knocking over a wire fence near the visitors' dugout. Perry managed to dismount safely just before the loose cayuse bowled over some chairs in the reserved section, hurdled rows of seats, and made a beeline for the concession stand at the top walk of the grandstand. The animal was finally cornered and lassoed and tied to one of the wooden beams supporting the roof. After it calmed down a bit, it was led away to the infield.

The rest of the show proceeded mostly as planned. Buck Steele and his son put a pair of Arabian stallions through their paces, jumping over barriers as smoothly as you please. For comic relief an orange jalopy chugged across the infield, stopping occasionally to rear up on its back wheels and disgorge a passenger. It also released a choking cloud of black smoke that hovered over the field for a long time.

The high points of the evening's entertainment—literally, the high points—were reserved for the finishing acts. Working without a net, a cool-as-ice tightrope walker cavorted high above the playing surface. Then, just to inject a bit more drama, he inserted both his feet inside a metal bucket and hopped across the wire, to great applause.

Finally, a pair of young men calling themselves the Aerial Snyders performed acrobatic maneuvers at the top of a precarious swaying pole more than 100 feet in the air. The Snyders put the exclamation mark on their spine-tingling display by having one of them do a one-armed handstand on a bar while the other performed a no-handed headstand on a small trapeze.

As the crowd filed out into the night, no one felt cheated. The only displeasure seemed to be expressed by attorney Harry Zaidins, the Milwaukee Brewers representative, who moaned, "It will cost at least $1,200 to get the field in shape. Those horses ruined the place."

44

Hail to the Victors

In the 12th season of the American Association, the Milwaukee Brewers brought their first pennant home to Athletic Park. This was a pleasant surprise to local fans because the ball club in 1912 had finished a poor fifth and the 1913 edition did not appear markedly better. The major change was that manager Hugh Duffy was fired and his duties assumed by fiery third baseman Harry "Pep" Clark. Duffy had been a great hitter in his day (his .440 average in 1894 stands as the record) and had managed the Brewers in 1901, their one season in the American League before the franchise became the St. Louis Browns. He was aloof from his players, though, and from president Agnes Havenor, who inherited the team when her husband died on April 3, 1912. Mrs. Havenor became the first female president of a minor league ball club. She said she would resign her position after the Brewers won a pennant. She kept her word, stepping down on October 10, 1913.

Clark's flag-winning club was not a world-beater. They didn't hit much, but their defense was sound and their pitching good enough to carry them. Their best hurlers, Cy Slapnicka and Ralph Cutting, won 25 and 21 games, respectively. Slapnicka made history as the scout who signed teenaged Bob Feller to a contract in 1936. Cutting earned his everlasting fame by purchasing a goat named Fatima in May of 1913. Fatima became the Brewers' mascot, roaming the outfield during off-hours and bedding down in the press area at night. Animal mascots were all the rage in those days. In 1915 the Brewers ballplayers kept a black bear cub for good luck throughout the season until October, when it grew too big and they had to give it to the Washington Park Zoo.

The Brewers did not have anyone in the lineup who hit as high as .290, at least not for the full season. They did have a .350 hitter for 85 games, but in July, outfielder Larry Chappell upgraded and signed with the Chicago White Sox for a then-exorbitant $18,000. Unfortunately for Chappell, he suffered a series of setbacks that derailed his promising career. In spring 1914 he broke in a new pair of shoes in an exhibition game. A tight left shoe rubbed the skin off his foot, which became septicemic. Chappell hovered near death for days. Doctors told him they needed to amputate his leg to save his life. Chappell refused, and ultimately he regained his health, although with a limp. On February 14, 1916, Chappell was one of three players traded by the White Sox to Cleveland, along with $31,500, for Shoeless Joe Jackson, the most expensive deal in baseball up until that time. Chappell later fought in World War I. He died from the Spanish flu epidemic in France two days before the Armistice.

The Brewers game in Athletic Park on May 8 demonstrated how tough they were. The Brewers and Minneapolis Millers had been bench-jockeying and jawing back and forth all afternoon. In the seventh inning, Millers shortstop Dave Altizer slid hard into third baseman Pep Clark with spikes high. One foot opened a deep gash on Clark's forehead that required stitches. The other punctured the manager's chest. Immediately Clark retaliated with a flurry of punches, mostly to Altizer's head. After the two combatants were separated and ejected, their faces were bloodied and bruised. But Clark was back at his position the following afternoon.

Milwaukee won 100 games in earning their first pennant. A few of those were memorable, and two occurred in Athletic

The Milwaukee Brewers won their first American Association pennant in 1913. It gave them an excuse to get all cleaned and dressed up. PHOTOGRAPH COURTESY OF THE MILWAUKEE COUNTY HISTORICAL SOCIETY

Park on consecutive days. On July 15, Columbus pitcher Leonard Cole, commonly called King Cole, tossed a no-hitter against the Brewers. Cole was a former Chicago Cub who started Game Four of the 1910 World Series. The next day the two clubs played again—they *really* played again. The Brewers scored two runs in the ninth to tie the score at five. Nearly two hours later it was still 5–5. Finally in the 19th inning Lena Blackburne scored on a perfect squeeze bunt to end the longest game in the history of the American Association. Four Brewers pitchers combined for the victory, but Jack Ferry went the distance for Columbus, to no avail.

In 1913 the American Association scheduled no official post-season. Instead the champions were free to play a best-of-seven series against the champions of some other league. The Brewers took on the Denver Grizzlies of the Western League, defeating them in the Colorado snow, four games to two.

Milwaukee won the pennant again in 1914, then had to wait until 1936 to capture another one. Unlike Pep Clark's scrappers, the '36 Brewers were loaded with hitters. They boasted nine men who batted .288 or above, with six of them exceeding .300. The leader of the list was Rudy York, the American Association's Most Valuable Player. York batted .334 with 37 home runs and 385 total bases. He was one-eighth Cherokee, so in the style of the day, he was called demeaning names on the field and in the newspapers, names like Chief and Pocahontas. One scribe disparaged York's fielding skills by writing that he was part Indian, part first base-man. But nobody questioned his prowess with the bat.

Also swinging the heavy lumber for the Brewers was Chet Laabs, popular native son of Milwaukee's heavily Polish south side. Laabs not only matched York's offensive numbers, he sur-passed them, with 42 homers and 388 total bases. Both men were destined to make their marks in the big leagues. In August 1937 York would shatter Babe Ruth's record for home runs in one month, blasting 18 four-baggers and driving in 49 runs, which eclipsed Lou Gehrig's record. Laabs would never enjoy that level of success, but he did smash a pair of home runs on the final day of the 1944 season to help put the St. Louis Browns into the World Series for their only time.

Besides their outstanding run producers, the Brewers also ben-efited from the defensive play of shortstop Wimpy Wilburn and the strong pitching of their mound staff. Tot Pressnell, Joe Heving, and Luke Hamlin each won 19 games, while number four starter Clyde "Mad" Hatter notched 16 victories. Hatter, a hard-throwing lefty, struck out 17 Columbus Red Birds in Borchert Field on July 13, giving him 30 strikeouts in a two-game span.

The 1936 Brewers started slowly, but they took over first place on August 4 and never looked back. At their peak they led by 11 ½ games. Even a 3–13 finish could not tarnish their great season. By winning the pennant, Milwaukee earned the top spot in the

Shaughnessy playoffs. Invented by International League president Shag Shaughnessy to help boost attendance during the hard times of the Great Depression, this postseason format matched the first-place team against the third place, the second against the fourth. The American Association was testing the system for the first time.

The Brewers swept through the Shaughnessies without breaking a sweat. They captured four straight wins from the Kansas City Blues before taking four of five from the Indianapolis Indians. The Milwaukee team completed its mission by blitzing the Buffalo Bisons in five games in the Junior World Series. Game Two in Borchert Field was pivotal. The Bisons could have evened the Series by winning, and they came close. But Lin Storti's two-run home run in the bottom of the ninth tied the score at four and kept the Brewers in the game. In the last of the 10th the Brewers had two out and nobody on when Tedd Gullic knotted the score again with a home run. Storti's second homer of the night earned a 6–5 victory for Milwaukee and essentially drove a stake through the heart of the Bisons.

Right-handed pitcher Tot Pressnell recorded three of the four victories for the Brewers. Laabs led the way in the final game by blasting two home runs. When the Series ended, more than a few experts were proclaiming that the 1936 Milwaukee Brewers might be the best minor league team ever.

If the 1936 championship postseason was a cakewalk, the 1947 playoff run was a dogfight. To begin, the 1947 season demonstrated both the good side and the bad side of Shaughnessy's brainchild. It kept half a dozen teams in contention until the final week, but it also sent a ball club that barely won more games than it lost during the season into the Junior World Series. That team was the Milwaukee Brewers.

Manager Nick Cullop's Brewers won 79, lost 75, and finished the regular season a distant third, 14 ½ games behind the first-place Kansas City Blues. Throughout the year the Milwaukee club played at a mediocre pace. The reason was simple: their pitching was weak. No Brewers hurler won more than 14 games, and none achieved an earned run average below 3.58. What success they did enjoy could be traced to their hitters—not sluggers like the 1936 champions, but reliable men (team average, .286) who could get on base and keep a rally going. Their leading home-run hitter, Carden Gillenwater, swatted a mere 23 home runs despite his home park's short fences.

The Brewers' strength was their infield. Third baseman Damon "Dee" Phillips batted .303. Their second sacker, Whistlin' Danny Murtaugh, hit .302. Rookie of the Year Alvin Dark played a solid shortstop, batted leadoff, and led the American Association in runs scored (121) and doubles (49). Utility man Skippy Roberge couldn't find a permanent defensive position but still batted .315. Most of all, first baseman Heinz Becker led the league with a .363 batting average and (although this statistic lay far in the future) an on-base percentage of .472. The popular Becker was a native of Berlin, Germany, and was a favorite of Milwaukee's Germanic populace.

By virtue of finishing in third place, the Brewers earned the chance to take on the league's best, the KC Blues, in the best-of-seven playoff opening series. Surprisingly Milwaukee captured the first two games in Kansas City, separated by a pair of rainouts, on their way to eliminating the Blues in six games. In the championship round of the American Association playoffs, the Brewers went the full seven games in defeating second-place Louisville. The decisive blow in the deciding game was a dramatic three-run homer by Heinz Becker.

As the Milwaukee players rode the train bound for Syracuse to begin the Junior World Series against the champions of the International League, all the talk was about money—more specifically, the lack of money. As each Brewer had boarded the train, he had received a check for his share of the revenue from winning the American Association playoff championship. It came to $162. In addition, each man was provided with meal money when the team was traveling, to the tune of $3.75 a day. Cullop's men felt shortchanged. They knew the Syracuse ballplayers had each received a $200 savings bond and $5.00 a day for food.

In Syracuse the Brewers lost the first two games, then rescued a 4–3 tussle in 10 innings before returning to Borchert Field for the duration. The Series went the full seven games, with Milwaukee ultimately coming out on top. The crucial contest, though, was Game Five on October 2. Twice the Brewers staged valiant comebacks to escape the brink of elimination.

Brewers southpaw Ewald Pyle was in full command as he breezed through the first six innings, allowing just two harmless singles. Meanwhile, his teammates were scoring a pair of runs. Alvin Dark accounted for the initial one by stealing home in the first inning. They added another to stake Pyle to a 2–0 lead. In the seventh, though, he lost his control, walking three batters. Mixed in with two singles and a throwing error, the inning produced four runs and a 4–2 lead for the Chiefs.

In the eighth inning, center fielder Carden Gillenwater evened the score with a two-run home run over the left-field boards. That score, however, was short-lived. A single, a base on balls, and a double put the visitors back on top, 5–4.

Dark led off the bottom of the ninth by lining a shot toward the gap in left center. The Syracuse shortstop leaped and speared it for the first out. Murtaugh kept hopes alive with a base hit, bringing up left fielder Tom Neill. He golfed a low fastball across Seventh Street to give the Brewers a thrilling 6–5 victory. Fans poured out of the seats and onto the playing field. The Junior World Series title was technically two nights away, but now it was a foregone conclusion.

45

Lights, Camera...

On April 14, 1962, fans of the Milwaukee Braves saw something they had not seen before. Their favorite team was on television. In their first nine seasons after moving the franchise from Boston to the Beer City, the Braves had not allowed even one of their games to be televised, even network telecasts, with the obvious exception of World Series and playoffs. Milwaukee was the last

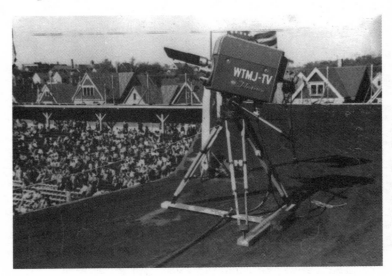

This is the Channel 3 TV camera that video photographer George Kasdorf used in televising Brewers games from the roof of Borchert Field in 1948 and 1949. COURTESY OF JIM NITZ

club in the major leagues to cross the barrier and utilize the small screen. It may not have been worth the wait. Warren Spahn gave up 13 hits and the Dodgers beat the Braves, 5–4, in the Los Angeles Coliseum.

Braves owner Lou Perini's aversion to TV is hard to explain. He spoke of not wanting to saturate the minds of potential paying customers, but his understanding of cranial physiology would be hard to support with science. Perini was no fool, though. While his Braves were chasing pennants between 1954 and 1959, his construction company was creating the St. Lawrence Seaway. Nevertheless, Perini had once been a proponent of televised baseball.

In August 1946 Perini was president and majority ownership partner of the Boston Braves when he purchased the Milwaukee Brewers from Oscar Salenger for $270,000. Television did not yet exist in Wisconsin, but radio broadcasts from Borchert Field were a surprisingly longstanding Milwaukee tradition. The first ballgame sent out over the airwaves from what was then called Athletic Park occurred on a Wednesday afternoon, June 9, 1926. The Brewers defeated the Minneapolis Millers, 12–4, as Dinty Gearin outpitched Bill Hubbell (no relation to Carl). Announcer Sam Levy, a local baseball writer, described the action from the press coop on the roof of the ballpark. The historic account was carried over station WHAD, operated jointly by the *Milwaukee Journal* and Marquette University. The broadcast facilities were located inside the new *Journal* building at Fourth and State Streets. A year later the FCC issued the call letters WTMJ (standing for "the Milwaukee Journal") to the newspaper.

No one knew how broadcasting the ballgames would be accepted by the public. Brewers owner Otto Borchert, fearing the worst, said a few days before the initial broadcast, "Radio will ruin me!" His thought was, why would fans pay to come to the game when they could listen to it for nothing?

Then again, what if people chose not to tune in? As recently as one year previous, Milwaukee's entire radio schedule consisted of two nights a week, Tuesday and Friday. There was dance music from the rooftop ballroom of the Wisconsin Hotel, a theater stage show, and a half-hour studio show of mostly idle chatter. Beyond that—static.

As it turned out, all the worry was unwarranted. Baseball on the air was greeted with wild enthusiasm. Phone calls and letters of praise cascaded into the radio station. It didn't hurt that Milwaukee's first radio game happened to be the Brewers' 16th consecutive victory—this from a club picked to finish last by the so-called experts. Officials quickly announced that Saturday's game and the Sunday doubleheader would also be available over WHAD. Contrary to Otto Borchert's concern, more than 15,000 packed the park for the twin bill. And for the record, the Brewers extended their winning streak to 20 by sweeping Sunday's pair. The Brewers continued to broadcast their games until 1944, when World War II temporarily forced them off the air.

On December 3, 1947, the miracle of television landed in Wisconsin and changed the landscape forever. Beginning at eight o'clock on that Wednesday night, WTMJ Channel 3 became the 11th television station in the United States by sending pictures across the ether and into the 400 TV sets stationed across the Milwaukee area. Most of the TVs resided in bars and restaurants, but giant-screen sets, eight inches by ten inches, were made available without charge to whoever could crowd into the WTMJ Radio City auditorium and the lobby of the library-museum building on Wisconsin Avenue.

The original two-and-a-half-hour program was a melange of introductory chatter, newsreels, college football films, a style show, various nightclub acts, and even a golf demonstration by the club pro from Blue Mound Country Club. From that time forward the station broadcast regularly, Wednesday through Sunday, a total of 19 hours a week. By the end of the month the number of Wisconsin TV sets receiving this programming had nearly doubled.

And who should be most eager to test the new technology and its application to sporting events? Brewers owner Lou Perini, of course. Barely three months after television came into existence in the Badger State, Perini announced that all 77 of his team's 1948 home games would be televised, at no cost to the sponsors. Declaring TV a wonderful thing, Perini explained, "We would not know what to charge and with comparatively few television sets here, the fee could not be very large."

So it was that on the afternoon of April 27, 1948, the hometown Brewers and the Toledo Mud Hens did battle not just inside Borchert Field but also on TV screens across southeast Wisconsin. A raucous Opening Day crowd, the largest in a decade, spilled out of the grandstand and bleachers and stood 10 deep on the grass in left-center field. The governor and the mayor led the host of dignitaries on hand for the historic occasion. WTMJ announcer Larry Clark, who had joined the station's staff a week after they went on the air, recounted the balls and strikes for listeners and gave them his description of the contest. Two TV cameras mounted on the stadium roof captured the action, one in a special booth directly behind home plate, the other 20 feet toward first base angled to cover the infield and outfield.

Clark was truly Milwaukee's pioneering sportscaster. Besides the Brewers games, he broadcast the first televised Green Bay Packers game from Chicago's Wrigley Field on November 14, 1948. In addition, Clark called play-by-play for Marquette University and UW Badgers football games. Later he did Braves baseball and basketball for the Milwaukee Hawks and Marquette. For his work on Brewers telecasts he earned $10 per game.

Milwaukee's first televised ballgame turned out to be both successful and exciting. The Mud Hens took the lead in the first inning when Hank "Bow Wow" Arft singled home a run. In the third inning Milwaukee left fielder Nanny Fernandez banged a triple that scooted along the right-field fence and drove in two teammates to put the Brewers ahead, 2–1. Toledo smacked lefty hurler Glenn Elliott repeatedly and in the sixth inning, with five straight hits, forced him out by scoring four runs for a 5–2 advantage. Milwaukee got one back in the sixth but still trailed, 5–3.

In the last of the seventh the Brewers loaded the bases with a double and a pair of walks, bringing up third baseman Damon Phillips. He was a veteran infielder with major league experience. In 1944 he had been the regular third sacker of the Boston Braves. He was in the lineup at Crosley Field on August 10, 1944, in the shortest nine-inning night game (one hour 15 minutes) in major league history. That was also the game in which Phillips's teammate Red Barrett set a record by throwing a complete game with just 58 pitches.

Phillips took ball one, then connected with the second pitch, driving it into the wind with enough force to clear the fence in left-center for a grand slam. Relief pitcher Cy Buker held the Hens in check in the final two innings, and the fans streamed happily out of the park, rejoicing in a 7–5 victory.

Of course television made this a day of firsts. The initial Milwaukee batter to be shown on camera was shortstop Johnny Logan. The first home run witnessed on the small screen in Wisconsin was the Phillips four-bagger. The first winning pitcher of a televised game in his home state was Greenwood native Cy Buker. And so forth.

Later in the season, in another game with the Mud Hens, Clark told his viewers that a first-inning fly ball was caught by Brewers outfielder Marv Rickert. A short time after that a note was delivered to Clark in the press coop. It was from a tavern owner across the street from the ballpark. The message informed Clark that Rickert had not caught that long fly in the first inning.

The barkeep was sure of that because Rickert was sitting across the bar from him drinking a beer.

The technical aspect of televising a game was not entirely without problems. The distant parts of the outfield proved difficult for the cameras to find. The lighting was inconsistent, sometimes distorted by reflections from houses and automobiles. At one point the screen went black and stayed that way for nearly half an inning. Overall, though, viewers were pleased.

WTMJ continued to televise all of Borchert Field's home games through the rest of 1948 and all of the following season. After that, station officials decided they were showing too much baseball, so they stopped. No more American Association games were televised after 1949.

46

Yatcha

The first Milwaukee ballplayer ever to bat on television was Brewers rookie Johnny Logan. He also recorded the first error witnessed by Channel 3, a low throw to first base. Brewers manager Nick Cullop was notoriously prejudiced in favor of baseball veterans, but he had been enthusiastic about Logan almost from the first day of spring training in Austin, Texas, when the young shortstop showed up sporting a bright green tie and matching socks. "Green is my favorite color," Johnny explained simply.

The array of talent in that Brewers camp was interesting. A towering, ambidextrous first baseman named Joe Bauman was hoping to impress Cullop with his towering home runs. Bauman, whose wife had nicknamed him Peony, was trying to make the leap from the Class C West Texas–New Mexico League to the Triple A level. He had some credentials, namely 86 home runs in the two previous seasons. He was destined for even bigger numbers. From 1952 through 1955 in the Longhorn League he would blast 221 home runs, including an Organized Baseball record 72 big flies in 1954. Big Joe made the team with Milwaukee but lasted just one at-bat before being sent back to the low minors. He would enjoy his greatest success playing semipro ball in Texas and owning and operating a Texaco station along Route 66.

Feisty Johnny Logan was Milwaukee's shortstop for 14 consecutive seasons, beginning in Borchert Field in 1948. FROM THE AUTHOR'S COLLECTION

By all accounts the most promising rookie in the Brewers camp was 18-year-old catcher Delmar Crandall. The recent high school graduate was tabbed for future stardom by all the scouts and coaches who watched him behind the plate. Cullop admired the young backstop's fielding and arm strength but teased him relentlessly about his "Hollywood" hairstyle (Crandall went and got a crewcut) and his fair complexion, calling him Pinky. Cullop was probably responding in kind for the baseball nickname he had been saddled with: Old Tomato Face. Crandall was simply too inexperienced to stick. He was assigned to the Leavenworth Braves of the Western Association.

Logan, meanwhile, in just his second season of pro ball, began working with the first-string infielders at the start of spring training and didn't relinquish the job. His teammates at the bases were veterans: first baseman Heinz Becker and third baseman Damon Phillips had been in organized ball for nine seasons apiece, and second sacker Gene Markland had played for five.

The fact that Logan earned a place in the Brewers lineup surprised no one who knew his background. As a kid in Endicott, New York, Johnny was all sports, all the time. When he was 12 years old, he skipped school one day and ran nine miles to the ballpark in Johnson City to see the New York Yankees play an exhibition game against their Binghamton farm club.

The Bronx Bombers who played in that game included some of the all-time greats: Red Rolfe, Lefty Gomez, Bill Dickey, Lou Gehrig. Johnny arrived at the park without any money, not realizing he needed a ticket to get in. He watched the game through a crack in the center-field wall, but that was perfect. The ballplayer he most wanted to see stood right in front of him—center fielder Joe DiMaggio, the Yankee Clipper. Joltin' Joe slammed a home run and drove in four runs in the contest. Afterward Logan ran back home in time to eat dinner with his folks. When his mother asked him how school had been, he just said, "Excellent."

In high school Johnny starred in nearly every sport. The whole town proudly followed his exploits and called him by his childhood nickname, Yatcha, a corrupted form of a Russian word used by his mom to calm him down when he was small. In football his senior year he scored 18 touchdowns, earned all-state honors, and received a number of scholarship offers.

Instead Uncle Sam drafted him into the army in the final months of World War II. He played on the baseball team at Camp Wheeler, Georgia, where he said he learned the fundamentals of the game from Bobby Bragan. After being honorably discharged and then trying college under the G.I. Bill, Johnny signed a contract with the Boston Braves organization. He spent 1947 with the Class B Evansville Braves. He slammed a triple in his first game there and an inside-the-park homer the next day. He batted .331

for the season and achieved rave reviews with his glove. That's how he earned a shot at the starting job as the Brewers shortstop in 1948.

At Evansville he had also learned an important lesson from manager Bob Coleman. Johnny got spiked one day at second base. The team doctor suggested Johnny sit out for three or four days. When Johnny told his manager, the skipper said, "If you listen to doctors you'll never be a ballplayer." Logan played in every game that season.

Unfortunately, in 1948 he lacked the consistency that experience later brought him. Case in point: a doubleheader in Borchert Field on May 16 against the Kansas City Blues. Johnny got two hits in each game, including a triple in the opener, and drove in a run in both games. He also made two errors in the first game and one in the second. In addition, though, he made a game-saving circus catch of a short fly off the bat of Al Rosen in the ninth inning. Red Thisted of the *Milwaukee Sentinel* called it "the best play of the season." Manager Cullop thought Logan needed more seasoning, so they farmed him out, first to Dallas, then to Pawtucket.

The next year he was back in Milwaukee. Heeding the good counsel of Bob Coleman, Johnny played every game for the next two years. In 1951 he established an American Association record for shortstops by playing 46 straight games without an error, handling 209 chances successfully.

Also in 1951, in a game against Kansas City, he got tangled up at second base with Blues catcher Clint Courtney. Somehow, in the scrum, two of Johnny's front teeth got knocked out. He exchanged words with the pugnacious Courtney, whose well-earned nickname was Scrap Iron. No satisfaction was achieved, so the two combatants agreed to settle the matter after the game under Borchert Field's old wooden grandstand. They did, and according to an eyewitness, Johnny punched the catcher's lights out. Until Johnny's dental appliance was installed, his teammates gleefully serenaded him with choruses of "All I Want for Christmas Is My Two Front Teeth."

In December 1951 Logan's career in the Braves organization appeared to be over. *Milwaukee Journal* beat writer Sam Levy, reporting from the minor league convention in Columbus, revealed that the Braves and Phillies had agreed on a trade. Boston would send its ace left-hander Warren Spahn along with Logan to Philadelphia in exchange for—get this—shortstop Granny Hamner and a right-handed pitcher called Bubba Church. In a stroke of good fortune or sense, the Braves called off the deal at the last moment and were spared the shame of the worst deal since Babe Ruth left the Red Sox. Church went on to win 13 more games in his career; Spahn enjoyed 255 more victories. Logan played in four All-Star Games; Hamner was selected for three.

Although he spent the final three months of the 1951 season with the Boston Braves, Logan began 1952 back in Milwaukee. When Charlie Grimm received the call to manage the Braves at the end of May, his first personnel move was to send for Logan. Johnny played his last game in Borchert Field as a Brewer on May 23, 1952. He belted a farewell home run in the fifth inning and added a single. However, he played the game in a fog—literally.

With the score tied, 1–1, and the Minneapolis Millers batting in the sixth inning, a low-hanging cloud descended on the diamond. Home-plate umpire Mike Briscese should have called off the game, but he refused. In the top of the seventh, Millers second baseman Ron Samford lined a ball down the left-field line that hooked foul. Umpire Harry King couldn't see it, though, and he called it fair. By this time the outfielders were no longer visible from the press box. Shortstop Daryl Spencer lifted an easy fly that should have been a routine third out. Instead left fielder Luis Marquez never saw the ball. It fell for a double, driving in two go-ahead runs.

In the Brewers' half of the seventh, the first two batters were retired quickly. Next up was Logan. He complained loudly to the umpire, "I can't see the ball when it's pitched." The man in blue finally suspended play. After an 82-minute delay, the action resumed and Logan struck out. Ten minutes later the heavy mist returned. Clint Hartung of the Millers stroked a fly ball to center that Billy Bruton could not locate until it landed near him. It went for a double and drove home an insurance run. Jim Basso hit a similar invisible double in the ninth to drive in a run for Milwaukee, but the game finally ended 10 minutes before midnight. The Millers won, 4–2.

Johnny Logan vanished into the fog. He would reappear in Borchert Field a few months later for one final time. On August 18 he and Eddie Mathews and the rest of Charlie Grimm's Boston Braves visited Milwaukee for an exhibition with the Brewers. Logan slapped a base hit in three trips, but the Brewers beat their parent club, 3–1.

47

Teenaged Catcher

Every ball club needs a good catcher. In 1947 the Milwaukee Brewers struggled most of the season to find one. They auditioned five different guys wearing the "tools of ignorance" before finding one they really liked. Somehow they won the Junior World Series anyway.

In 1948 they thought the problem had been solved. Norm "Duke" Schlueter, the best of the lot from the previous year, was a 31-year-old veteran with three big-league seasons behind the mask, two with the White Sox and one with the Indians. He offered little threat as a hitter, but his work behind the plate made up for it. His handling of Milwaukee's pitchers was credited with Milwaukee's surprise win in the 1947 Series.

At Toledo in the fourth game of the 1948 season, Mud Hens third baseman Don Richmond swung hard at a fastball and inadvertently struck Schlueter on the head. Catchers did not wear helmets in those days. Duke was hospitalized and advised to stay in bed for three or four days. X-rays showed, though, that it was "only" a concussion, so he climbed out of bed and, despite some headaches, rejoined his team.

With Schlueter hurt, 24-year-old Paul Burris took over. The nervous rookie twice threw into center field on successful stolen

On the day he stopped being a teenager, Del Crandall blew out his birthday candles at spring training in Bradenton, Florida. To his right is Larry Pennell, who starred in TV shows like *Ripcord* and *The Beverly Hillbillies*. Behind Pennell is 18-year-old Eddie Mathews. FROM THE AUTHOR'S COLLECTION

base attempts in his first inning, but gradually he settled down. In his fourth game he was hit on the wrist with a pitch and was replaced—by Schlueter. Two days later in Indianapolis Schlueter suffered a bump on the head in a pepper game and could not play. He tried again the next day, but after the game he was bothered by dizzy spells. His career ended immediately.

Burris returned and performed admirably as the regular catcher, with 30-year-old Billy Kerr filling in as needed. At the beginning of September, Milwaukee also called up from Class C Leavenworth an 18-year-old prospect just out of high school. His name was Del Crandall. He was there to observe and learn.

A native of California, Crandall had been signed by scout Johnny Moore (who one year later recruited Eddie Mathews) as a can't-miss prep athlete out of Fullerton Union High School, the same school attended by Hall of Famers Walter Johnson (yes, the Humboldt Thunderbolt) and Arky Vaughan.

On a mild Wednesday evening the young phenom sat idling in the Milwaukee dugout, watching the third-place St. Paul Saints pummel his second-place Brewers. Taking it in with great interest from the grandstand were Brooklyn Dodgers president Branch Rickey and his son "the Twig," as well as coaches Jake Pitler and Clyde Sukeforth, all there to scout Saints hurler Harry Taylor. In the third inning the home pitcher, Norman "Schoolboy" Roy, began to take exception to the strike zone of umpire Sandy Sandt. Roy came off the mound to protest and was quickly joined by manager Nick "Old Tomato Face" Cullop and catcher Burris. The man in blue was in no mood to debate. He chased all three of the plaintiffs.

Without warning, the lanky teenager was directed to put on the chest protector. Crandall proceeded to catch a flawless game, slap a single for one of his club's four hits, and throw out the only base runner audacious enough to trying stealing against him. His American Association debut went so well that the fans instantly loved him and he earned a few more starts in the next week.

The Brewers were firmly ensconced in second place on September 9 when the parent club, the pennant-bound Boston Braves, called up Paul Burris, making Billy Kerr the starting catcher. When the Columbus Red Birds took the field at Borchert to begin the playoffs, southpaw Jim Prendergast was on the mound and Kerr was crouched behind the plate—but not for long.

In the fifth inning a foul tip off the bat of center fielder Bill "Hopalong" Howerton split the pinkie finger on Kerr's throwing hand. At once Crandall was not only the best available catcher but also the only one. In an emergency the Brewers would need to activate 41-year-old coach Ray Berres, who had once been a catcher. Kerr, meanwhile, was expected to be incapacitated for a week.

Crandall filled in admirably for four-plus innings, although Milwaukee lost to Columbus, 4–1. The following night he caught the full nine innings and contributed a base hit and two runs scored in a 10–3 triumph. The format of the best-of-seven series called for the first three games to be played in Milwaukee, with the remainder of the necessary games played in Columbus. Having divided the first two in Milwaukee, the Brewers needed to win Game Three or go on the road facing a daunting two-games-to-one deficit.

The last Borchert Field contest of the Junior World Series took place on the night of September 16. Crandall's battery mate was 23-year-old right-hander Ray Martin, a 10-game winner during the season. Martin's career had been and would remain unremarkable except for a few gulps of coffee with the Boston Braves. His moment in the sun had been a complete-game, 2–1 victory over the National League champion Brooklyn Dodgers on the penultimate day of the 1947 season. Martin had failed to go the distance in his last seven starts with the Brewers. On this night he again did not have great stuff, giving up a pair of runs in the top of the first. Assisted considerably by four double plays, however, he survived into the eighth inning, thanks also to some lusty bat support.

The Brewers roughed up Red Birds starter Kurt Krieger for four runs in the first inning. Reliever Harvey Haddix had to be summoned just to get the third out. The Milwaukee fans received an even bigger jolt of excitement in the bottom of the fifth. Their sun-bleached California catcher blasted a home run with a teammate on base to put the Brews ahead by a comfortable 9–3 margin.

In the Columbus eighth, Martin quickly squandered the sense of comfort. He faced four batters and retired none of them. With the bases full, a run in, and nobody out, manager Cullop called Prendergast from the bullpen. Before the carnage ended, several line drives and some shoddy fielding (each Milwaukee infielder committed an error in the game) had produced a seven-run inning and a 10–9 lead for the visitors. They tacked on one more in the top of the ninth.

Trailing 11–9 in their final at-bats, the Brewers appeared doomed. Shortstop Dee Phillips atoned for his fielding miscue by singling. Center fielder Marv Rickert did the same. Columbus skipper Hal Anderson changed pitchers, bringing in Clarence Beers, who had beaten the Brewers just 48 hours previous. Beers failed to locate the strike zone and walked first baseman Heinz Becker to load the bases. With the crowd now standing and jeering wildly, Beers walked left fielder Nanny Fernandez to force in a run.

Anderson yanked Beers and sent for Ray Yochim, last night's losing pitcher. Yochim had no better luck than Beers had. As the crowd hooted its delight, he walked right fielder Jim Gleeson, forcing in Rickert with the tying run. That brought up Crandall.

It's likely the young signal-caller had never before experienced such a tumultuous situation, but with the poise of a veteran, he did what he was supposed to do. He stood with the bat on his shoulder as the flustered pitcher fired four consecutive errant pitches. Brewers win! Brewers win! Brewers win! ...

Crandall's walk-off walk put his club ahead in the Series, two games to one. Unfortunately they traveled to Columbus and lost the Series in seven games. Billy Kerr recovered sufficiently to catch the final two games, which had twice been delayed by rain.

Nine months later Crandall began his major league career with the Boston Braves. During his 13 years with the Braves, he appeared on the cover of *Sports Illustrated*, won the first two NL Gold Glove awards for catchers, and earned eight all-star selections.

48

The Buck Stops Here

One of the most iconic photos in American journalism appeared on November 3, 1948. In the picture a grinning President Harry Truman joyfully displays the front page of the *Chicago Daily Tribune*. The headline reads, "Dewey Defeats Truman."

The headline, of course, was wrong. So was the cover of *Life* magazine dated March 22 of that year. It featured a close-up of Truman's mustachioed Republican challenger, Thomas E. Dewey, with the caption, "The next President of the United States." Whoops.

These gaffes occurred for a variety of reasons. Pollsters and pundits overestimated the depth of support for Dewey, the popular governor of New York, and their overconfidence may have caused many of his backers to skip the voting booth and stay home. Besides that, Dewey was made to look publicly foolish by two widely circulated characterizations of him. Dorothy Parker described Dewey as looking "like the little man on the wedding cake." Another wag called Dewey "the only man who could strut sitting down."

Truman, on the other hand, emerged as a down-to-earth hero of the ordinary working folks, people who would sit outdoors on splintering wooden seats in the 35-degree chill of an October night in Milwaukee. Nineteen days before Election Day, on

President Harry Truman and his wife, Bess, along with Wisconsin's acting governor, Oscar Rennebohm, and his wife, arrived by train from Madison for the president's campaign speech in Borchert Field. PHOTOGRAPH COURTESY OF THE MILWAUKEE COUNTY HISTORICAL SOCIETY

October 14, 1948, Truman visited Borchert Field and delivered the first address in the city by a US president since Woodrow Wilson spoke in the Milwaukee Auditorium on January 31, 1916. Several presidents had traveled to Milwaukee since then, but none gave speeches. Truman himself had spent one day of his honeymoon in Wisconsin's largest city in 1919, arriving from Chicago by boat.

The presidential train carrying Truman on whistle stops around the Badger State arrived at the North Western depot near the lakefront at 7:27 p.m. An enthusiastic crowd of 2,000 greeted the president, his wife, Bess, and his daughter, Margaret, as they detrained about a half hour later. From there Truman rode on the back of an open car along a circuitous three-mile course through the streets of Milwaukee: west on Wisconsin Avenue, north on Third Street to Center, west on Center to Eighth Street, north to Chambers, then into the ballpark. An estimated 50,000 people lined the route of the 25-vehicle motorcade, waving and shouting as the commander in chief passed by at eight miles an hour. "Harry, come in and have a beer with us!" a group of Schlitz brewery workers entreated from outside their workplace, but the offer was not accepted.

A small army of security personnel guarded Truman the entire time. According to the newspaper accounting, 497 of MPD's finest and 105 firefighters supplemented 20 Secret Service agents and 20 railroad police in keeping the chief executive safe from harm. Nevertheless, the thought of a president in an open car, at night, along an announced parade route, sounds inconceivable today.

A loud cheer erupted as Truman's car entered Borchert Field and parked in the infield. The crowd had waited patiently for nearly two hours, listening to a 100-piece concert band of volunteer AFL union musicians, followed by campaign speeches from two congressional candidates.

Carl Thompson, the Democratic candidate for governor, introduced the president. Once Truman began to speak, the audience was friendly and respectful, probably interested more in who was speaking than in what was being said. The president's chosen subject, however, was a solemn one.

"Tonight I'm going to talk about something that ought not to be in politics at all," Truman began, "but the Republican candidate has brought it in."

The subject was atomic energy. Having made the momentous judgment to drop atomic bombs on Hiroshima and Nagasaki three years earlier, Truman qualified as something of an expert on the matter. "It was the hardest decision I have ever had to make," he said. "But the president cannot duck the hard problems—and he cannot pass the buck."

He explained, "I decided the bomb should be used to end the war quickly and save countless lives, Japanese as well as American."

Truman proceeded to issue a warning to the Soviet Union that the United States was still ahead in atomic weapons and would not make any "one-sided sacrifice" or share atomic know-how.

"The world knows," the president added, "that the United States will never use the atomic bomb to wage aggressive war. But in the hands of a nation bent on aggression, the atomic bomb could spell the end of civilization on this planet. That must never happen."

Because this was a campaign speech, the president also made a point of attacking Dewey and the opposition party. "Powerful, selfish groups within the Republican Party are determined to exploit the atom for private profit."

He then earned his loudest applause of the night by shouting, "I shall fight this effort with all my strength!"

At the conclusion of his 20-minute address, the unassuming, plain-spoken leader of the free world climbed back into his chauffeured automobile. The driver made a large circle around the inside of the ballpark, then steered out the left-field gate and headed south on Eighth Street toward a private gathering of party members at the Pfister Hotel.

What did the president of the United States think about his visit to Borchert Field? "Very good," he told reporters, smiling, "very good."

Eighteen months later, on April 18, 1950, President Truman again made history in a ballpark. As was the presidential custom, he tossed the ceremonial first pitch on Opening Day in Griffith Stadium in Washington, DC. Truman, though, became the first to hurl two pitches—one left-handed, one right-handed.

49

Art Imitates Baseball

One of Hollywood's most popular baseball-themed movies of all time is *The Natural,* based on Bernard Malamud's novel of the same name. The 1984 film, starring Robert Redford, is a mythic work of fiction, but a half dozen of its characters resemble or parallel real-life ballplayers and their exploits. What's more, these players are all connected in some way to Borchert Field. Let's look at the dramatis personae and see who they are.

Two ballplayers could have served as models for protagonist Roy Hobbs, portrayed by Redford. First is Billy Jurges, who enjoyed a 17-year big-league career as a shortstop with the Chicago Cubs and New York Giants. He was not much with the bat, but his slick fielding helped the Cubs win three pennants during the 1930s. Jurges suffered a serious injury in 1940 when he was beaned by Bucky Walters. He missed more than 90 games after the incident but recovered and had six more productive seasons. On September 1, 1931, in Borchert Field as a member of the Louisville Colonels, Jurges slammed a two-run homer off bespectacled hurler Merton Nelson of the Brewers.

In 1946 with the Cubs, one of Jurges's teammates was a smooth-swinging, fancy-fielding first baseman named Eddie Waitkus, the second possible inspiration for Hobbs. The son of Lithuanian immigrant parents, Waitkus was not your typical ballplayer. He could read Latin and spoke four languages. He was suave, soft-spoken, and always impeccably dressed. He had signed with the Cubs shortly before World War II, then earned four battle stars in the Philippine Islands and New Guinea in some of the bloodiest fighting in the Pacific theater. Returning home from the war, he became one of Chicago's most popular players. He was a slap hitter, not a slugger, but he hit for a good average and became a two-time National League All-Star first baseman. Having been traded to the Phillies after the 1948 season, Waitkus was a key part of Philadelphia's Whiz Kids, who won the 1950 pennant.

In Borchert Field on May 6, 1946, the Cubs played an exhibition game with the Brewers. The number three hitter in the Chicago lineup was Eddie Waitkus. Against Milwaukee right-hander Eddie Karas, Waitkus went 0-for-2 before leaving the game, replaced by former Brewer Heinz Becker.

The day before the Borchert Field game with the Brewers, the Cubs had played a doubleheader with the Phillies in Wrigley Field. The Chicago lineup in both games included Jurges, Waitkus, and a third notable ballplayer, Harry "Peanuts" Lowrey, third baseman and leadoff batter. Lowrey had been a Milwaukee Brewer for a short stay during the 1942 season.

The fourth member of our cast, Carvel Rowell, shared a first name with an ice cream franchise, but no one called him that. He was always known by a contracted form of his home state— Bama. He spent most of his baseball career in the Boston Bees/ Braves system, including five of his six seasons in the National League. He was also part of the blockbuster trade that brought Eddie Stanky to the Braves in 1948.

On the night of June 29, 1950, Rowell was involved in one of the most unusual plays in Borchert Field's long history. Batting for the visiting Minneapolis Millers in the fourth inning, Bama lifted an easy fly ball toward right fielder Bob Jaderlund. Without warning, a pair of nighthawks swooped in and attacked the baseball. Their pecking was sufficient to change the line of flight, and the ball fell untouched between Jaderlund and center fielder Bob Addis. With help from the birds, Rowell arrived safely at second, credited with a double. He soon scored what proved to be the winning run in a 4–3 Millers victory.

Fifth on the list is versatile Sebastian "Sibby" Sisti, who spent 13 years in the big leagues, all with the Braves. After serving in the US Coast Guard for the better part of World War II, he returned home to find his positions filled—all of them, each one except pitcher and catcher. He was assigned instead to the Indianapolis club of the American Association, where he blossomed, batting .343 for the Indians. *The Sporting News* named him their Minor League Player of the Year for 1946. In 1948 Sibby filled in for the injured Eddie Stanky and helped the Braves secure their first pennant since 1914.

In the second game of a doubleheader in Borchert Field on June 9, 1946, Sisti drew a walk with two out and nobody on base. He then stole second and scored on a single by right fielder Joe Bestudik, giving the Indians a 4–2 lead. They won the game by the score of 7–4 in 10 innings.

After earning his way back to the majors, Sibby returned to Borchert Field on August 18, 1952, when the Boston Braves played an exhibition with their Triple-A affiliate, the Milwaukee Brewers. With two on and nobody out in the eighth inning, Sisti drew a walk to load the bases. Milwaukee hurler Billy Allen then fanned the next three batters. The Brewers won the game, 3–1.

The sixth and final ballplayer in our review of *The Natural* is right-handed pitcher Francis "Spec" Shea, who earned his nickname not because he wore glasses but because his fair complexion caused him to acquire a face full of freckles (also known as speckles). He burst onto the American League scene as a spectacular New York Yankees rookie in 1947. Spec won 14 games, lost only five, earned the win in the All-Star Game, and led Joe DiMaggio and his teammates to the World Series championship with two victories. He would have captured the American League Rookie of the Year Award if there had been one at the time.

On his way to the big leagues, Shea pitched for the Kansas City Blues. On July 14, 1942, against the Brewers in Borchert Field, he worked the opener of a doubleheader. Shea had always possessed a live fastball, but sometimes its flight path was unpredictable, as on this day. Shea struck out the first two batters, walked the next three, then fanned Tedd Gullic to get out of the inning.

The game was tied at 2 in the bottom of the sixth when Shea's control abandoned him. With one out he walked Eddie Stanky, Hal Peck, and Frank Secory in order. Manager Johnny Neun called in a relief man, who promptly walked Heinz Becker, forcing home Stanky with the deciding run. Shea took the loss.

So there they are: Jurges, Waitkus, Lowrey, Rowell, Sisti, and Shea. With these six characters in hand, film director Barry Levinson went about recrafting Malamud's dark novel as an upbeat tale of redemption and romance in which good triumphs over evil. Both the novel and the film have as their central event the shooting of a star ballplayer by a woman in a Chicago hotel room. Malamud died in 1986 without revealing the genesis of his tale, so the model for his protagonist, Roy Hobbs, portrayed in the film by Robert Redford, could be either of two men, or perhaps both.

On July 6, 1932, Billy Jurges was shot in room 509 of the Carlos Hotel near Wrigley Field by his ex-lover, Violet Popovich Valli, who was toting a .25-caliber pistol. Violet was a former chorus girl who had previously dated Leo Durocher and Al Lopez, among others. She was distraught because Jurges had broken off their relationship. "To me life without Billy isn't worth living," she wrote in an intended suicide note, "but why should I leave this earth alone? I'm going to take Billy with me."

She and Jurges wrestled for the gun. In the struggle he was shot twice, she once. When the case reached a courtroom, Jurges

Eddie Waitkus was a solid ballplayer but is remembered primarily for being shot by a crazed admirer. NATIONAL BASEBALL HALL OF FAME LIBRARY, COOPERSTOWN, NY

refused to testify and the charges were dropped. Violet went back to work, billing herself in nightclubs as "Violet (What I Did for Love) Valli, the Most Talked About Girl in Chicago."

The judge who dismissed Valli's case did so reluctantly, and he said, "I hope no more Cubs get shot." Technically he got his wish.

In Chicago's Edgewater Beach Hotel, room 1297A, on June 14, 1949, Phillies first baseman Eddie Waitkus, who had been traded to Philadelphia by the Cubs exactly six months before, was shot by a delusional 19-year-old woman named Ruth Steinhagen. She lured him to her hotel room with a cryptic note, then shot him in the chest with a .22-caliber rifle. The two had never met. The obsessive young lady had built a shrine in her bedroom filled with pictures and clippings about Waitkus. She had even tried to learn to speak Lithuanian because she had read that it was the language of Waitkus's parents.

The day after the shooting, Steinhagen granted a long interview to a reporter. Among other bizarre statements, she was quoted as saying, "I liked Eddie because he was clean cut and I liked the way he played baseball." She went on to say, "I guess I got the idea to shoot him because he reminded me of my father."

Eddie Waitkus was hospitalized for a month after the shooting and would not play ball again until the 1950 season opener. Ruth Steinhagen was tried and found legally insane. She was incarcerated and received electric shock treatments over a two-year period. She was pronounced cured and released from the Kankakee State Hospital in April 1952. She lived more than 60 years after that and more than 40 years after Waitkus's death.

Friends of Steinhagen revealed that before she turned her full attention to Waitkus, she had previously had a crush on other public figures, including actor Alan Ladd and Waitkus's Cubs teammate Peanuts Lowrey. Fortunately for those two men, Ruth Steinhagen's affection was only temporary.

An important early scene in *The Natural* portrays young Roy Hobbs in an impromptu pitching matchup in which he strikes out a heavy-set slugger called "the Whammer," clearly based on Babe Ruth. Lead actor Redford wanted to lend legitimacy and accuracy to the event, so he hired Spec Shea to teach him how to throw the way pitchers did in the 1930s.

One of the memorable moments in the picture shows Hobbs breaking out of a batting slump by smashing a gargantuan home run in Wrigley Field. The ball shatters the clock atop the scoreboard, showering glass on the outfielder below. This scene owes its inspiration to a similar event that occurred in Brooklyn's Ebbets Field on May 30, 1946. Boston Braves left fielder Bama Rowell drove a ball that struck the Bulova clock on the scoreboard, sending a spray of glass onto Dodgers right fielder Dixie Walker. The hands of the clock were struck at 4:25 p.m. At 5:25 they permanently stopped running.

Finally, Sibby Sisti served as a consultant on the film, helping the actors look and move like real ballplayers. He also portrayed the manager of the Pirates, Hobbs's opponents, in the climactic scene. In the final inning of the pennant-clinching game, Sisti's character makes a pitching change, calling in a fire-balling stud southpaw to face Hobbs with two out. Hobbs, of course, promptly makes the manager regret his decision by blasting a home run that shatters a bank of stadium lights, gives his team the victory, and sends the movie audience home smiling. Cue the dramatic music.

50

King of the Ring

Professional wrestling was a major attraction at Athletic Park since its earliest days. On July 16, 1888, while the baseball team was out of town, an enterprising promoter had a six-foot-high platform, 34 feet square and stuffed with sawdust, erected in front of the grandstand for a match between a local weightlifter named Otto Wagner and a challenger named McMillan. Outweighing his opponent 184 pounds to 176, McMillan had all the better of it.

On July 21, 1889, in the ballpark, American wrestling champ Evan "the Strangler" Lewis took on Charles Green, the top-ranked British wrestler of the time. The match was delayed nearly an hour because the Englishman objected to wrestling on a platform. Eventually he agreed to the setup and the bout proceeded. Neither man could be described as nimble, but the two giants put on an impressive display of strength and ferocity. In the end the United States entry prevailed, which met with the crowd's approval.

The grappling seems to have been legitimate. As the sport evolved and grew in popularity, gymnastics and histrionics took larger roles. Soon everyone knew it was scripted, but accounts of the matches still appeared in the sports pages, not with the drama reviews. What's more, fans attending the exhibitions displayed genuine emotion when reacting to the unbridled villainy and mayhem visited upon their heroes and favorites.

Whether or not the outcome was preordained, no one doubted the athletic prowess of these large, powerful men that the newspapers condescendingly referred to as "grunters." Some of them, like the legendary Lou Thesz, had been stars in amateur (legitimate) wrestling. Others, like Bronko Nagurski, had demonstrated their talent in football before entering the wrestling ring.

On April 18, 1949, a young man named Verne Gagne signed a contract with Minneapolis wrestling promoter Tony Stecher. Gagne had been a four-time Big Ten champion and had won two consecutive NCAA heavyweight wrestling championships at the University of Minnesota while also excelling in football. Stecher said at the signing, "Verne Gagne has more possibilities in the professional ranks than any of the other amateur wrestlers I've signed."

Two weeks later Gagne made his professional debut in the Minneapolis Auditorium against one of the sport's most dastardly heavies, Abe "King Kong" Kashey. The derisive headline in the *Minneapolis Star* the next day told part of the story: "Gagne Passes Screen Test as Wrestler." The article explained how he had won the match. The bad guy was disqualified after nearly 23 minutes for repeatedly stomping on Gagne's body as the rookie lay sprawled across the canvas.

Gagne, however, had more than wrestling in mind for his career. He aimed to follow the example of previous University of Minnesota grads, including Nagurski, who combined a wrestling career with professional football. This was more than wishful thinking. Gagne had been selected in the 1947 NFL draft by the Chicago Bears. In August of 1949 Gagne played for the College All-Stars against the defending NFL champion Philadelphia Eagles in the annual charity game in Soldier Field in Chicago. Following the exhibition Gagne was expected to report to the Chicago Bears' training camp. He and owner/coach George Halas could not agree on salary, though, so Halas dismissed

Gagne, making him a free agent. On the last day of August he began workouts with the Green Bay Packers. He appeared briefly in an intrasquad scrimmage in Marinette, then played sparingly in preseason games against the New York Bulldogs and Washington Redskins.

Years later Gagne said of his NFL experience, "I'd played about four games with the Green Bay Packers [three, actually, counting the scrimmage] and it was pretty well agreed that I would do well if I stuck with the team."

Legendary Green Bay coach Curly Lambeau saw it differently. Three weeks after Gagne started practicing with the Packers, six days before the season opener against the Chicago Bears, Lambeau released him on waivers.

With football out of the picture, Gagne turned his full attention to the wrestling ring. On December 16, 1949, in Houston, he defeated Leo Newman for the Texas heavyweight championship. When the Milwaukee Arena opened in April 1950, the first sports event in the new building was a wrestling match between Gagne and the evil Fritz von Schacht. In November in the Milwaukee Auditorium, Gagne pinned Billy Goelz to earn the National Wrestling Alliance's version of the World Junior Heavyweight title.

On the night of July 14, 1951, Gagne appeared as the protagonist in the main event of a wrestling card in Borchert Field put together by longtime promoter Henry Tolle. The grappling commenced at 8:30 with a preliminary match between Tommy Martindale and Carl Engstrom that ended in a draw. This was followed by a so-called Australian Tag Team match pitting evil-doers Leo Kirilenko and Al Williams against Al Szasz and Walter Palmer. The good guys prevailed in a free-for-all, winning two out of three falls. In the semi-windup, local favorite Goelz prevailed over nefarious Gypsy Joe, also by a two-falls-to-one margin. During this contest a large woman, incensed by the shady tactics of the Gypsy, left her ringside seat and tried to enter the ring, purse in hand, to

Heavyweight wrestler Verne Gagne, shown here sporting one of his championship belts, was a Milwaukee favorite at several venues, including Borchert
Field. LOREGA/MINNESOTA HISTORICAL SOCIETY

offer her assistance. She was intercepted and led away by one of
Milwaukee's finest.

At last the featured contest of the evening arrived, the one most
of the crowd had paid their buck and a half to see. Lightning-quick
hero Verne Gagne, he of the flying dropkick and the sleeper hold,
faced the Mighty Atlas (whose wrestling moniker sounded more
fearsome than his actual name, which was Morris Shapiro). To
make certain no one mistook his role in the match, Atlas wore a

thick black mustache. Mr. Atlas ("May I call you Mighty?") had an interesting background. His father had been a strongman in a Russian circus in Minsk. The younger Atlas had appeared as a stuntman in an Abbott and Costello film entitled *Here Come the Coeds.*

Atlas and Gagne were physically mismatched. The former Green Bay Packer was outweighed by a good 30 pounds. To compensate, the terms of the match required that Atlas pin Gagne twice in 60 minutes while Gagne only needed to subdue the larger man once.

The two headliners exchanged holds, kicks, punches, and acrobatic rough stuff for 45 minutes before Atlas succeeded in pressing his smaller opponent's shoulders to the mat for the requisite count of three. He was unable to pin Gagne a second time, however, so the clean-cut hero's arm was raised in victory by the referee. The crowd of 4,724 cash customers seemed satisfied as they filed out into the warm summer night.

Gagne went on to enjoy a long and lucrative career as a wrestler, appearing hundreds of times in Wisconsin. After that he became a successful trainer and promoter. Unfortunately fate delivered him a cruel blow late in his life. He developed either Alzheimer's-related dementia or possibly chronic traumatic encephalopathy from being struck countless times on the head.

On January 26, 2009, Gagne attacked a 97-year-old fellow nursing home resident with whom he had argued. The frail victim received severe injuries when Gagne apparently applied a wrestling hold called a Boston crab. The elderly man died of his injuries 19 days later.

Gagne was not charged criminally because it was determined that he lacked the mental capacity to understand his actions. He died on April 27, 2015, in Bloomington, Minnesota. He was 89.

51

The Real M & M Boys

Eddie Mathews and Mickey Mantle were separated at birth—by one week and less than 200 miles.

On October 13, 1931, Mathews entered the world in Texarkana, on the Lone Star side of the Texas-Arkansas line. Four years later his impoverished parents took their little boy and fled west from the Dust Bowl, like so many others, looking for a new life in sunny California.

Mantle was born in rural Spavinaw, a bleak town of a few hundred residents situated in the northeast corner of Oklahoma. Mantle's dad, called Mutt, considered moving to California before trying his hand as a tenant farmer and ultimately a lead and zinc miner around Commerce, Oklahoma.

Both fathers had played semipro baseball, and both aspired to have their sons play in the big leagues. Mutt Mantle named his son Mickey in honor of the great Philadelphia Athletics catcher Mickey Cochrane, perhaps unaware that Cochrane's actual first name was Gordon. Edwin Lee Mathews named his son after himself.

Both Mickey Mantle and Eddie Mathews excelled in high school football and baseball. Both signed professional baseball contracts at age 17 (actually, their fathers had to sign them) right after graduation, Mantle with the soon-to-be World Series

Eddie Mathews (left) and Mickey Mantle (right) had parallel careers. They played against each other for the first time in Borchert Field in an American Association game. FROM THE AUTHOR'S COLLECTION

champion New York Yankees, Mathews with the reigning National League champion Boston Braves. Both young men were fast and powerful and handsome and, everyone agreed, destined for stardom.

In 1949 both Mathews and Mantle became infielders for Class D ball clubs. Mathews became the third baseman for the Hi-Toms in High Point–Thomasville, North Carolina. He batted .363 and belted 17 home runs in half a season. Mantle, meanwhile, filled the shortstop position for the Independence (Missouri) Yankees, batting .313 with seven homers. The next season he advanced one step in the Bronx Bombers' farm system to Class C Joplin, where he broke loose and batted a league-leading .383 with 26 homers.

A sensational spring training in 1951 made Mantle the hottest young prospect in baseball. Just 19 years old, the ex-shortstop from Oklahoma joined Joe DiMaggio in the Yankees outfield. Mathews might have made a similar jump to the big leagues following a 32-home-run season with the Atlanta Crackers. The Korean War was under way, however, and rather than wait to be drafted, Eddie and a handful of high school buddies had enlisted in the US Navy a few days after Christmas. (Mantle was 4-F.)

The two young sluggers both enjoyed long, successful careers that propelled them to Cooperstown. Each retired in 1968, Mantle after playing in the Yankees' second-to-last game of the regular season, Mathews after playing for the Detroit Tigers as they defeated the St. Louis Cardinals in the World Series.

At retirement Mantle ranked third on the all-time home-run list with 536, behind only Babe Ruth and Willie Mays. Mathews had two dozen fewer four-baggers than Mantle and stood at number six on the list. Along the way, their home-run totals were never far apart. The two muscular stars led their respective leagues in total home runs during the decade from 1951 through 1960.

Mantle had a one-year head start, but Mathews caught him at 45 homers on June 16, 1953, then moved ahead in July. The Milwaukee Braves third baseman stayed in front of Mantle for eight years. On August 6, 1961, Mantle went back into the lead with 361.

The two long-ball specialists exchanged places on the home-run list five times over the next four seasons. Nineteen sixty-six found Mantle and the Yankees in 10th place in the American League, Mathews and the Braves in Atlanta, and the two living legends tied (on June 29) with 483 home runs apiece. Mantle homered that day and never again relinquished his advantage.

Mantle and Mathews competed against each other in nine All-Star Games, two World Series, and six regular-season games after Mathews joined the Detroit Tigers late in his career. They never homered in the same game. In their six league games against each other, only once did both get a hit in the same game. It occurred on September 19, 1968, at Tiger Stadium, the game in which Denny McLain famously grooved a home-run pitch to the Mick as a tip of the hat for a great career.

The first time these two heroic home-run hitters met on the playing field, however, was a product of unique circumstances, and it occurred in Borchert Field.

A month or so into the 1951 season, Mantle began striking out with alarming frequency. In a Decoration Day doubleheader at Fenway Park, he made five plate appearances and fanned each time. By mid-July his average had dipped to .260 and Casey Stengel had lost patience with his spring phenom. The Yankees sent Mantle down for more seasoning with their Triple-A farm club, the Kansas City Blues.

Mantle caught up with the Blues in Milwaukee on July 16. Six days prior to that, a teenaged third baseman had been added to the Milwaukee Brewers roster, a youngster whose tape-measure blasts in the Southern Association in 1950 had stamped him with a can't-miss label.

The youthful slugger was, of course, Eddie Mathews. After just half a year of a four-year navy commitment, he had been granted a dependency discharge because his father was seriously ill with tuberculosis.

On July 16 Mantle made his Borchert Field debut. He walked, beat out a bunt, flied to left, took a third strike, and lined out to the third baseman. Mathews watched from the bench as the Brewers defeated the Blues, 7–5.

The next night the two future Hall of Famers opposed each other for the initial time. Truth be told, neither used his bat to much effect. Mantle went hitless in four trips against Brewers right-hander Bert Thiel. Mathews, in his first official at-bat with Milwaukee, pinch-hit for Thiel in the last of the ninth and lined out to right field to end the ballgame.

Kansas City won the game, 5–4, paced by four runs batted in by Bob Cerv, the top power hitter in the American Association that year. Cerv was the beneficiary of Borchert's short foul lines. He hit a towering 265-foot pop fly that barely cleared the left-field fence for a two-run homer in the fourth inning.

Despite failing to hit, Mantle demonstrated for the crowd of 10,400 why he was so special. With one out in the ninth, the speedy Oklahoman raced to the center-field bleachers, leaped at the railing, and robbed Al Unser of a game-tying home run.

Five days later, on July 22 in Borchert Field, Mathews smashed a pinch-hit grand slam to beat the Minneapolis Millers. The pitcher who served up Mathews's bases-loaded blast was Dave Barnhill, one of the finest hurlers in the Negro Leagues from 1938 through 1949. Barnhill was the first African American Mathews had ever faced at the plate. After the game, manager Charlie Grimm informed Eddie that he was being sent back to the Atlanta Crackers.

On August 24 in Cleveland, Mantle rejoined the Yankees. In his six-week sojourn with Kansas City he had batted .361 with 11 homers and 50 runs batted in.

52

Say Hey to Borchert Field

Not many people remember who won the 1934 All-Star Game. What they may remember is Carl Hubbell, the New York Giants southpaw master of the screwball, striking out, in order, Babe Ruth, Lou Gehrig, Jimmie Foxx, Al Simmons, and Joe Cronin.

That second annual midsummer classic was played in Hubbell's home park, the Polo Grounds. Fifteen years later, on May 29, 1949, Hubbell, the Giants' director of player development, sat in the stands at the Polo Grounds and watched a doubleheader between the Birmingham Black Barons and the New York Cubans of the Negro American League. Hubbell liked what he saw that afternoon. After the second game he signed two of the Cubans, Ray Dandridge and Dave Barnhill, to minor league contracts.

The player Hubbell liked most, however, he could not sign. The center fielder of the Black Barons had amazing defensive skills and a great arm. In addition, he belted a home run. The problem was that he was still in high school. Even though he had helped Birmingham reach the 1948 Negro World Series he was off-limits for another year. Hubbell's scouting report made clear his impressions of the young outfielder, though; he called him "the best goddamn baseball player I have ever seen in my life."

The Barons' young fly-catcher was Willie Mays. He was a year away from graduation at Fairfield Industrial High School outside

Four days after Mays smiled for this photo, he visited Borchert Field for the first and only time. Six days after that, he made his major league debut with the New York Giants. ST. PAUL DISPATCH & PIONEER PRESS/MINNESOTA HISTORICAL SOCIETY

Birmingham, Alabama. He was enrolled in courses that would lead to a productive career in dry cleaning. Although he was a conscientious student, young Mays truly excelled in athletics. He was the leading scorer on the school's basketball team and the star pitcher on the baseball team. In the summer he played for the Black Barons in Rickwood Field, the club's venerable home park when the white Birmingham team was on the road.

Willie's father, William Howard Mays, worked in the toolroom of a steel mill in Birmingham and played on its baseball team in the industrial league. His exceptional quickness earned him the nickname Cat. It was Cat Mays who introduced his son to Piper Davis, player-manager of the Black Barons.

Davis had first learned about baseball by listening to radio accounts of Southern Association games on Birmingham station WBRC. The announcer on those broadcasts was Bull Connor, who gained notoriety in 1963 as the Birmingham Public Safety Commissioner who ordered fire hoses and police dogs to disperse civil rights demonstrators. The brutal tactics so outraged TV viewers that President John F. Kennedy remarked, "The civil rights movement should thank God for Bull Connor. He's helped it as much as Abraham Lincoln."

Thanks to Davis's managerial leadership and the outfield artistry of 17-year-old Mays, the Black Barons defeated the Kansas City Monarchs to win the Negro American League pennant. Black Barons general manager Eddie Glennon had thought initially that Mays could be a pitcher because of his strong right arm, but his myriad talents were too great not to utilize every day. In what turned out to be the final Negro World Series, Mays and his Birmingham teammates were defeated by the Homestead Grays.

On May 25, 1950, Mays graduated from Fairfield High. A few weeks later the New York Giants paid the Black Barons $10,000 for his contract. The Giants assigned Willie to their Trenton farm club in the Class B Interstate League, where he was the first African American. In a little more than half a season, he batted .353.

The next season Mays was ready for stiffer competition. He joined the Minneapolis Millers, the Giants' Triple-A farm club. On Saturday, May 19, the Millers visited Milwaukee for a three-game series with the Brewers. There was little doubt that this would be Mays's only trip to Wisconsin. His batting statistics shouted that he was ready for the National League.

Mays entered Borchert Field with a 10-game hitting streak and an incredible .475 batting average. When he left town on Sunday, he had raised it to .493. Thirty games into the American Association schedule, the Brewers and Millers were locked in a battle for second place, behind the Kansas City Blues. All eyes, however, were on Mays.

In the series opener the Brewers broke out of a batting slump and pounded Minneapolis hurlers for 16 hits. Milwaukee won the contest despite the individual heroics of Mays. The 20-year-old phenom had not yet mastered the strike zone, but he belted everything thrown to him. He struck out in the first inning but singled in his next two trips. In the sixth he smashed a home run into the center-field bleachers to put the Millers two runs ahead. After the Brewers scored three runs to retake the lead, Mays tripled off the scoreboard and scored on a fly ball to tie the score in the eighth inning. An inside-the-park homer by center fielder Jim Basso put Milwaukee ahead in the bottom of the inning. They added one more run and held on for a 10–8 victory.

In the Sunday doubleheader Basso and Mays slugged it out again. Basso hit the big blast, a bases-loaded job in the sixth inning that made Art Fowler a winner by the score of 6–4. Wondrous Willie did his best, though. He ripped three doubles, driving in a run with each. In the eighth inning he was robbed of a likely triple by Basso's leaping grab in front of the scoreboard.

Mays turned the tables in the nightcap. Racing far to his right, he speared Paul Burris's long drive in front of the bleachers. "Nobody else catches the ball," wrote Red Thisted of the *Milwaukee Sentinel*. "[Mays] is simply out of this world." Mays also chipped in a single and a solo home run as the Millers took the finale, 3–1.

Nine hits in 14 plate appearances in three games at Borchert Field may have provided the final persuasion for the New York Giants management. After a quick stop for three games in Kansas City, Mays made his big-league debut in Philadelphia's Shibe Park on May 25, 1951. The date marked the one-year anniversary of his high school commencement ceremony. Before long he would show the baseball world what manager Leo Durocher meant when he called Mays "Joe Louis, Jascha Heifetz, Sammy Davis, and Nashua rolled into one."

53

Quiet Pioneer

By the time the Milwaukee Braves made the franchise shift from Boston, George Crowe was 32 years old. He still possessed big-league batting skills, but he had no place to ply his trade on a regular basis. The Braves' first baseman, Joe Adcock, was an iron man who played every game in 1953 (157, including three ties). Crowe never started one game the whole season, playing just 21 innings and pinch-hitting 37 times. The next year, rather than let him collect moss on the bench, the Braves sent Crowe to their Triple A Toledo farm club, where he played every day, batted .334, and led the league in hits, doubles, and runs batted in.

Crowe was no stranger to having doors closed to him. He was an African American athlete ready for professional sports before they were ready for him. He was born in 1921 and grew up in a part of Indiana where one of every four adults claimed Ku Klux Klan connections. After a sensational high school basketball career at Franklin High School, he was named the original Mr. Basketball for that basketball-crazy state. He wanted to continue on and play at the collegiate level, but large universities were not recruiting black players, no matter how talented. Instead George attended Indiana Central College, a small institution affiliated with the United Brethren in Christ.

Graduation was followed by three years in the army, 16

Jackie Robinson described George Crowe as "the most articulate and
far-sighted Negro in the majors. Younger Negroes turned to him for advice."
COURTESY OF PAUL F. TENPENNY

months of which involved World War II combat duty in the
China-Burma-India theater. After the war when Crowe drove
one of his younger brothers to California to begin college, he
happened to pick up a newspaper and saw an announcement of
tryouts for an integrated Los Angeles basketball team called the
Red Devils. Among the squad members were Jackie Robinson
and future Yankee Irv Noren. Crowe tried out and made the cut,
but the team quickly folded for lack of funding.

Crowe then pursued the only path accessible to him. For the
next three years he played two professional sports. During the
summers he was the first baseman of the New York Black Yankees, a Negro Leagues team that played in the House That Ruth
Built when DiMaggio and the other Bronx Bombers were on
the road. During the winters he was a forward on a legendary

all-black hardcourt quintet called the New York Rens (short for Renaissance, the ballroom and casino inside which their home court was located).

On August 6, 1947, Crowe visited Milwaukee for the first time. His New York Black Yankees defeated the Chicago American Giants in a Negro Leagues exhibition in Borchert Field, 11–7. Crowe's baseball excellence was evidenced by his selection in August 1948 to the third annual Negro Leagues All-Star Game in Yankee Stadium. He contributed two hits and scored two runs as his National League team triumphed, 6–1.

The world of professional basketball in which Crowe competed consisted primarily of two parts: the all-white National Basketball League, a forerunner of the NBA, and the various barnstorming teams, many of them all black, like the Rens and the Harlem Globetrotters. These two factions converged once a year from 1939 through 1948 in the World Professional Basketball Tournament, an invitational playoff series sponsored by the *Chicago Herald American* newspaper.

The first tournament champions were the New York Rens, who defeated the Oshkosh All-Stars, 34–25. The last were the fabled Minneapolis Lakers, led by George Mikan, who beat the Rens, 75–71, on April 11, 1948. The six-foot 10-inch Mikan, who scored 40 points in the game, was simply too big and too strong to be defended by front-court players like six-foot two-inch George Crowe.

On January 27, 1949, the Rens, now calling Dayton, Ohio, their home base, took part in a pro basketball doubleheader in the Milwaukee Auditorium (the Arena was still under construction). In the second matchup of the night, the Rens took on a local aggregation calling themselves the Milwaukee Bright Spots. Early in the contest the Rens' top scorer, Pop Gates, became embroiled in a struggle with Milwaukee favorite John Schimenz under the basket. Punches were thrown and Gates (but not Schimenz) was ejected. Crowe took up the slack, scoring a game-high 23 points, and the Rens were victorious, 60–56.

After the basketball season, Crowe received his biggest break. The Boston Braves, who like a dozen other big-league clubs had never put a black player on the field, signed George to play minor league ball in Pawtucket, where he hit .354. The next year he batted .353 at Hartford and became the first African American voted the league's most valuable player.

During the 1950–51 off-season, Crowe played winter ball for the Caguas team in Puerto Rico, batted .375, and won the batting title. While he was in the Caribbean, his immediate future was being decided for him back in the States. He had been invited by the Triple A Milwaukee Brewers to attend their spring training in Austin, Texas. Civic authorities in Austin, however, according to *The Sporting News*, "served notice that Negroes would not be allowed on the field with white players." Instead Crowe and the Brewers' other two black players, Len Pearson and Buzz Clarkson (the first two black men to play for the Brewers) trained elsewhere, Crowe in Bradenton with the Braves, the others in Myrtle Beach, South Carolina. Even after the Braves broke camp and made their way north, Crowe was not permitted to play exhibition games in two Louisiana towns, Shreveport and Monroe.

In February 1951 the Kansas City Monarchs offered the Brewers the contract of another player from the Negro Leagues, Jim LaMarque. On March 9 Harry Jenkins, farm director of the parent Boston Braves, responded to the Monarchs on team letterhead. In refusing the offer, Jenkins wrote, "The truth is we now have three colored boys at Milwaukee, and if we take another, I am fearful that the club would get top-heavy." He went on to say, "I am certain you can recognize this is a factor to be considered."

Of course, Crowe made the Milwaukee ball club, led the American Association in several batting categories, and helped the Brewers win the Junior World Series. He also was voted unanimously to the all-star team. On July 24 he hit for the cycle in a game in Indianapolis.

On August 6, 1951, Crowe and his teammates hosted an exhibition game with the Chicago Cubs in Borchert Field. Because they were the closest major league franchise, the Cubs were very popular in Wisconsin, as attested to by the crowd of more than 11,000 who watched them play the Brewers. Milwaukee skipper Charlie Grimm was a former Cubs player and manager as well. In fact, Phil Cavarretta, the recently appointed Chicago field boss, had made his debut as a teenager in 1934 when Grimm was the player-manager of Wrigley's club.

The Cubs (surprise, surprise) did not have a strong team—they finished last in 1951—but they had some interesting ballplayers that Milwaukee fans were willing to pay to see. Handsome Ransom Jackson was a solid third baseman, a future all-star at the position. Lumbering outfielder Hank Sauer was a consistent 30-home-run man who would win the MVP in 1952. The catcher was pudgy, sweet-swinging Smoky Burgess, in his first full season. When he retired 16 years later he would be the leading pinch hitter of all time. In addition, the Cubs outfield featured Hal Jeffcoat, who three years later would be reborn as a pitcher.

For historic value, the Cubbies also showcased 35-year-old backup catcher Mickey Owen. Owen had been suspended from Major League Baseball from 1946 to 1949 for playing in the outlaw Mexican League in 1946. He was best remembered, though, for a notorious mistake he made in the fourth game of the 1941 World Series. As the catcher for the Dodgers, with Brooklyn leading 4–3 and two out in the ninth, he let the game-ending third strike get away, allowing Tommy Henrich to reach first base. The Yankees then scored four runs and won the game. Owen became the goat for all time. Ironically, he had set a record that season of 508 errorless fielding chances by a catcher.

One other Cub worthy of mention was their first baseman that day, Kevin Connors, who got one hit in three at-bats. He stood six and a half feet tall, and basketball was probably his best sport. He had played pro basketball with the Rochester Royals and Boston Celtics. In 1952 he played his final season with the Los Angeles Angels in the Pacific Coast League. It was a fortuitous venue for his final year. He changed his name to Chuck Connors and embarked on a movie career, appearing in his initial film with Katharine Hepburn and Spencer Tracy. By far his greatest Hollywood success was achieved between 1958 and 1963 when he portrayed the title role in the TV western series *The Rifleman*.

And George Crowe? He gave the home fans plenty to cheer about. He ripped a pair of singles and a double, drove in a run, and scored three. The Brewers cruised to an easy 8–1 victory over Johnny Klippstein and the Cubs.

54

Et cetera

Big Dan Brouthers stood six-foot-two and weighed more than 200 pounds. In the latter part of the 19th century, that was a big man. In a sandlot ballgame when he was 19 years old, Brouthers was involved in a violent collision at home plate. The catcher was rendered unconscious with a traumatic brain injury. Five weeks later he died. Brouthers was grief-stricken but was absolved of any blame for the tragedy.

Playing in the days before grounds crews manicured the infield, when infielders had to rake the diamond for themselves, Brouthers was a first baseman and baseball's first great slugger. He slammed 106 home runs before the dawn of the 20th century and from 1887 to 1889 held the career home-run record. Honus Wagner told of walking five miles each way, several times when he was a boy, just to watch Brouthers play ball in Pittsburgh. Big Dan won the league batting title four times, and his .342 lifetime average exceeded that of Babe Ruth by a tiny fraction.

An estimated crowd of 3,000 came out to see the powerful Brouthers in Milwaukee's Athletic Park on September 19, 1891, as the hometown Brewers, newly enrolled in the big-league American Association, took on the league-leading Boston Reds. No home run was forthcoming, but the man with the big bat slapped a double and a single and boosted his league-leading average another point. The next afternoon he managed only one single in four times at bat.

Twenty years later Brouthers was the night watchman in New York's Polo Grounds. In 1945 the veterans' committee elected him to the Hall of Fame.

~

First baseman Dan McGann was a rough-edged brawler, a drinking buddy of John McGraw who followed the pugnacious manager to New York. McGann was considered the finest first baseman in the National League. He led league batters six times in being hit by a pitch. On May 27, 1904, he became the first base runner to steal five bases in a game, a record that lasted for 70 years. In 1905 he was a key member of McGraw's Giants, the first National League team to win a World Series.

McGann's career was in decline when he joined the Milwaukee Brewers in 1909, but the big guy contributed mightily to Milwaukee's strong run that fell just short of the pennant. He started on Opening Day with a single, a double, a stolen base, and two runs scored as the Brewers defeated the St. Paul Saints in Athletic Park. That night McGann and many of his new teammates celebrated by attending the Majestic Theater for a performance of *Stealing Home*, a one-act play written by and starring actress Mabel Hite and her husband, Mike Donlin, a former teammate of Dan's with the Giants.

In Athletic Park on September 3, in the first game of a doubleheader against Kansas City, the Brewers were losing, 6–5, with two out in the ninth and nobody on base. A walk and a safe hit brought McGann to the batter's box. He worked the count to 3 and 2. Then he ripped a single up the middle. The center fielder threw home too late to shut off the tying run. The catcher fired down to third base, but the ball got away and the winning run scored. Milwaukee also won the second game, so at the start of play on Labor Day, the Brewers led the league by four and a half games. Perhaps the most interesting aspect of the victorious day, however, was the description of McGann's decisive hit in the flowery prose of the time, as written by an unnamed journalist in the *Milwaukee Journal*: "Dan laid his fateful willow along the seam of the pellet and the sphere whistled through the second base opening."

McGann's two-year stay in Athletic Park had a tragic epilogue. On December 13, 1910, he took his own life with a handgun in a hotel room in Louisville. His 38 years had been marked by violence, alcohol binges, and clinical depression.

~

Bill Terry became the last National Leaguer to hit above .400 when he batted .401 in 1930. That was the same year he collected 254 hits, still tied for the league record more than 80 years later. Terry was a brusque, no-nonsense man who openly admitted that he played baseball strictly for money, not pleasure. He clashed frequently with his autocratic manager, John McGraw of the New York Giants. For more than two years the two men never spoke a word to one another, but when McGraw retired in 1932, he recommended Terry for the position of player-manager. The following season Terry took the Giants to the World Series title.

In 1923, as the first baseman of the Toledo Mud Hens, Terry made several trips to Milwaukee's Athletic Park. On July 17 he rapped four singles off three Brewers pitchers in a 17–16 slugfest won by the home team. Two days later he got just one hit in five at-bats, but it was a mammoth blast that cleared a house across Seventh Street and landed in somebody's backyard.

When the Hens returned for the final time that year, Terry had replaced Possum Whitted as manager. It didn't affect Terry's hitting, though. In a doubleheader sweep by his last-place

Toledo club, Terry went 3-for-5 in each contest. In the first game he slammed two homers and a triple.

~

Few baseball people generated more controversy than Leo "the Lip" Durocher. He was ejected from ballgames 95 times, and he was suspended for a full season by Commissioner Happy Chandler because of an unseemly personal life and ties with gamblers and underworld characters. Yet Durocher also played an important role in breaking down racial barriers in baseball, most notably as the manager of Jackie Robinson. Leo has long been characterized by his statement that "nice guys finish last." He was reviled as a vicious bench jockey. His lengthy managerial career was marked by both failure and success, the latter especially in 1954 when his New York Giants swept the Cleveland Indians in the World Series. As a ballplayer he was the stereotypical "good field, no hit" shortstop whom his teammate Babe Ruth famously referred to as "the All-American out." Nevertheless, Durocher was voted into the Hall of Fame as a manager in 1994.

On June 30, 1927, Durocher was the shortstop of the St. Paul Saints when they took on the Milwaukee Brewers in Athletic Park. He went to bat five times, producing three singles and a sacrifice bunt. He led off the 10th inning with a bouncer over the third baseman's head and scored the winning run in a 9–8 Saints victory that knocked the Brewers out of second place.

On September 25, the last day of the season, the Saints and Brewers split a doubleheader in the rain and mud of Athletic Park (on its final day of being Athletic Park). As a result Milwaukee finished tied for second place, two games behind the champion Toledo Mud Hens. Durocher contributed three hits in seven tries. Perhaps of greater note, he took part in three double plays as the Saints established a record total of 213 twin-killings for the season. Almost 15 years later Durocher made one last appearance in Borchert Field as manager of the Brooklyn Dodgers. In an exhibition game on July 8, 1942, Durocher's club defeated the Brewers, 7–6, behind three RBIs by Ducky Medwick.

~

Born under czarist rule in Odessa, in the Ukraine, Charles "Buckets" Goldenberg immigrated to Wisconsin at age four. In high school he discovered that he had a knack for football, that it perfectly suited his temperament and physique. On November 12, 1927, Goldenberg helped his West Division team defeat rival Washington High in Athletic Park in front of a standing-room crowd of 11,000 and claim the City Conference championship. On the opening possession Washington was driving toward a score when Goldenberg forced and recovered a fumble by fullback Harry Max. West promptly took the pigskin the length of the field for a touchdown. Behind Goldenberg's bone-crushing blocking, West scored four TDs that afternoon and won convincingly.

Following an All–Big Ten football career with the University of Wisconsin Badgers, Buckets accepted a contract offer from Curly Lambeau's Green Bay Packers. In Borchert Field on Sunday, October 1, 1933, the third contest of his rookie year, he made a long kickoff return and generally ran and blocked well. His play was one of the few bright spots for Green Bay as the Packers fumbled away the game to the New York Giants, 10–7. Goldenberg went on to lead the NFL in touchdowns that season with seven.

Goldenberg enjoyed a 13-year career as a Green Bay Packer but never again played football in Borchert Field. He wasn't finished there, however. Drawing on the name recognition he had acquired on the gridiron, Goldenberg embarked on an off-season professional wrestling career. Outdoor rasslin' was popular at Borchert Field, and Buckets was a good drawing card. On Saturday night in the ballpark, July 31, 1937, Goldenberg subdued Jack Ross with an armlock and a half-nelson. When referee Art "Whataman" Shires stuck his nose in to try to separate the two combatants, Goldenberg gave him a biel throw across the ring and separated the ex-Brewer's shoulder.

~

Over the years the Brewers had better ballplayers than Tedd Gullic but probably none more popular. To the adoring fans who flocked to Borchert Field to watch him, Tedd was known as Old Reliable. In 10 seasons with the club (not counting his fraction of a season when he first joined them in 1931), Tedd averaged .314 with 24 home runs. He batted above the .300 mark for eight successive years. Most of the time the lanky Gullic patrolled center field, but when asked he moved without complaint to one of the other outfield positions, to first base, to third base, even pitching four innings when called upon one time in 1940 (and hurling a five-inning stint in an exhibition between the Brewers and a bunch of old-timers on August 4, 1941).

Tedd was a classic example of a ballplayer whose ability peaked just below the major league level. He had a couple of season-long trials with the St. Louis Browns, 1930 and 1933, but he only hit .250 and .243, respectively. Today those numbers might keep him in the big leagues, but in offense-minded 1930, the American League average was .288. The National League's average hitter that season batted .303, the highest in history. Tedd was out of his league.

Old Reliable made a successful big-league debut in 1930, in the first game after the 1929 stock market crash. He started in right field and went 2-for-4 with a home run. Then within a week and a half he slipped into mediocrity and below, at one stretch going 0-for-30-something. Inexplicably, Gullic enjoyed his greatest success in the majors against New York Yankees right-handed Hall of Famer Red Ruffing. In five plate appearances against him, Tedd

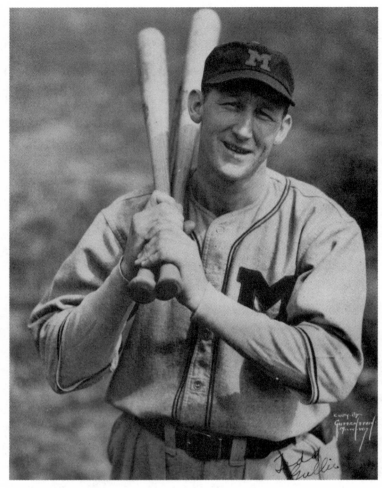

Slugger Tedd Gullic was a Milwaukee fan favorite for more than a decade, 1931 through 1942. RICHARD LULLOFF COLLECTION

roughed him up for a single, a triple, a home run, a sacrifice, and a base on balls.

With the Brewers, though, Tedd produced more highlights than he could count. Perhaps the most dramatic of those occurred on a foggy night in Borchert Field on September 18 in Game Three of the 1936 postseason playoffs. Some questionable umpiring had given the Indianapolis Indians a brace of runs that deeply upset the crowd and placed the Brewers in a 6–4 hole in the ninth inning. Then with one out and runners on first and second, Gullic lofted a majestic home run off Dizzy Trout. The homer sent the spectators into fits of euphoria. They hugged and kissed each other as if rehearsing for V-E Day. They swarmed onto the playing field and nearly crushed the breath out of poor Tedd in their enthusiasm to thank him. Afterward the ever-modest Gullic gave all the credit to a lucky penny a lady had given him a few nights before.

Even that moment, however, pales in comparison to Gullic's signature achievement. Like many of the Brewers during the season, he rented a room near the ballpark. His was directly across Eighth Street from Borchert Field, in full view of the diamond. One day he belted a home run that cleared the street, shattered a window, and landed in his own living room. For a long time after that, when their favorite center fielder stepped up to the plate, the home fans would exhort him to "hit it where you live, Tedd."

Maurice Tillet was born to French parents in 1903 in the Ural Mountains of Russia. He was such a sweet, handsome young boy that he acquired the family nickname "the Angel." After he reached adulthood, however, his body and face began a horrifying, gradual disfigurement. Over time his thick-boned body grew squat and powerful while his head grew to enormous proportions—his hat size was 11 ¾—with a pronounced jaw and misshapen mouth and forehead.

Tillet was a victim of acromegaly, a malfunction of the pituitary gland. He was intelligent and sociable, but his distorted features made a normal life impossible. For a short time he was employed as a sailor, but his life's path led him to the United States, where he became a professional wrestler known, with no small irony, as the Angel.

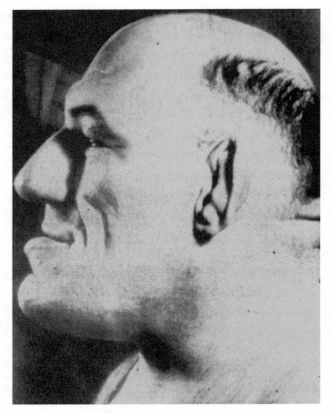

Maurice Tillet overcame a horrible disfiguring disease and
made a career out of his menacing appearance. PUBLIC DOMAIN

Anthropologists at Harvard University examined and studied
Tillet extensively. They described him as a throwback to Nean-
derthal Man. Other people afflicted with Tillet's disorder became
freaks in carnival sideshows. Instead, the Angel adapted to a life
on the canvas, grappling with other oversized men. He lacked
style or agility, but his terrifying looks attracted crowds of curi-
osity seekers, and his powerful bear hug made him a formidable
foe in the ring.

Exactly four months before the Japanese attacked Pearl
Harbor, the Angel wrestled for the first time in Borchert Field.

Three thousand cash customers came out to see for themselves the person billed as "the ugliest man in the world." The Angel's opponent was Ole Olson, a local product of little repute. Each fighter achieved one fall before the Angel ended the match with his patented bear hug.

Tillet made one more ring appearance in Borchert Field. On July 2, 1942, he traded holds and grunts with Wladek Talun, the Polish Giant, who clocked in at 307 pounds, some of it muscle. The attendance on this night was just 1,200. The novelty of pitiful ugliness had grown old. Each man won one fall before the clumsy, lackluster exhibition ended mercifully in a draw.

~

In Borchert Field on the afternoon of August 28, 1933, the Brewers hosted the Minneapolis Millers. The visitors' catcher, Joe Glenn, belted a three-run homer and Minneapolis won the game, 6–3. It was not Glenn's first shining moment against the Brewers that summer. On July 21 in Nicollet Park, he had pinch-hit a three-run blast that beat Milwaukee, 7–6.

So who was Joe Glenn? He was one of the thousands of men who have played major league baseball but are now lost in the fog of time. His birth name was Gurzensky. His nickname was Gabby, probably for the same reason a large man is called Tiny. But like nearly every ballplayer who ever reached "the show," Glenn did something unique and unexpected.

On October 1, the last day of the 1933 season, Babe Ruth pitched for the final time in the major leagues. He had begun his career as a pitcher, but as the years passed, he rarely took the mound. In fact, he had pitched only once since 1921, on the final day of the 1930 season. That was in Braves Field against his former team, the Boston Red Sox. Now in 1933, with the pennant race already decided, he again faced the Red Sox, this time in Yankee Stadium, the House That Ruth Built. He did not pitch particularly well, allowing five earned runs, but he worked the complete game and earned his 94th career victory, 6–5. He hit a home run to help his own cause. His catcher, just up from the minor leagues, was Joe Glenn.

Fast forward to August 24, 1940, in Fenway Park. In the first game of a doubleheader, the Red Sox were being thrashed by the Detroit Tigers, 11–1. Rather than waste a relief pitcher in a lost cause, Bosox manager Joe Cronin brought in his left fielder to hurl the eighth and ninth innings. It was Ted Williams, in what would be the only pitching appearance of his 19-year career. He gave up three hits and one run in two innings. When Cronin brought Williams to the mound, he also decided to rest his starting catcher, Jimmie Foxx. The substitute catcher he brought in to catch Teddy Ballgame was Joe Glenn.

⌒

In an era when pro football was almost an afterthought among sports fans and baseball was still the national pastime, the Los Angeles Rams were glamorous. After the franchise shifted from Cleveland in 1946, the Rams were the first major sports franchise on the West Coast. They played in the vast L.A. Coliseum and became the first pro team since 1933 to include black athletes on its roster. The first two of these pioneers were Kenny Washington and Woody Strode. On the night in 1950 when Richard Nixon nervously awaited the voting results of his race for the US Senate in California, he spent the night listening to music in Kenny Washington's Los Angeles home. Strode, after a short football career, became a Hollywood film star.

In October 1951 the Rams traveled to Milwaukee to play the Green Bay Packers. For three days they held workouts in Borchert Field. Among the Rams players were five future Hall of Famers: Tom Fears, Elroy "Crazy Legs" Hirsch, Andy Robustelli, and quarterbacks Norm Van Brocklin and Bob Waterfield. They also had "Mr. Outside," 1946 Heisman Award winner Glenn Davis. In addition they included two of the great African American running backs of that time, Deacon Dan Towler and Paul "the Tank" Younger. As befits a team from Tinseltown, Waterfield was married to screen star Jane Russell, Davis was married to starlet Terry Moore, and Crazy Legs would appear in several films in the next half dozen years.

On Thursday, October 18, the day the Rams arrived, they held a spirited two-hour workout in the Borchert Field mud in a pouring rainstorm. They were clearly taking nothing for granted against Gene Ronzani's downtrodden Packers in their Sunday game in State Fair Park. They needn't have bothered getting soaked. The Rams smothered the Packers, 28–0.

55

Best for Last

The Milwaukee Brewers were charter members of the American Association when it was formed in 1902. In their half-century history, the Brewers' best ball clubs may have been the last two, in 1951 and 1952, also the final years of Borchert Field.

Nineteen fifty-one began with low expectations. The previous season had been awful. Manager Bob Coleman had little talent from which to build a team except for outfielder Bob Addis, who came over from the Dodgers organization and won the batting crown. Milwaukee finished in sixth place, 14 games behind fifth-place Louisville. Attendance and hopes were both down. It looked like 1951 would be another dismal year. But as Yogi Berra explained, "In baseball you don't know nothing."

In 1951 Charlie Grimm returned to manage the Brewers. Charlie made them winners again, but he didn't do it with magic or rare strategy. He was blessed with an infusion of fresh talent. In 1950 the Brewers had exactly one man from their roster, Addis, on the league all-star team. In 1951 Addis had been called up to the parent Boston Braves, but seven Brewers earned selection as all-stars. Among those was slugger George Crowe, a 30-year-old rookie voted the American Association's outstanding freshman in 1951. Crowe batted .339 and smashed 24 homers. Some observers thought Crowe also should have been chosen the league's

Popular manager Charlie Grimm pauses between pregame fungoes in Borchert Field. RICHARD LULLOFF COLLECTION

MVP. That honor went instead to another new Brewer, catcher Al Unser.

The association's best pitcher, hands down, was lanky Brewers right-hander Ernie Johnson, who won 15 games, lost only four, and turned in a league-leading earned run average of 2.62. He was new to the club. All-star third sacker Billy Klaus and center fielder

Jim Basso had been added. So had a flock of strong non-all-star contributors, including pitchers Bert Thiel (14–9) and Virgil Jester (13–6) and fly-chasers Bob Thorpe and Luis Olmo. It was essentially a whole new team.

The Milwaukee home opener showed what kind of season it was going to be. George Crowe went 4-for-4, including a home run; 11,001 fans yelled themselves hoarse; and the Brewers won the game and stayed in first place. For the next two months the standings remained tight as the Brewers and the Kansas City Blues jockeyed back and forth, never more than a game or two separating them. Then in the second half of July Milwaukee won 13 of 15 games and lengthened their advantage to five games. Two weeks later the Brewers were sitting on a 10-game lead and it was all over but the shouting. On September 1 they rallied with two outs and nobody on in the ninth. Appropriately, 37-year-old Al Unser, recently named the league's most valuable player, pinch-hit for Billy Klaus and lined a single to right field for what many years in the future would be called a walk-off base hit. It clinched the pennant.

In the postseason playoffs, the Brewers easily subdued the third-place Kansas City Blues, winning the best-of-seven series in five games. Milwaukee suffered its only loss in Game Three on a chilly night in Borchert Field. Future Milwaukee Braves hurler Lou Sleater pitched a five-hit shutout for the visitors. Having dispatched KC, the Brewers proceeded to defeat second-place St. Paul, four games to two. The deciding game matched the two ball clubs' best pitchers, but it turned out to be no contest as Ernie Johnson and his heavy-hitting henchmen swamped Joe Black and the Saints, 17–2.

By eliminating the visitors from Minnesota, the Brewers qualified to challenge the International League champion Montreal Royals, the Brooklyn Dodgers affiliate, in the Junior World Series. The first three games were played in icy Montreal. Two games had to be postponed because of squall-like conditions and wintry blasts. When the two teams did play, the Brewers' only victory on Canadian soil came in Game Two. A pinch single by "Rootin' Tootin' Junior Wooten" tied the game in the ninth, and Wooten promptly scored the winning run. The Brewers returned to Milwaukee trailing two games to one.

But not to worry. In Game Four Milwaukee shortstop Buzz Clarkson slammed a three-run homer to give his club all the offense it needed as Grimm's team knotted the series at two games each. The next night Ernie Johnson fired a four-hit shutout for his fifth postseason victory and 20th of the season. The Brewers needed just one more win.

The Royals had other ideas. In Game Six they jumped on Milwaukee starter Sid Schacht for a single, two doubles, and a triple, scoring three runs before the pitcher could register the second out. His relief man, Charlie Gorin, allowed a pair of runs in the second inning. In the third the Royals blasted Murray Wall for five runs on six hits. After two and a half innings, Montreal led, 10–2. The outlook wasn't brilliant for the Brewers nine that day.

Jim Basso clubbed a two-run homer in the bottom of the third to make it 10–4. In the top of the fifth inning, one of baseball's time-honored protocols may have altered the complexion of the contest. Brewers left-hander Dick Hoover threw a fastball in the vicinity of Al Gionfriddo's cranium. Whether Hoover was instructed to do that is unclear, but in the Royals' wild third inning, when Charlie Gorin took a full windup, Gionfriddo stole home. When a base runner did that to "show up" the pitcher, a beanball was usually in order. That was how the game was played.

Gionfriddo, also following the custom of the times, then bunted down the first-base line, hoping to catch Hoover at the bag and spike him. First baseman Crowe failed to field the ball in time, though, preventing Gionfriddo from executing his nefarious plot. To avoid a collision, Hoover put his hands lightly on the runner's back as he crossed behind him. Gionfriddo was furious.

The Milwaukee Brewers won the Junior World Series in 1951. From left: Billy Klaus (3B), Bob Thorpe (LF), Buzz Clarkson (SS), George Crowe (1B), Jim Basso (CF), Billy Reed (2B), Luis Olmo (RF), Paul Burris (C), Al Unser (C), Bert Thiel (P). FROM THE AUTHOR'S COLLECTION

Foul words ensued. Very quickly, Virgil Jester of the Brewers and Royals pitcher Tommy Lasorda joined the fracas. The brouhaha lasted for five minutes with no serious punches landed. The level of emotion in the game changed, however.

In the bottom of inning number five, Milwaukee exploded. Two Montreal errors, two walks, and two solid hits produced five runs and brought the Brewers within a run. Al Unser smacked a home run in the sixth that tied the score. Luis Olmo tripled off Lasorda with the bases loaded in the seventh to put Milwaukee on top. Thanks to four innings of shutout relief by Virgil Jester, the Brewers prevailed, 13–10, and took home the Junior World Series title for the third time. Manager Charlie Grimm called it "the biggest thrill of my life." The Brewers ballplayers, after dividing their Series winnings into shares, were each richer by $880.35.

When you're the defending champion, people automatically pick you as the favorite the following year. So it was with the Brewers. Of course the nature of minor league baseball is that your best players leave you. Ernie Johnson and George Crowe were the biggest losses to the roster. The best new players were outfielders Billy Bruton and Luis Marquez, along with catcher Dewey Williams and first sacker Hank Ertman. A surprising bonus for Milwaukee was the breakout season of seldom-used southpaw Don Liddle, who became the ace of the pitching staff and won 17 games.

Charlie Grimm was back at the helm, but he too was destined to move up the ladder. On Memorial Day weekend the woeful Boston Braves fired manager Tommy Holmes and replaced him with Grimm. With no ready successor for Grimm waiting in the wings, the Brewers installed general manager Red Smith as an interim replacement. Smith won the only seven games he managed. On June 7 new skipper Bucky Walters took the reins. George Estock welcomed him by throwing a one-hitter at Louisville, the Brewers' eighth win in a row.

Grimm was a tough act to follow, but Walters was a good choice. He was a veteran baseball man with a long list of accomplishments. He had managed the Cincinnati Reds for nearly a season and a half. As a ballplayer he had pitched 198 victories with the Phillies and Reds. He had also played, in the big leagues, every position except catcher and shortstop. He was the winning pitcher in the first televised game, August 26, 1939, and he received the Most Valuable Player Award in the National League that season.

When Grimm went to Boston to manage the Braves, he took shortstop Johnny Logan along, a gesture Logan appreciated all his life. Grimm helped offset Logan's loss to the Brewers by returning Buzz Clarkson to Milwaukee, as well as sending them towering right-hander and two-sport star (also basketball) Gene Conley. Conley won 11 games for the Brewers.

Little Don Liddle, who was 17–4 for the Brewers in 1952, takes his warm-ups before a contest in Borchert Field. RICHARD LULLOFF COLLECTION

In many ways the 1952 Brewers season mirrored 1951. They stayed almost even with the Kansas City Blues for much of the season before pulling away in the dog days of summer. The Boston Braves were in seventh place in the National League and going nowhere when they shipped George Crowe back to Milwaukee on August 16 to help their farm club win the pennant. The day Crowe arrived, the Brewers defeated the Blues, 3–2, in Borchert Field and moved a half game ahead of them in the standings. Seventeen days later the Brewers led Kansas City by 12 full games. In the final 27 games of the regular season, Big George drove in 29 runs and batted .351. On September 1 Gene Conley tossed a six-hit shutout at the Blues to clinch the pennant on the same date as in 1951. Bucky Walters's club finished their schedule with a 101–53 record, 12 ahead of the Blues.

The Brewers made short work of the St. Paul Saints in the semifinal playoff round, sweeping them in four games. In the final round, they played their old nemesis, the Blues, for the right to compete in the Junior World Series. Whenever Milwaukee played KC, something unusual seemed to happen. This best-of-seven battle turned out to be no exception.

Game One was played in Borchert Field on the night of September 15. The Brewers were winning, 3–2, with two outs in the top of the ninth and a full count on pinch hitter Bob Marquis. Needing one strike to win, Brewers hurler Gene Conley served up a two-run single that proved decisive for the Blues, 4–3. Brewers pilot Bucky Walters protested the game, though. In the first inning, first-base coach Mickey Owen, who also was one of KC's two catchers, left the coach's box and ran to home plate to complain about a called third strike on Don Bollweg. By rule, Owen should have been automatically ejected. He was not. Because he was not tossed, he was available for catching duty in the ninth inning. As a result, Marquis was able to pinch-hit for catcher Roy Partee, and Marquis drove in the winning runs.

American Association president Bruce Dudley was in attendance and witnessed what happened. In ruling on Walters's protest, he agreed, as did the umpires, that Owen should have been thrown out. Dudley disallowed the protest, however, saying it should have been lodged in the first inning when the offense occurred. In other words, yes, you're right, but tough luck. Blues win the game.

Milwaukee won the next evening to tie the series, and the venue shifted to Kansas City for Game Three. The Brewers won a slugfest, 10–8, with a pair of home runs by outfielder Pete Whisenant. The big story of the night, though, was that a runner was caught stealing second base and the catcher was the one who tagged him out.

Here's how it happened. In the third inning, Brewers second

baseman Gene Mauch was on first base. He got hung up between first and second when George Crowe struck out swinging. The catcher, Roy Partee, ran toward Mauch, faking a couple of throws as he did. With nowhere to hide or run, Mauch stood his ground. Partee eventually reached the stranded base runner and put the tag on him. The frustrated Mauch tried to knock the ball out of the catcher's mitt. Partee took offense, setting off a brief skirmish. The two combatants were separated, and the game continued.

In the fifth inning Mauch came to bat. Before a pitch was thrown, Partee offered a rude remark, his mask came off, and a flurry of punches followed. Mauch seemed to be the victor, landing a hard right to the chin. Both pugilists were kicked out of the game. Mauch followed his opponent to the home clubhouse and the punch-up resumed. The details of the bout went unreported, but the following day Partee was sporting an impressive shiner.

The teams split the next two games played in KC. Returning to Borchert Field, the Brewers needed to win just one of two games to take the series. Shoddy fielding sent them to a 10–4 defeat in Game Six, making the game on Sunday, September 21, a sudden-death affair. To the utter dismay of the 6,427 fans who came to cheer their Brewers heroes, it was death.

Kansas City sluggers Bill Renna, Don Bollweg, and Moose Skowron (nicknamed in childhood because his parents thought he looked like Mussolini) each slammed a home run to build an 8–2 cushion for right-hander Eddie Erautt. Renna's blast narrowly missed clearing the back wall of the center-field bleachers.

But the Brewers hadn't won 101 games by being quitters. Down six runs in the ninth inning, they fought back. Buzz Clarkson started the rally with a base hit. An out, two more singles, and two KC errors made the score 8–5. Billy Bruton tried bunting for a base hit but popped out to pitcher Dave Jolly. Two down. Mauch reached first on a walk. Crowe ripped a double. Luis Marquez singled to center, driving home both runners. It was now a one-run game, and the spectators were beside themselves with glee.

Alas, there was no Hollywood ending. After fouling off a couple of pitches, Billy Klaus lifted a routine fly to Renna in center. The series, the season, and the stadium came to an abrupt end. The splintered old park that folks liked to call Borchert's Orchard was now closed and would soon be just a memory.

In pace requiescat.

By mid-June 1953, all that remained of Borchert Field were the skin portion of the infield and countless memories. MILWAUKEE SENTINEL PHOTO, © 2015 JOURNAL SENTINEL INC., REPRODUCED WITH PERMISSION

Notes

1. This Old House

As Minneapolis Millers owner Mike Kelley: Sam Levy, "Ghosts of Old Borchert Field," *Milwaukee Journal*, January 15, 1952, p. 14.

An "immense" crowd of 6,000: "Athletic Park Dedicated," *Milwaukee Journal*, May 21, 1888, p. 4.

His final words were: "Otto Borchert Dies Speaking at Banquet," *Milwaukee Sentinel*, April 28, 1927, p. 1.

"The end of Borchert Field": R. G. Lynch, "Borchert Field to Be Condemned Soon," *Milwaukee Journal*, November 7, 1935, pt. 2, p. 6.

Bill Topitzes, who as a youngster: Bill Topitzes, interview with author, December 3, 2008, West Milwaukee, WI.

2. Pioneer in a New Park

The *Milwaukee Journal* proclaimed: "Athletic Park Dedicated," *Milwaukee Journal*, May 21, 1888, p. 4.

On July 8, 1888, the sports world: Pete Ehrmann, "Boxing Flashback: Hattie Leslie," *OnMilwaukee.com*, December 12, 2010, http://onmilwaukee.com/sports/articles/hattieleslie.html; "A Female Prize Fight," *Milwaukee Sentinel*, July 9, 1888, p. 2.

As the unnamed baseball writer: "Won in the Rain," *Milwaukee Sentinel*, July 9, 1888, p. 2.

3. Gay Nineties

As the *Milwaukee Sentinel* aptly: "An End of Baseball," *Milwaukee Sentinel*, July 8, 1892, p. 2.

"The sleeping volcano begins to smoke": "Last Days of Pompeii," *Milwaukee Sentinel*, September 11, 1892, p. 2.

"Houses fall and the great": John Gurda, "Milwaukee Loves Its Oohs and Ahhs!" *Milwaukee Journal Sentinel*, August 5, 2007, p. 2E.

4. Major League

After returning to the mainland: Lyell D. Henry Jr., *Zig-Zag-and-Swirl* (Iowa City: University of Iowa Press, 1991), 30.

As rival Charlie Comiskey said: Brownie, "Baseball Guff," *Milwaukee Journal*, August 25, 1904, p. 5.

As the *Milwaukee Journal* scribe: "Orioles Also Victims," *Milwaukee Journal*, September 17, 1891, p. 7.

As the *Milwaukee Sentinel* described it: "Sporting Notes," *Milwaukee Sentinel*, October 13, 1891, p. 4.

5. Tragedy of the Rube

Writer Lee Allen wrote: Michael Lalli, "An Athletic You Should Know: Eccentric Madman Rube Waddell," *Philly Sports History*, July 19, 2011, http://phillysportshistory.com/2011/07/19/an-athletic-you-should-know-rube-waddell/.

The Sporting News described him: "Faces Death Just as He Did Batters," *The Sporting News*, April 9, 1914, p. 3.

He proceeded to throw five shutout innings: Alan H. Levy, *Rube Waddell: The Zany, Brilliant Life of a Strikeout Artist* (Jefferson, NC: McFarland & Co., 2000), 61.

Interviewed afterward by a *Milwaukee Sentinel*: "Rube Waddell at a Fire," *Milwaukee Sentinel*, August 22, 1900, p. 7.

Although the "lively" new ball: Brownie, "Continued Slump of the Brewers Is Agitating Milwaukee Fandom," *Milwaukee Journal*, June 3, 1911, p. 11.

According to *Sporting Life*: "Waddell in Sorry Plight," *Sporting Life*, November 22, 1913, p. 3.

6. Send in the Clowns

"There is no room in baseball": Bob Uecker and Mickey Herskowitz, *Catcher in the Wry* (New York: Jove Books, 1982), 25.

On July 4, 1912, the American flag: "Bone Domed Work," *Milwaukee Journal*, July 5, 1912, p. 11.

The unseasonably frigid weather: "Brewers Win Last," *Milwaukee Journal*, May 11, 1904, p. 7.

During a game in Cleveland: David Jones, ed., *Deadball Stars of the American League* (Dulles, VA: Potomac Books, 2006), 552.

"I am Germany Schaefer," he said: Dan Holmes, "Germany Schaefer," Society for American Baseball Research Biography Project, www.sabr.org/bioproject.

When Grimm went to Boston: Bob Buege, "Johnny Logan," *Society for American Baseball Research Biography Project*, www.sabr.org/bioproject.

Schaefer's reputation as a comedian: Billy Evans, "Why Wasn't Sheriff on the Job?" *Milwaukee Journal*, September 13, 1911, p. 13.

Nothing Schaefer ever accomplished: Lawrence Ritter, *The Glory of Their Times* (New York: Vantage Books, 1985), 35.

Because outfielders have lots of free time: Marvin Tonkin, "Home Brews' Opener Like Real Circus," *Milwaukee Sentinel*, April 29, 1932, p. 4.

In the late innings of an exhibition: "Brewer Pick-Up," *Milwaukee Journal*, June 18, 1932, p. 10.

In December 1931 for a charity: "Cuckoo Christensen Mimics Al Jolson," *Milwaukee Sentinel*, December 17, 1931, p. 13.

What Price developed during those years: "American Association," *The Sporting News*, September 7, 1944, p. 23; "Johnny Price," Oakland Oaks website, http://oaklandoaks.tripod.com/price.html; Vince Guerrieri, "Jackie Price: Baseball's Sad Clown," April 15, 2014, http://didthetribe winlastnight.com/blog/2014/04/15/jackie-price-baseballs-sad-clown/.

No discussion of baseball clowns: "Negro Ball Clubs Play Here Tonight," *Milwaukee Journal*, August 18, 1941, pt. 2, p. 5; "Indianapolis Clowns Always Thrill Fans," *St. Petersburg Times*, April 20, 1960, p. 10B.

On June 23, 1942, the Clowns: "Negro Teams Open Season," *Milwaukee Journal*, June 23, 1942, pt. 2, p. 7.

7. Iron Man

His exaggerated sidearm motion: Sam Levy, "His Feats Are Baseball Legends," *Milwaukee Journal*, August 26, 1941, pt. 2, p. 1.

On September 29, 1906, and again: Associated Press, "New York 6–0, St. Louis 2–1," *Milwaukee Sentinel*, September 30, 1906, pt. 2, p. 1; "New York 4–4, St. Louis 3–3," *Milwaukee Sentinel*, August 1, 1907, p. 10.

The game was twice threatened: Brownie, "Stoney M'Glynn Pitched a Great Game Against Saints," *Milwaukee Journal*, May 3, 1909, p. 9; Manning Vaughan, "M'Glynn's Pitching Wins from Saints," *Milwaukee Sentinel*, May 3, 1909, pt. 2, p. 2.

It was a 14-year-old: "Has Brewers' Hoodoo Been Discovered in Snowball?" *Milwaukee Journal*, June 14, 1909, p. 9; "Brewers' Mascot Refuses to Be Fired," *Milwaukee Sentinel*, June 15, 1909, p. 8.

The Brewers had a precedent: "Has Brewers' Hoodoo," 9.

In 1909 Snowball also failed: Ibid.

On July 21 McGlynn made: "M'Glynn's Pitching Wins Double Bill," *Milwaukee Sentinel*, July 22, 1909, p. 8.

However, in the first inning: Brownie, "Stoney M'Glynn Hurt; Brewers Crippled," *Milwaukee Journal*, September 17, 1909, p. 13.

He made his last return: "Hurler McGlynn Services on Friday," *Milwaukee Sentinel*, August 27, 1941, p. B3.

8. Wordsmith

In the earliest days of: "Sport Fans Mourn Death of Manning Vaughan," *Milwaukee Sentinel*, April 8, 1932, p. 13.

Vaughan covered a variety of athletic: "M. Vaughan, *Journal* Sport Writer, Dead," *Milwaukee Journal*, April 7, 1932, p. 6.

In a quarter century of chronicling: "Manning Vaughan Has Been a Baseball Writer Since 1906," *Milwaukee Journal*, May 19, 1929, p. 7.

Among all those thousands of innings: Ibid.

Writing about a game in Athletic Park: Manning Vaughan, "Brewers Lose, 6–2; Tom Jones Injured," *Milwaukee Sentinel*, August 19, 1911, p. 6.

He described a ninth-inning base hit: Manning Vaughan, "Duffydils Held to One Hit by Liebhardt," *Milwaukee Sentinel*, May 2, 1912, p. 8.

On August 18, 1911, Brewers: Vaughan, "Brewers Lose," 6.

Describing Brewers pitcher Joe Hovlik: Manning Vaughan, "Timely Hits Win Two for Brewers," *Milwaukee Sentinel*, September 2, 1913, p. 8.

In another game he called Hovlik: Manning Vaughan, "Sting Champs, 6–5, in Eleven Rounds," *Milwaukee Sentinel*, June 19, 1912, p. 11.

Perhaps more than anything else: Sam Levy, "Manning Coined Nicknames for Athletes," *Milwaukee Journal*, April 8, 1932, pt. 2, p. 1.

In the days before political correctness: Manning Vaughan, "Introducing the Pigtail to Boxing," *Milwaukee Journal*, August 11, 1926, p. 18.

One other of his Deutschisms: Ibid.

Sometimes the verbally playful Vaughan: Manning Vaughan, "Rain Stops Game; Double Bill Today," *Milwaukee Sentinel*, June 20, 1912, p. 10.

As much as any baseball writer: Vaughan, "Timely Hits," 8.

On another occasion Vaughan painted: Vaughan, "Brewers Lose," 6.

9. Georgia Peach

In 1897 Jennings was beaned: Tom Stanton, *Ty and the Babe* (New York: St. Martin's Press, 2007), 67.

For example, on July 12, 1911: "Athletics Held to Four Lone Bingles," *Milwaukee Sentinel*, July 13, 1911, p. 7.

A heckler named Claude Lueker: Jack Lessenberry, "Nothing New, or Original, About Going After the Fans," *The* (Toledo) *Blade*, November 26, 2004, sect. A, p. 13.

They refused to take the field: Ibid.

Predictably, in the Athletic Park exhibition: "How Did Ye Like Cobb, Seems to Be the Popular Question Today," *Milwaukee Journal*, October 3, 1914; Manning Vaughan, "Ty Cobb Defeats Our Brewers, 6–5," *Milwaukee Sentinel*, October 3, 1914, p. 6.

10. A Touch of Ginger

On Wednesday night, November 28, 1951: Gerald Kloss, "History of Athletics Comes Alive for Boys," *Milwaukee Journal*, November 29, 1951, p. 22.

Gridiron standouts Pat O'Dea: Ibid.

The most poignant moment of the evening: Ibid.

Born in 1876, the son: "Diamond Dust," *Milwaukee Journal*, August 29, 1898, p. 8.

While at Waupun he was spotted: Sam Levy, "Beaumont Recalls Days as Star," *Milwaukee Journal*, April 29, 1938, p. 9.

Mack auditioned Beaumont in a pair: Norman Macht, *Connie Mack and the Early Years of Baseball* (Lincoln: University of Nebraska Press, 2007), 151–152.

One week after his Western League: "Diamond Dust," *Milwaukee Journal*, August 30, 1898, p. 8.

Eddinger, however, ordered Lewis off: "Umpire Is Whipped by Brewer Player," *Milwaukee Sentinel*, October 1, 1911, pt. 2, p. 2.

What ensued, though, was by one newspaper: "Saints, by Poor Sportsmanship, Stall Way into First Division," *Milwaukee Journal*, October 2, 1911, p. 11.

11. Eight Men In

Those "eight men out," as author: Eliot Asinof, *Eight Men Out* (New York: Henry Holt, 1987).

Even after his lifetime ban: Stoney McGlynn, "Felsch's Four Hits Win for Bucher's, 4–1," *Milwaukee Sentinel*, May 22, 1933, p. 13.

So great a hitter was Shoeless Joe: Brother Gilbert and Harry Rothgerber, *Young Babe Ruth* (Jefferson, NC: McFarland & Co., 1999), 136.

The White Sox arrived in Milwaukee: "Indians Forfeit Game," *New York Times*, September 10, 1917, p. 10.

The host All-Stars elected: Manning Vaughan, "White Sox Trim All-Stars, 15–6," *Milwaukee Sentinel*, September 13, 1917, p. 8.

Despite the lopsided score: "Sox Prove Magnet," *Milwaukee Journal*, September 13, 1917, p. 15.

Local scribe Manning Vaughan declared: Vaughan, "White Sox Trim," 8.

12. Loose Cannon

On the opening day of the 1914: "City Leaguers Ready to Open," *Milwaukee Journal*, April 26, 1914, pt. 2, p. 1.

Cannon occasionally pitched sandlot ball: "Ray Cannon, a 'Ringer,' Turns Back Tars in Fray at Athletic Park," *Milwaukee Sentinel*, August 4, 1918, pt. 2, p. 2.

On the last day of August 1919: "Judges Are Chosen," *Milwaukee Journal*,
   August 28, 1919, p. 18; "Athletic Park Will Be Scene of Life and Pep,"
   Milwaukee Sentinel, August 31, 1919, pt. 3, p. 1.
Cannon's committee deemed 19-year-old: "Milwaukee's Best Amateur Ball
   Tossers," *Milwaukee Journal*, September 2, 1919, pt. 3, p.1.
Cannon's law practice continued to grow: "Judge Cannon—A Man in the
   Middle," *Milwaukee Sentinel*, August 31, 1966, pt. 2, p. 1.
With this weighing upon him: "Want Cannon as Ball Union Head," *Milwau-
   kee Sentinel*, August 16, 1922, p. 12.
Five of the banished Black Sox: "Ray Cannon Pitches No Hit, No Run
   Game," *Milwaukee Sentinel*, June 23, 1922, p. 9.
He took part in the Chicago Cubs: J. J. Delaney, "The Morning After," *Mil-
   waukee Sentinel*, February 16, 1922, p. 14.
Cannon had his enemies: "Ray Cannon's Case on Day to Day Docket,"
   Milwaukee Journal, August 18, 1944, pt. 2, p. 1; Donald Gropman, *Say It
   Ain't So, Joe* (New York: Carol Publishing Group, 1995), 202.

13. Wet and Wild

His renown grew from the day: "'Buster' Braun Dies; Sheboygan Land-
   mark," *Milwaukee Journal*, June 19, 1966, pt. 2, p. 5.
In 1902 a man named George Hildebrand: Jack Smiles, *Big Ed Walsh: The
   Life and Times of a Spitballing Hall of Famer* (Jefferson, NC: McFarland
   and Co., Inc., 2007), p. 29.
Then he complained bitterly: "Ed Walsh Is Dead at 78," *Milwaukee Journal*
   Final, May 26, 1959, p. 2.
If he is destined to be remembered: Frank Russo and Gene Racz, *Bury My
   Heart at Cooperstown* (Chicago: Triumph Books, 2006), ebook.

14. Sweet Science

The range operator later explained: "Barred from Using Golf Driving Range,
   Plaint by Negroes," *Milwaukee Journal* Final, August 4, 1947, p. 1; "Action
   Stayed in Racial Case," *Milwaukee Journal*, August 5, 1947, pt. 2, p. 1.

15. Frozen Tundra South

Racine arrived with a caravan: "Pro Gridiron Teams to Play for State Hon-
   ors," *Milwaukee Journal*, December 4, 1921, pt. 3, p. 1.
Running back Johnny Mohardt had been: Ibid.; Sam Levy, "Sport Peri-
   scope," *Milwaukee Journal*, December 5, 1921, p. 14.
One often-related story about Blood: William Povletich, *Green Bay Packers:
   Trials, Triumphs, and Tradition* (Madison: Wisconsin Historical Society
   Press, 2012), 23.

16. The Rock

The moment of his death was described: Ray Robinson, *Rockne of Notre Dame* (New York: Oxford University Press, 1999), 82.

By coincidence, Marquette's third-string quarterback: Ibid., 111.

Taugher had been a Marine: "Taugher Rites Today; Former MU Grid Star," *Milwaukee Sentinel*, February 12, 1963, pt. 2, p. 3.

"The hospitality which has been accorded": "We Want to Come Back Here—Rockne," *Milwaukee Sentinel*, November 21, 1921, p. 7.

17. Up, Up, and Away

That evening a special holiday radio: "Salute to Hero Dead," *Milwaukee Sentinel*, May 30, 1922, p. 1.

Milwaukee's own Brig. Gen. William: "Accident to Bar Entry in Balloon Race," *Milwaukee Sentinel*, May 29, 1922, p. 1.

The afternoon air show was marred: "Plane Crashes into Lake," *Milwaukee Sentinel*, May 31, 1922, p. 1; "Recounts Plunge in Army Airplane," *Milwaukee Sentinel*, June 1, 1922, p. 4.

Not everyone in town flocked to: "Can't Watch Bags Take Off," *Milwaukee Sentinel*, May 30, 1922, p. 1.

The oldest entrant, also from St. Louis: "Who's Who in Race," *Milwaukee Journal*, May 31, 1922, p. 1.

The first pilot, Roy Donaldson, knew: "Big Gas Bags Off to Cheers of Thousands," *Milwaukee Sentinel*, June 1, 1922, p. 1.

Upson said he had tried to reach Buffalo: "Upson Leading Balloon Race; Six Remain Up," *Milwaukee Sentinel*, June 2, 1922, p. 1.

One of the landings near Fulton, Missouri: "Crippled Balloon, Occupants Exhausted, Continues 20 Hours," *Milwaukee Sentinel*, June 3, 1922, p. 1.

Westover and his assistant reported: "Tells Thrilling Tale," *Milwaukee Sentinel*, June 4, 1922, p. 1.

Westover said that during the night: Ibid.

18. Grid Showdown in Athletic Park

Paul Robeson was among the most accomplished: *Paul Robeson: Here I Stand* (video). New York: WNET Television and Menair Media International. American Masters TV series, 1999.

Robeson caused a firestorm and received: "Faces of the Harlem Renaissance: Paul Robeson," *Drop Me Off in Harlem*, http://artsedge.kennedy -center.org/interactives/harlem/faces/paul_robeson.html.

Camp called Robeson "a veritable superman": Paul Robeson Jr., *The Undiscovered Paul Robeson* (New York: Wiley, 2001), 30.

On this afternoon Harvard's overmatched opponents: "Ten Biggest Upsets in College Football History," *Mean Green Cougar Red*, September 7, 2007, http://indotav.blogspot.com/2007/09/ten-biggest-upsets-in-college -football.html.

The famous Native American athlete: "The Greatest Athlete," *Time*, April 6, 1953.

Coach Warner did not hesitate: Lars Anderson, *Carlisle vs. Army* (New York: Random House, 2007), 278.

The injury was serious enough that: Ibid., 315.

The heralded matchup between Jim Thorpe: "Thorpe-M'Millin Fight Great Duel," *Milwaukee Sentinel*, November 20, 1922, p. 7.

Thorpe completed several long passes: "Badgers Trim Thorpe's Team," *Milwaukee Journal*, November 20, 1922, p. 16; "M'Millin Stars as Badgers Beat Indian Eleven," *Chicago Tribune*, November 20, 1922, p. 27.

Much of the damage was inflicted: "McMillan [sic] and Local Pros Beat Indians, 13–0," *Wisconsin News*, November 20, 1922, p. 14.

McMillin tattooed Eagle Feather with a crushing block: Ibid.

For the next several seconds, spectators: Robeson, *The Undiscovered Paul Robeson*, 69.

"The Thorpe-McMillan [sic] three ring circus": "McMillan [sic] and Local Pros Beat Indians, 13–0."

The *Milwaukee Journal* said Robeson: "Badgers Trim Thorpe's Team."

Despite playing in a losing cause: "McMillan [sic] and Local Pros Beat Indians, 13–0."

Fritz Pollard simply described it as: Sheila Tully Boyle and Andrew Bunie, *Paul Robeson: The Years of Promise and Achievement* (Amherst: University of Massachusetts Press, 2001), 109.

19. Tigers and Bears

"Local Darkies Win Opener," proclaimed: "Local Darkies Win Opener from Cuban Giants," *Milwaukee Sentinel*, April 29, 1923, sports section, p. 1.

The anonymous *Sentinel* reporter wrote: "American Giants Play Milwaukee 2 Games Sunday," *Chicago Defender*, May 5, 1923, p. 10.

The entourage totaled nearly two dozen vehicles: "On to Milwaukee," *Chicago Defender*, May 5, 1923, p. 10.

Besides Foster and Schorling, the drivers: Ibid.

Twenty-six African Americans, including women: "Negroes: Less Lynching," *Time*, January 7, 1924, p. 5.

The *Milwaukee Journal* the next day: "Negro Hanged, Coeds Look On," *Milwaukee Journal*, April 30, 1923, p. 1.

The Tigers' opening doubleheader on Memorial Day: "Milwaukee Negro Nine in Debut Wednesday," *Milwaukee Journal*, May 27, 1945, pt. 2, p. 7.

20. Papa Bear
He joined the base's football team: "Great Lakes Grid Squad Wins Title," *Milwaukee Sentinel*, January 2, 1919, p. 10.

Halas impressed the New Yorkers sufficiently: "George Halas," *Retrosheet .org*, www.retrosheet.org/boxesetc/H/Phalag101.htm.

On September 17, 1920, he and a group: Jeff Davis, *Papa Bear: The Life and Legacy of George Halas* (New York: McGraw-Hill, 2005), 50.

According to the *Milwaukee Journal*: "Badger Pros Lose to Bears but Play Well," *Milwaukee Journal*, September 20, 1926, p. 19.

The Bears won the game, 10–7: Ibid.

21. Tall Tactician's Team
Second, this game offered Mack his first: Gerald Kloss, "History of Athletics Comes Alive for Boys," *Milwaukee Journal*, November 29, 1951, p. 22.

Twenty-two years later a celebration: Bob Warrington, "A 1944 Tribute to Connie Mack," Philadelphia Athletics Historical Society, http://philadelphia athletics.org/history/macktribute.htm.

The fact that the evening's festivities: Ibid.

At the conclusion of the pregame: Ibid.

The two former Milwaukeeans attracted: "Kansas City Blues in Town for 4 Games," *Milwaukee Journal*, September 1, 1923, p. 6.

During the investigation Milwaukee attorney Henry: Mark Alvarez, "Say It Ain't So, Ty," *The National Pastime* (Cleveland: Society for American Baseball Research, 1994), 23.

A New York Giants outfielder walloped: "Great Honus Wagner Dies," *Calgary Herald*, December 6, 1955, p. 24.

After the first three balls: "Big Leaguers Haven't Anything on Our Brewers," *Milwaukee Journal*, October 4, 1913, p. 10.

The youngsters carried a large banner: Photo, *Milwaukee Journal*, October 13, 1930, pt. 2, p. 1.

Following Foxx's example, Simmons also pitched: Manning Vaughan, "Large Crowd Welcomes Al Simmons Back Home," *Milwaukee Journal*, October 13, 1930, pt. 2, p. 1.

22. Galloping Ghost
The *Cleveland Plain Dealer*, for example: Raymond Schmidt, *Shaping College Football: The Transformation of an American Sport* (Syracuse: Syracuse University Press, 2007), 75.

Even his beloved coach, Bob Zuppke: Ibid.

Grange was a pariah and: John M. Carroll, *Red Grange and the Rise of Modern Football* (Champaign-Urbana: University of Illinois Press, 1999), 96.

In May 1925 he had accepted an invitation: "Grange Given Movie Lesson," *Milwaukee Journal*, May 13, 1925, p. 2.

The tour was brutal, but from it: Lars Anderson, *The First Star: Red Grange and the Barnstorming Tour That Launched the NFL* (New York: Random House, 2009), 206.

What's more, Grange also became the first: Carroll, *Red Grange and the Rise*, 113.

The team was described as an "unofficial member": "Pro Football Coming Here to Stay," *Milwaukee Journal*, September 7, 1930, pt. 3, p. 2.

Center George Trafton, the first to hike: Anderson, *The First Star*, 204.

23. Better Than Thorpe

Football legend Glenn "Pop" Warner: "A Football Legend, Nevers, Dies at 72," *Milwaukee Journal*, May 3, 1976, pt. 2, p. 11.

24. Bully in Blue

Suddenly the Major was toe-to-toe: Arthur Daley, "Farewell to the Maje," *New York Times*, October 20, 1966, p. 54.

As the two men shouted vehemently: Bruce Nash and Allan Zullo, *Baseball Hall of Shame* (New York: Simon and Schuster, 1989), 153.

Magerkurth was heard to tell Griffin: "Battling Umpire Let Out by Hickey," *The Sporting News*, May 5, 1927, p. 3.

The hulking Magerkurth demanded an apology: "Wife of Star Is Witness to Cruel Attack," *Milwaukee Sentinel*, April 25, 1927, p. 11.

The sports editor of the *Milwaukee Sentinel* wrote: George Downer, "Following Through with Downer," *Milwaukee Sentinel*, April 27, 1927, p. 11.

25. Bambino Comes to Beertown

The biggest laugh their act produced: Paul Adomites and Saul Wisnia, "Babe Ruth's Barnstorming," entertainment.howstuffworks.com/babe-ruth24 .htm.

After the game the Babe said: Manning Vaughan, "Ruth Hits Home Run to Beat Gehrig's, 5 to 4," *Milwaukee Journal*, October 29, 1928, p. 16.

At 75 cents a head: Bob Buege, "Babe Ruth in Milwaukee," *Baseball in the Badger State* (Milwaukee: Society for American Baseball Research, 2001), 25.

26. Whataman

Afterward the self-proclaimed "Art the Great" said: "Shires (The Great) Dies of Lung Cancer at 60," *Milwaukee Sentinel,* July 14, 1967, pt. 2, p. 1.

The fistic display lasted the scheduled five: Morris Siegel, "Big Man Trafton, Gridder—Lover!" *The Sporting News,* September 27, 1950, section 2, p. 1.

At the time of the transaction: "Shires Best Player I Ever Sent to Minors," *Milwaukee Journal,* November 29, 1930, p. 8.

27. Father and Son

Tony the elder made such an impression: Ronald McIntyre, "Between You and Me," *Milwaukee Sentinel,* April 29, 1931, p. 19.

Bob Connery, the owner of the St. Paul: Sam Levy, "Bob Connery Studies Tony Kubek," *Milwaukee Journal,* May 22, 1931, sports section, p. 3.

In a game in Toledo against Casey: Red Thisted, "Southpaw Holds Hens Safe; Mates Win, 5–4; Kubek Is Hitting Star," *Milwaukee Sentinel,* April 21, 1931, p. 15.

28. *Nowiny Polskie*

"I wanted him to play with the Brewers": Sam Levy, "Sports Chatter," *Milwaukee Journal,* May 9, 1935, pt. 2, p. 7.

When he was reassigned to Longview: Ibid.

To honor Brief in Borchert Field: Zyg Kaminski, "Polish Idol Given Auto, Other Gifts," *Nowiny Polskie,* August 21, 1928, p. 6.

Milwaukee Journal baseball writer Manning: Manning Vaughan, "Remarkable Tribute Paid Bunny Brief," *Milwaukee Journal,* August 21, 1928, pt. 2, p. 6.

29. Nats in Town

Clark Griffith's Nationals had a reputation: Charles Dryden, *Washington Post,* June 27, 1904, quoted in *Izquotes,* http://izquotes.com/author/Charles-Dryden.

Of all the players who paraded: Michael Feldberg, "The Riddle of Moe Berg," American Jewish Historical Society–New England Archives, February 7, 2011, www.ajhsboston.org/2011/02/07/the-riddle-of-moe-berg/.

One of his teammates, when told: Nick Acocella, "Moe Berg: Catcher and Spy," Sportscentury Biography, *ESPN Classic,* www.espn.go.com/classic/biography/s/Berg_Moe.html.

When Berg was first evaluated by: Nicholas Dawidoff, *The Catcher Was a Spy* (New York: Pantheon Books, 1994), 50.

Berg later claimed that his films: Ibid., 135.
Armed with a pistol and a cyanide capsule: Ibid., 201.
If someone did touch one: Ibid., 69.

30. Hot Enough for Ya?

Within the 24-hour period preceding: "13 Murderers Put to Death," *Milwaukee Sentinel*, July 11, 1936, p. 2.
At Coushatta, Louisiana, three men described: Ibid.
Huntsville, Texas, in a rare spirit: Ibid.
The accompanying drought motivated Archbishop: "Prayers for Rain Will Be Made in Catholic Churches," *Milwaukee Journal*, July 11, 1936, p. 1.
Eighteen women employed by the WPA: "Heat Fells Women of WPA; 18 Collapse; 30 Quit Work," *Milwaukee Journal*, July 10, 1936, p. 1.

31. Deans Cause a Riot

The most enduring memory of that: "Dizzy Dean," *Baseball-Reference.com*, http://baseball-reference.com/players/d/deandi01.shtml.
After the game, promoter Stumpf: Sam Levy, "Judge Landis to Get Report from Stumpf," *Milwaukee Journal*, October 16, 1934, pt. 2, p. 2.

32. Stars of the Negro Leagues

Catcher Josh Gibson was often called: Larry Whiteside, "Nobody Could Hit Like Ol' Josh," *Milwaukee Journal*, February 9, 1972, pt. 2, p. 1.
His Hall of Fame plaque, dedicated: "Judy Johnson," Baseball Hall of Fame, http://baseballhall.org/hof/johnson-judy.
Connie Mack told Johnson: Dick Clark and Larry Lester, eds., *The Negro League Book* (Cleveland: Society for American Baseball Research, 1994), 45.
The 1974 Hall of Fame plaque of James: "Cool Papa Bell," Baseball Hall of Fame, http://baseballhall.org/hof/Bell-Cool-Papa.
One oft-remembered Cool Papa Bell: Joe Posnanski, "No. 99: Cool Papa Bell," December 3, 2013, http://joeposnanski.com/no-99-cool-papa-bell/.

33. No Runs, No Hits

They called him "the spaghetti king": "Polli Champ Jockey," *Milwaukee Journal*, December 11, 1932, pt. 2, p. 4.
A newspaper photo of Polli: Tom Simon, ed., *Green Mountain Boys of Summer* (Shelburne, VT: New England Press, 2000), 131.
Polli's given name was Louis Americo: Lawrence Baldassaro, *Beyond DiMaggio* (Lincoln: University of Nebraska Press, 2011), 104.

At Goddard Seminary on June 3: Simon, *Green Mountain Boys of Summer*,
128.

The contest offered an unusual incentive: Sam Levy, "Polli, Riddle Figure in
Scrap," *Milwaukee Journal*, May 27, 1934, pt. 2, p. 1.

By consensus of 1932 American: "Polli Champ Jockey."

"I almost froze in left field": "One-Base Hits," *Milwaukee Journal*, June 7,
1934, pt. 2, p. 6.

The first time that owner Otto: Sam Levy, "Made Otto Gasp," *Milwaukee
Journal*, May 20, 1951, pt. 3, p. 2.

Fourteen years and one day later: Manning Vaughan, "Brewers Take Both
Ends of Double Bill," Milwaukee Journal, August 22, 1926, p. 2, p. 1.

In an odd display of what: Ibid.

He eventually struck out Don: Red Thisted, "Thiel Knew He Had It," *Milwaukee Sentinel*, August 17, 1951, pt. 2, p. 3.

34. Out of Darkness

Milwaukee's morning newspaper called the Stratton: Ronald McIntyre,
"Night Baseball Sole Salvation for Brews," *Milwaukee Sentinel*, June 7,
1935, p. 13.

The Milwaukee Sentinel described him: "Bearded Nine Beats Red Sox," *Milwaukee Sentinel*, June 6, 1931, p. 20.

35. Added Attractions

Perhaps the level of the Davids' performance: "Brewers Nose Out 'Daves' in
16th, 7–6," *Milwaukee Sentinel*, August 29, 1933, pt. 2, p. 1.

Stephens captured the gold medal: Edward Seldon Sears, *Running Through
the Ages* (Jefferson, NC: McFarland Co., 2008), 187.

"People say that it was degrading": Jacqueline Edmondson, *Jesse Owens: A
Biography* (Santa Barbara, CA: Greenwood Publishing Group, 2007), 57.

37. Goober Zuber Beans Splinter

Ted Williams's oft-repeated goal in life: Mike Gee, "Ted Williams Today:
Profile of a Legend," *Boston Phoenix*, April 12, 1983, p. 6.

"Bill Zuber and the strike zone": John Henshell, "Bill Zuber," Society for
American Baseball Research Biography Project, www.sabr.org/bioproject.

As a child he had experienced: Ibid.

In Borchert Field's tiny visitors' locker room: Red Thisted, "Brewer Notes,"
Milwaukee Sentinel, August 4, 1938, p. 11.

38. Men in Pinstripes

Hoag is perhaps best remembered for: "Myril Hoag," *Baseball-Reference.com*, www.baseball-reference.com/players/h/hoagmy01.shtml.

Stadium announcer Art Truss went into: Sam Levy, "Homer Lifted by Mapes Goes over Scoreboard," *Milwaukee Journal*, June 1, 1947, pt. 3, p. 1.

39. Jack and Bunny

He changed his surname after: "'Make It Brief,' Said Boss, and 'Brief' It Has Been to This Day," *Pittsburgh Press*, May 12, 1915, p. 27.

Jack Kloza arrived at his professional: Lou Chapman, "Scouting the Sand-lots," *Milwaukee Sentinel*, June 4, 1950, pt. B, p. 2.

It is available at more than 800: Gina Thorsen, Vice President of Marketing and Sales, Stormy Kromer company, email to author, October 13, 2014.

"I went to Blytheville": Manning Vaughan, "Kromer's Boys Making Good," *Milwaukee Journal*, September 28, 1930, pt. 2, p. 2.

He taught his young hitters: Ibid.

They established a dubious record: "Stormy Kromer Visions State Baseball League," *Milwaukee Sentinel*, December 8, 1929, p. 5C.

"I have spent 10 years": Sam Levy, "Tough Luck Plagues Jack Kloza," *Milwaukee Journal*, April 17, 1936, p. 9D.

Their philosophy of teaching boys: "Kloza, Former Brewer and Friend of Boys, Dead After Heart Attack," *Milwaukee Journal*, June 12, 1962, pt. 2, p. 1.

40. No Tie

On that day a syndicate of: Sam Levy, "Brewers Sold for $100,000," *Milwaukee Journal*, June 23, 1941, pt. 2, p. 3.

At that same time the younger Veeck: Bill Veeck and Ed Linn, *Veeck—as in Wreck* (New York: G.P. Putnam's Sons, 1962), 43.

Veeck consulted with his most-trusted: Sam Levy, "Harry Grabiner: His Death Deprives Veeck of Long Time Friend," *Milwaukee Journal*, October 25, 1948, pt. 2, p. 3.

Grimm was a musician of long standing: William Fay, "Good-Time Charley," *Chicago Daily Tribune*, March 16, 1947, p. H7.

Novikoff was happy to leave Wrigley: Jim Vitti, *The Cubs on Catalina* (Darien, CT: Settefrati Press, 2003), 156.

With the cooperation of Abe Saperstein: R. G. Lynch, "Firm of Veeck and Schaffer Starts with a Splash," *Milwaukee Journal*, December 9, 1942, pt. 2, p. 10.

The outcome might have been different: Veeck and Linn, *Veeck—as in Wreck*, 75.

41. Ladies Days

The league even had an official song: Official Website of the AAGPBL,
www.aagpbl.org/index.cfm/

Eventually they were officially dubbed: Ibid.

That contest was held in Chicago's: "Wisconsin Girls Win Star Softball Tilt,"
Milwaukee Sentinel, July 2, 1943, pt. 2, p. 4.

On May 29 Thelma "Pigtails" Eisen: Millie Keene, "Milwaukee Girls Win in
12th," *Milwaukee Sentinel*, May 30, 1944, pt. 2, p. 3.

42. The Mighty Casey

As he told the Kefauver committee: "Casey Stengel Testimony: July 8, 1958,
Senate Anti-Trust and Monopoly Subcommittee Hearing," *Baseball Almanac*,
www.baseball-almanac.com/quotes/Casey_Stengel_senate_testimony
.shtml.

Nothing in his career as a funnyman: "Casey Stengel—Clown and Hero,"
http://sports.jrank.org/pages/4598/Stengel-Casey-Clown-Hero.html.

Stengel argued long and loudly: "One-Base Hits," *Milwaukee Journal*, August
23, 1926, p. 14.

In Borchert Field on May 2: Manning Vaughan, "Error by Electric Scorer
Starts Row," *Milwaukee Journal*, May 3, 1931, pt. 2, p. 1.

Vitriolic sports columnist Dave Egan: Quoted in Robert Creamer, *Stengel*
(New York: Simon and Schuster, 1984), 197.

Pittsburgh Pirates manager Frankie Frisch: Ibid., 195.

The jovial, fun-loving Grimm: "American Association," *The Sporting News*,
June 1, 1944, p. 24.

On September 11 Stengel announced: R. G. Lynch, "Stengel Announces He
Won't Be Back," *Milwaukee Journal*, September 11, 1944, pt. 2, p. 4.

43. Life and Limb

Staples was a genuine cowboy: "Cowboys Swarm Where Brewers Used to
Frolic," *Milwaukee Journal*, August 2, 1945, p. 22.

The only displeasure seemed to be: "Court Returns Rodeo Funds," *Milwaukee Sentinel*, August 8, 1945, p. 5.

44. Hail to the Victors

She said she would resign: "Milwaukee Woman Ball Team Owner Becomes
Bride, Now on Honeymoon Trip," *Milwaukee Journal*, October 11, 1913,
p. 1.

45. Lights, Camera . . .

Brewers owner Otto Borchert, fearing: "When Baseball First Met Radio in Milwaukee," *Milwaukee Journal*, August 20, 1944, pt. 8, p. 14.

Beginning at eight o'clock on that: "TV Has Grown Rapidly Since Milwaukee Debut," *Milwaukee Journal*, October 17, 1951, p. 41.

Barely three months after television: "Perini to Give Television No-Fee Test in Milwaukee," *The Sporting News*, March 17, 1948, p. 2.

Declaring TV a wonderful thing: Ibid.

Clark told his viewers: William Janz, "CPR Gave TV Pioneer the Rest of His Life," *Milwaukee Journal*, November 15, 1991, p. 19A.

Later in the season, in another game: Ibid.

46. Yatcha

Brewers manager Nick Cullop was notoriously: Sam Levy, "Logan Doesn't Sound Russian, but It's Logan's Russian Name," *Milwaukee Journal*, March 10, 1948, pt. 2, p. 8.

When his mother asked him: Johnny Logan, interview with author, December 6, 2005, Milwaukee, WI.

He played on the baseball team: Johnny Logan, interview with author, May 17, 2006, Milwaukee, WI.

When Johnny told his manager: Levy, "Logan Doesn't Sound Russian."

Red Thisted of the *Milwaukee Sentinel*: Red Thisted, "Elliott Faces Millers Tonight," *Milwaukee Sentinel*, May 17, 1948, pt. 2, p. 4.

Somehow, in the scrum, two: Sam Levy, "In Slump," *Milwaukee Journal*, June 26, 1951, pt. 2, p. 7.

Milwaukee Journal beat writer Sam Levy: Sam Levy, "Brewers' Hopes Fade for Return of Logan," *Milwaukee Journal*, December 5, 1951, pt. 2, p. 4.

However, he played the game in a fog: Sam Levy, "Brewers Beaten by Fog and Millers," *Milwaukee Journal*, May 24, 1952, p. 8.

He complained loudly to the umpire: Ibid.

47. Teenaged Catcher

During his 13 years with the Braves: *Sports Illustrated* cover, April 21, 1958.

48. The Buck Stops Here

Dorothy Parker described Dewey as: Maureen Dowd, "In Praise of Insults," *Victoria Advocate*, July 21, 1997, p. 10A.

Another wag called Dewey: Paul Greenberg, "The Me-Too Democrats," *The Bryan Times*, April 26, 1990, p. 4.

Truman himself had spent one day: "Honeymoon First of Six Truman Milwaukee Visits," *Milwaukee Journal*, May 2, 1952, p. 12.

From there Truman rode: "Milwaukee's Turnout Pleasing to President," *Milwaukee Journal*, October 15, 1948, p. 2.

"Harry, come in and have a beer": Ibid.

"Tonight I'm going to talk": "Full Text of the Talk President Gave Here," *Milwaukee Journal*, October 15, 1948, p. 10.

"It was the hardest decision": Ibid.

He explained, "I decided the bomb": Ibid.

"The world knows," the president added: Ibid.

"Powerful, selfish groups within the Republican Party": Ibid.

He then earned his loudest applause: Laurence C. Eklund, "Truman Tells Atomic Policy," *Milwaukee Journal*, October 15, 1948, p. 3.

What did the president of the United States: "Milwaukee's Turnout Pleasing," p. 2.

Truman, though, became the first: "Truman 'Hurls' Left, Right," *Milwaukee Sentinel*, April 19, 1950, pt. 2, p. 4.

49. Art Imitates Baseball

She was distraught because Jurges: "He Destroyed Our Romance," *Milwaukee Journal*, July 7, 1932, pt. 2, p. 9.

Violet went back to work: Jack Bales, "The Shootings of Billy Jurges and Eddie Waitkus," *Wrigley Ivy*, http://wrigleyivy.com/the-shootings-of-billy-jurges-and-eddie-waitkus/.

The judge who dismissed Valli's case: Ibid.

Among other bizarre statements: (As told to) Virginia Kachan, "Girl Who Shot Waitkus Planned to End Life," *Milwaukee Sentinel*, June 16, 1949, p. 4.

She went on to say: Ibid.

Friends of Steinhagen revealed that: "Love for Star Made Girl Leave Home, Set up Ed Waitkus 'Shrine,'" *Milwaukee Journal*, June 16, 1949, p. 15.

50. King of the Ring

Professional wrestling was a major attraction: *Milwaukee Journal*, July 17, 1888, p. 4; "Defeat of Otto Wagner," *Milwaukee Journal*, July 23, 1888, p. 4.

On July 21, 1889, in the ballpark: "International Wrestling Match," *Milwaukee Journal*, July 23, 1889, p. 4.

Stecher said at the signing: "Stecher Has High Hopes for Gagne," *Minneapolis Star*, April 19, 1949, p. 28.

The derisive headline in the *Minneapolis Star*: "Gagne Passes Screen Test as Wrestler," *Minneapolis Star*, May 4, 1949, p. 47.

Years later Gagne said of his NFL: Allen Ressler, "Verne Gagne's Great Cru-
sade," *Boxing Illustrated*, April 1960, p. 17.

Mr. Atlas . . . had an interesting background: "The Mighty Atlas," www.old
timestrongman.com.

On January 26, 2009, Gagne attacked: Bob Wolfley, "Gagne Focus of In-
quiry," *Milwaukee Journal Sentinel*, February 22, 2009, p. 2C.

51. The Real M & M Boys

It occurred on September 19, 1968: "The Day the Tigers Tipped Pitches for
the Mick," *New York Times*, May 9, 2009, p. D3.

After just half a year of a four-year: Eddie Mathews and Bob Buege, *Eddie
Mathews and the National Pastime* (Milwaukee: Douglas American
Sports Publications, 1994), 44.

52. Say Hey to Borchert Field

Hubbell's scouting report made clear: John Klima, *Willie's Boys* (Hoboken,
NJ: John Wiley & Sons, 2009), 4.

The brutal tactics so outraged: William A. Nunnelley, *Bull Connor* (Tuscalo-
osa: University of Alabama Press, 1991), 28.

"Nobody else catches the ball": Red Thisted, "St. Paul Opens 3-Game
Stand," *Milwaukee Sentinel*, May 21, 1951, pt. 2, p. 3.

Before long he would show the baseball: George Plimpton, *Out of My
League* (New York: Harper Books, 1961), 44.

53. Quiet Pioneer

He was born in 1921: Cynthia Carr, *Our Town: A Heartland Lynching, a
Haunted Town, and the Hidden History of White America* (New York:
Crown Publishing, 2006), ebook.

Jackie Robinson described George Crowe [in caption]: Jackie Robinson,
Baseball Has Done It (Philadelphia: J.B. Lippincott Co., 1964), 55.

Civic authorities in Austin, however: "Crowe to Work with Braves," *The
Sporting News*, December 20, 1950, p. 25.

In refusing the offer, Jenkins: Larry Lester, *Black Baseball's National Showcase: The East-West All-Star Game, 1933–1953* (Lincoln: University of
Nebraska Press, 2002), 350.

54. Et cetera

In a sandlot ballgame when: Dave Fleming, "The Musial Triple Crown," *Bill
James Online*, March 22, 2013, www.billjamesonline.com.

Perhaps the most interesting aspect: 'Hick,' "Brewers Victors in Doubleheader Sunday," *Milwaukee Journal*, September 6, 1909, p. 9.

For more than two years the two men: Lew Freedman, *The Day All the Stars Came Out* (Jefferson, NC: McFarland & Co., 2010), 74.

As a ballplayer he was the stereotypical: Thomas Rogers, "Leo Durocher, Fiery Ex-Manager, Dies at 86," On This Day, *New York Times*, October 8, 1991, www.nytimes.com/learning/general/onthisday/bday/0727.html.

Afterward the ever-modest Gullic gave: Sam Levy, "Brewers Fans Mob Gullic After Homer in Ninth Defeats Indians, 7 to 6," *Milwaukee Journal*, September 19, 1936, p. 6.

One day he belted a home run: Lou Chapman, "Should've Quit 15 Years Earlier," *Milwaukee Sentinel*, June 18, 1968, pt. 2, p. 2.

Anthropologists at Harvard University: "The Angel," Life, March 4, 1940, p. 38.

Three thousand cash customers came out: "Cox May Wrestle Maurice Tillet," *Ottawa Citizen*, August 9, 1940, p. 11.

On the night in 1950 when: Woody Strode and Sam Young, *Goal Dust* (New York: Madison Books, 1990), 169.

55. Best for Last

But as Yogi Berra explained: "Yogi Berra Quotes," *Baseball Almanac*, www.baseball-almanac.com/quotations.

Manager Charlie Grimm called it: Bob Wolf, "Victory for Brewers," *Milwaukee Journal*, October 5, 1951, pt. 2, p. 11.

When Grimm went to Boston: Bob Buege, "Johnny Logan," *Society for American Baseball Research Biography Project*, www.sabr.org/bioproj/person/4140a710.

Kansas City sluggers Bill Renna: Richard Goldstein, "Bill Skowron, Slugger in Yankee Golden Era, Dies at 81," *New York Times*, April 28, 2012, p. D8.

Acknowledgments

The author expresses his gratitude to the following people for their contributions to this book: Tom Kaminski, Richard Lulloff, Jim Nitz, Rick Schabowski, Paul Tenpenny, and Gina Thorsen of the Stormy Kromer Company.

Index

Page references in **bold** refer to illustrations.

About the Author

Photo by Rick Schabowski

Bob Buege is the author of *The Milwaukee Braves: A Baseball Eulogy* and coauthor of *Eddie Mathews and the National Pastime*. He is president of the Milwaukee Braves Historical Association, secretary of the Wisconsin Old Time Ballplayers' Association, and a member of the Society for American Baseball Research.